From Scratch

From Scratch

Why I Walked Away
From My Life
and Built this Home

SALLY PARADYSZ

Deer Trail Publishing
Coopersburg, Pennsylvania

Deer Trail Publishing
Coopersburg, Pennsylvania

First edition: November 2015
Printed in the United States of America

ISBN: 978-0-9967070-0-8
Library of Congress Control Number applied for

Cover Image © and Design by Melanie Powell, Shybuck Studios
Interior Design by Melanie Powell, Shybuck Studios

To five women whose souls rest deeply within my heart.

Katherine H. Sharp, PhD, DD, always
Melanie J. Powell
Norma M. Elliott
Carol L. Wright
Emily P. W. Murphy

ALSO FROM SALLY PARADYSZ

Stories or essays in:

A Christmas Sampler
Sweet, Funny, and Strange Holiday Tales
Bethlehem Writers Group (2009)

65 Things to Do When You Retire
65 Notable Achievers on
How to Make the Most of the Rest of Your Life
Sellers Publishing, Inc. (2012)

70 Things to Do When You Turn 70
Sellers Publishing, Inc. (2013)

Once Around the Sun
Sweet, Funny, and Strange Tales for All Seasons
Bethlehem Writers Group, LLC (2013)

A Readable Feast
Sweet, Funny, and Strange Tales for Every Taste
Bethlehem Writers Group, LLC (2015)

Acknowledgements

I am deeply indebted to my friend Susan Richards for her love, wit, tenacity, and support. I took my first writing workshop from Susan, and I'll never forget her words to me on the last day of that perfect week. "If this memoir is important to you, go forward with commitment, don't be tossed away, and never doubt yourself again. Write with passion. Tell it!" I wrote that down on a piece of white birch bark I found at the lake at the end of her road. I have it nailed to the wall of my writing cabin. Thanks, Susan.

Carol, the facilitator of my writing group, and Emily, who did my very first edit, is a mother-daughter team, I am genuinely grateful for how much of your time and energy you gave so generously. This story, in part, is yours as much as mine.

My writing group and its original members have contributed to my finishing this memoir. Paul, Emily, Jo, Jerry, Ralph, Courtney, Jeff, and Ann, I owe you one. None of you ever came clean and said you couldn't read this manuscript one more time.

My sister, Norma, gives unconditional love on a continual basis. She offered feedback throughout the subsequent drafts, of which there were tons. Thank you, sis.

My friend, Julie, read my later manuscripts and gave me continual vision for where I was headed. She never wavered on her enthusiastic support. What a gem you are.

I feel blessed to know my friend, Kate, who read one of the first copies of this memoir. And then so willingly read the last edit, helping me even more with her fine tuning. A true friend I can always count on.

Dr. Barbara R. Keane gave me the original key to unlock my inner door and then willingly held my hand as we walked through together. This book wouldn't have been possible without her.

I've always had love and support from my three children. Christopher and his wife Angela, and their three children: Alexandra, Daniella, and Nicholas. Shelly and her husband Kevin, and their three children: Daniel, Emily, and Michael. Andrew and his wife Kathryn, and their two children: Amelia, and Abigail.

Mom and Dad, I love you always and still. Family, it's the best, or mine is.

Always love and full support to my partner, Melanie, for each and every day of building our home on our chosen land. What a ride!

Nothing represents building a new life, literally or metaphorically, better than building a new house. However, at sixty years old, that's probably not how most women would choose to start over. Sally Paradysz isn't most women, and building a house with her own hands is exactly what she did on the eve of her seventh decade.

Like all building projects, it began with finding the right piece of land and finding the right piece of land represented the first step in deciding where in this world Sally wanted to place herself. It was the first of many decisions for someone sorely out of practice in decision-making following a thirty-five year marriage where her opinions, on matters large or small, were not welcomed.

It is a wonderful thing to witness the emergence of a more authentic self, and in this sometimes instructive (we learn a lot about building a house) but often humorous memoir, we watch a gentle woman find her inner jack hammer. Apparently it's never too late to challenge yourself in physically daunting ways, but more importantly, it's never too late to challenge old beliefs and painful memories that define you in ways that are limiting or no longer true. If they ever were true. For if you begin in the "basement" and work your way up to the "roof" one nail at a time, surely you will discover the incredible stuff you're made of which has been there all along.

And so the rebuilding of Sally Paradysz takes place as we watch the house grow from its sturdy new foundation to its final cedar shake. An awful lot happens in between that makes the story of building this house all the more remarkable given Sally's particular challenges.

Awakenings are never gentle and, in rural Pennsylvania, summer is sweltering, fall is cold, and winter is colder for those who live high on ladders and scaffolding, trying to get the angles just right. But dealing with the weather might be easier than dealing with the sometimes amused, sometimes hostile attitudes of the male-dominated construction world Sally is forced to navigate. Ultimately, it is heart-warming to learn how many men go out of their way to help this white-haired, rogue carpenter achieve her dream. The book is peppered with big-hearted farmers and tree-hugging truck drivers who appear at just the right moment. The hole is dug. The tree is saved. The land is safe. Integrity wins the day again and again.

As the house rises, so too does Sally, from the remnants of a person derailed in her youth and hidden for the next forty years, even from herself. It is the story of so many women who grew up before The Feminine Mystique who found themselves narrowly defined, and so learned to silence their voices in order to please a mother, a father, a husband, a community. This is the story of one who built a house, and in the process, found herself.

Susan Richards
New York Times best-selling author of *Chosen By a Horse*
Kennebunkport, Maine
July 20, 2015

I went to the woods because I wished to live deliberately, to front only the essential facts of life, and see if I could not learn what it had to teach, and not, when I came to die, discover that I had not lived. . . . I wanted to live deep and suck out all the marrow of life, to live so sturdily and Spartan-like as to put to rout all that was not.

—Henry David Thoreau
Walden: Or, Life in the Woods

From Scratch

The Search

F resh snow covered the forest ground that January morning, and as it crunched beneath my boots, I admired the massive 200-year-old oaks. Throwing my arms around one of them, I realized that my fingertips didn't touch. Rough bark felt thick, tight, and healthy against my cheek. A good sign for an ancient tree. My head fell back and blue sky peeked through the topmost limbs as they waved in the gentle wind.

I noticed this three-acre lot had a slight fade, or downward slope, which was good for drainage. It sat close to the top of a hill, and was rectangular in shape. The age of the trees and absence of other human footprints told me I was standing on a virgin forest floor where only animals had walked. Observing the deer paths that cut through the snow, and the abundance of scat, I realized dozens of deer must live on this land, and I envisioned putting out bird feeders and corn for the deer and other ground animals, asking them if I could share this land.

Most of the property was wooded, but the back three-quarters of an acre remained open field. It would be easy to build there, but my heart longed for a house among those towering trees. They seemed to have a pulse of their own, offering me shade in summer, and warming me in winter with their deadfall for my woodstove.

I told myself not to get too excited until I had hiked every inch of the lot. As the cold winter sun rose to its height in the sky, I walked the land until I felt I knew every tree, every branch. Come noon I was in love. And if I loved this acreage in the winter, it would only be better in spring. My search might have ended.

I'm not sure why I was doing this investigation on my own when there were two of us in this venture. Two of us hunting to find land on which to build our home. When I thought about making any decision, my usual response was to avoid it, but not about this. I was in charge of the exploration, but still my choice to make decisions felt crucial. Plus, I was as qualified as the best of them in giving my assessment for purchasing this land.

Why did I say I'd do this? Why was this time different? My stomach was in knots, but complex as this moment seemed I felt I was taking another step in my self reconstruction. Here I was, at age sixty, using the love for the land that my father nurtured in me as a teenager to guide me as I scouted properties, his deep voice giving me direction. He was six feet tall, muscled, and always smiling. People in town called him white-top because his hair had been white for decades, and he had what was known at that time, as a butch haircut. Handsome, blue-eyed. Larger than life to me. He filled my heart with joy and I loved him. What I learned much later was how inadequate he felt, never having finished high school and working the family sawmill instead.

Ambitious and smart, my dad owned his own sawmill while I was growing up and I loved being a woodsman's daughter. We often worked side by side in a perfect dance between master sawyer and Sal, the lumber-girl. And at other times, when logs were needed, we walked the forest together. Trees to be cut were selected with awareness and with reverence. I loved riding on the hood of his jeep while he drove deep within these wooded areas. Usually we were on some kind of two-track, bumpy and filled with holes and debris that we'd have to stop and remove. Dad always had his shotgun with him and often he'd shoot a rabbit or partridge to bring home for the game dinners we shared with friends each month. The timber lots did not belong to my father. The timber rights to cut the trees on those acres did. Most times he went to the various owners and asked to buy the timber rights, but on occasion he purchased them by bidding against other sawmill proprietors.

Did this experience make me an expert in purchasing a three-acre parcel of land? A natural at choosing where to build a home, never mind how? No, but I learned how to love nature. I again wrapped my arms around one of the old growths and as I thought of my dad, I felt tears spring to my eyes. Excited and anxious about my choice, I pulled out my cell phone.

Melanie and I lived together and shared life. After two years at our quiet rented farmhouse we made a decision to build our own home. It was a risk, but one we were eager to share. Mel was an artist and I'd met her years ago at the home of my friend, minister, and spiritual teacher. She is shorter than

I at five-foot-four, a decade plus four years younger, and had dark brown hair falling to the base of her neck. Her smile is radiant and her eyes are dramatically blue. I marveled that such different women could share space so peacefully. Our life at the farmhouse was gentle and serene, two simpatico souls filled with consideration and love for each other. I felt blessed to have Mel in my life and we were partners in every sense of the word. Totally committed, one to another.

"Mel," I said when she picked up. "I think I've found it."

"Tell me where. I'll be right over."

Mel arrived in twenty minutes. "Let's get going," she said forging right into the woods. Her legs were shorter than mine, but she moved easily. Not an athlete, nor in great physical condition because of sitting in front of a desk full time, Mel made great efforts to keep moving.

We spent the next three hours hiking around in silence. I stood back so she might experience the land in her own way. I wanted to allow Mel to fall in love at her own speed. It was important to me to see if my life partner felt the same passion for this land that I did.

But what if she doesn't fall in love, I wondered. Or what if she does and we can't afford it?

Together we sauntered along the creek at the bottom of the field. The air was clear and cold with the smell of frost. I drew calm from the water as it gurgled over the stones. The snowy banks were alive with flocks of titmice, chickadees, winter wrens, and dozens of wild turkey.

When we returned to the large oaks, having toured the entire property, I studied Mel's face for her reaction. She stood with her hands on her hips and turned in a slow circle, surveying the land as the sun began to set over the field. She had crinkles at the corners of her eyes and slightly raised eyebrows, but I couldn't tell if she was happy, confused, or unimpressed. At last she turned to me and smiled. "It's extraordinary," she said letting out a deep breath. "We can build in the woods and still have a garden, fruit trees and a majestic view."

An explosion of joy galloped through my body, and I shivered with delight. We hugged one another and ran around the field in our sloppy boots, whooping it up. "It's just what we hoped for," I said standing in the closing glow of day. I felt love for the land and certainty that it must be ours, but what if we couldn't afford it? The land was expensive at $96,000. But then again, it was Bucks County, Pennsylvania. What did I expect?

Later that night, Mel and I sat down to discuss how we would pay for the property. Since I knew our friends Bill and Heidi had purchased their land next to this lot from the same farmer, I decided I'd give them a call. Bill picked up the phone on the second ring.

I asked him if he thought the farmer's lot beside him had gone down in price in the last year. "Not sure about that, but he may negotiate."

Bill told me the farmer's name and gave me his phone number. I hung up and told Mel. With calculators in hand we each figured out what we could afford for the land. It was far less than the asking price.

———

I called Steve, the farmer, early the next morning with our offer of $83,000. He said he'd have to think about it and promised to call me back. I waited, my stomach churning all day. It had been a long search—or at least it had felt like a long search. There were so many properties I'd looked at, some with not enough acreage, and others that fell short of the quiet space my heart longed for. One lot I especially liked because of the stream that ran through it, but the asking price was a lot higher. Each time the phone rang, I jumped, hoping—what? Could we, in fact, afford it? Were we, after all that time I spent searching, about to move forward?

We paced the floors, checked the phones, and catnapped. When he finally called late the next morning it was with a counter offer of $95,000, only a thousand off his asking price. I got a pad of paper and did more money juggling. It was no use.

"He wants too much for that land," I told Mel at dinner. "It's perfect, so we shouldn't be surprised. Maybe we can't afford perfection after all."

Mel nodded. "I double checked my math this afternoon. If we spend that much on the land, we'll have to cut our expenses in other places. The house might have to be smaller, or we may have to wait a little longer to start construction."

I dropped my fork onto my plate and pushed it aside. "Ugh," I moaned. "Over the last twelve months I've walked countless miles over so many acres."

"We could counter his counter offer," Mel said.

"Why not?"

I called him the next morning with our new proposal. We came up a little, but not as much as he wanted. He turned us down, but lowered the price. At least he wasn't giving up on us.

I phoned Mel at her art studio. "I'm calling Chris. Steve is still way out of line."

"Great idea. Let me know what he says."

Chris is my oldest son, an entrepreneur with a direct marketing services corporation in New York City. He's a master at negotiating so I asked him if he'd call Steve. He said yes, and called me back within the hour.

"He won't budge much, Mom. I talked him down a little, but he's sticking to $93,000. What price can you and Mel afford to pay for the land?"

I hesitated. "$83,000. Otherwise we'll have to compromise on the size of the house, and it's a small footprint already."

"I'll give you the extra $10,000. I'll put the check in the mail this afternoon. I can't wait to come over and walk on it with you. Maybe this weekend?"

I felt love and gratitude touch my heart. Chris's generosity—he meant this as an outright gift, not a loan—helped me understand that all three of my kids were pulling for me. When he stepped in to help, he meant it, and kept to his commitment. "Thank you, Chris, for believing in me. You've made all the difference. I love you." I knew he heard my tears over the phone.

"It's okay, Mom, you deserve it. I love you, too. I can't wait to come and see the land. I'll call in a few days to set up a time."

"Okay, sounds good." Crying, I hung up and called Mel. She, too, felt humbled by his gift.

Still I hesitated. The land was just what I'd hoped for, but it was so much money. Certainly such expenditure would mean sacrifices in the future. Beyond that, it was a gigantic step, and I'd never made a decision about that much money on my own.

Ever.

Despite the fact that I was only paying half of everything for this venture, Mel and I made that decision up front, I was still apprehensive. What was I thinking? But regardless of my fear, change was coming; I could feel it prickle my skin. It was time to make a choice, well equipped or not.

I meditated later that evening, as I often do when I'm faced with a dilemma. Afterward, remaining in the silence of my reflections, I went to bed and considered the decade that was ending. The 90's had been my time of searching. I left my husband of thirty-five years in 1995, and three years later our divorce was final. There are always two sides (or more) to every disagreement or misunderstanding, but after thirty-five years I'd reached the end of what I could give. I longed for autonomy and to be worthy of unconditional love. Free to go forward with the gifts God gave me, never again thinking of escape. The time had come for me to ease the anxiety caused by my deteriorating marriage. Bob didn't want the divorce, but he didn't want to modify his behavior either. A heartbreak for me because I felt he didn't love me enough all those years to want to change. I felt limited and wanted to understand why a woman shouldn't feel ambitious for herself. Often negative, he had the footprint of another life in his mind for me. One I could not survive any longer.

I was not lonely living on my own, but I was slightly fearful of how I'd survive, so I gave more effort to defining my spirituality. In 1990, after much research, I began the study of an ancient Eastern Path called Sant Mat. This path and its meditation practice helped me find balance and make tough decisions; nourished my soul and honed my self trust. My earlier meditation awakened something inside of me that night, so profound and passionate that I felt strengthened rather than terrified.

The next morning brought clarity.

I wanted those three acres of land.

I told Mel how energized I felt at breakfast over a cup of her special blend of hazelnut coffee. "I'm going to send a letter to Steve telling him we accept his offer, and include a check for a thousand dollars as part of the down payment."

Mel laughed, "Sounds good to me. I was secretly hoping you'd come around to my way of thinking, but I didn't want to influence you." What a pleasant contrast to my life with Bob.

I mailed it later that morning and waited a few days for it to arrive. Then I called. He said the land was ours, and asked us to come right over to work out the details. I waited to hang up the phone before screaming and doing my crazy dance. Mel, who had been listening, joined in my celebration. We made enough noise that Eli and Toby, our two Maine Coon kitties, bolted out of the kitchen. Who knew what they were thinking. They had crazy mommies, after all.

Once we dressed, Mel and I drove to the farm where Steve and his wife Gail lived. They were quiet and straightforward people, and I liked them immediately. We sat in their kitchen and talked about our plans and how we would proceed. The room was large and old, but clean and smelled of pie baking. The wooden table we sat around was well used and must have been witness to many discussions over the years.

"You can start by felling the trees for your driveway. Anytime you want. No need to wait for the bank to close the deal," Steve said shyly.

"Perfect." I laughed with relief, sat back in my chair, and felt as if I'd begun a new friendship based on a handshake and a thousand dollar check.

We left Gail and Steve's farm and drove straight to our new land. I wept while I walked into the woods toward the back field. Along the path I counted fifteen turkeys, three squirrels, two does, and one red fox. Hawks flew overhead.

It took my breath away.

Mr Wonderful

Before deciding where to put the driveway, we had to figure out where to put the house. "I have several sites in mind," I said to Mel one evening. "Do you think you can take some time off to walk them with me?"

Chickadees, wrens, and titmice followed me as I sauntered through the woods on that late January morning waiting for Mel to arrive. Hawks soared over the trees, their red tails glinting in the sun as they rode the thermals hunting for food.

With her artist's eye, Mel moved toward the locations I suggested. "See how it slopes off there?" she said, pointing. "Wouldn't it be easier to build on more level ground?"

It is amazing to have an existence that includes choices. For too much of my life, I'd denied myself the privilege—and the responsibility—of choice. I hated Bob's anger more than I hated not having a voice, so I chose not to articulate my opinion, or any opinion. Over the years, I tried to express myself when decisions had to be made, but they were either ignored or met with anger. All things considered, I embraced silence.

"I'd like to avoid cutting any more trees than necessary," I said, pushing my shoulders back. "The trees are thicker on this flatter ground. It's unfair to disturb the wildlife and some of these old growths just to make a home for us. I'd rather use the sites that have fewer trees."

Mel nodded and we moved on. I showed her several more spots, each with benefits and drawbacks.

"Perhaps we need professional advice," I said hours later, hoping Mel wouldn't take offense. "We need to find a contractor."

"I agree. Let's start calling as soon as we get back to the farmhouse."

It had been five years since I'd left my home and husband, yet I was still amazed by the fact that my opinion was not only welcomed, but valued. The two of us were giddy with excitement by the time we left what was almost our land. All we needed was a skilled builder who would not cut corners, let us save money by working alongside him, and respect both us and the land. That wasn't too much to ask, was it?

Two weeks later we wondered if such a builder existed. Mel and I had spoken with several contractors. No one was interested in working with two women who wanted to help with the construction, even after we assured them of our abilities. We protested, but it didn't help.

I wondered if it was my fault that we had not found a contractor. I have had difficulty working with men in the last few decades, and I wanted the one we chose to be worth the effort it would take on my part. Perhaps it was me who didn't like the ones we'd interviewed, and not the other way around.

And now, to build our house, we needed to find a contractor I could trust. The most puzzling contractors were those who wouldn't return our calls. I wondered if they passed because we said upfront on the messages we left that we wanted to work alongside them. There were many areas in my life in which I lacked self-confidence, but my ability to do physical labor and to work on the land was not one of them. As a teen I'd labored hard with my father in his lumber business. We felled trees, dragged them away with his tractor, and sweated in fear each time one took a wrong fall. We'd accomplished a lot. I'd stayed in shape and wondered why it couldn't work that way now.

On a weekend in early February, Mel and I took a ride through the country. Snow covered the ground, but the sun was shining and I smelled spring coming early. My car window was down and I hunted for any indication of new construction. If a contractor's sign was posted at the end of a newly cut driveway, I wrote down the contact information so I could call on Monday.

Miles went by and my list grew. I found five new builders. Satisfied with our effort I suggested we go to Lake Nockamixon to relax and take a walk. It was only two miles away and I loved it there. Mel parked the car and I walked to the water's edge, taking a deep breath of the crisp air. Canada geese swam by at the lake's shoreline where the ice had melted.

Mel's boots crunched on the snow behind me and I turned my head. "I just remembered!" she exclaimed. "Twenty years ago I had a builder come to my house. I wanted him to raise the roof so I'd have more room on the second floor. His name was Kim Ziegler. Even though I never followed through on the project, I liked him a lot. I can't believe I didn't think of him sooner!"

"Call him," I said.

"Now?"

"Why not?" I answered pulling the cell phone from my pocket and handing it to her.

She dialed 411 for his number. "Yikes. After twenty years he's still in the book," she said, as the call connected.

I squeezed close trying to press my ear to the phone. It rang three times before a man's voice answered. Despite my best efforts I couldn't make out his words, so I stood back in order not to distract Mel.

She spoke into the phone while I danced from one foot to the next in apprehension. At last she laughed. "Yes, I still make the same hazelnut coffee." She paused and listened. "Yes, we'd love to meet with you." She met my eyes and gave me a thumbs up. "The sooner the better." She nodded. "Of course. We can drive to your office and be there in about twenty minutes." She grinned at me, then laughed again and shook her head. "Yes, I promise to bring you a pound of coffee."

Mel handed the phone back. We raced to the car as if our feet were on fire.

The trip took fifteen minutes. I was restless with trepidation as Mel drove to the garage that housed Kim's office. I bit my lip and felt a chill that was independent of the winter temperature. A new and different choice loomed. Finding and choosing the person who will help us make our dream a reality.

My past has kept its grip on me after sixty years. Feeling restrained in any way left me claustrophobic. Even leaving large Bandaids on my skin for too long made me sweaty and short of breath because I felt too confined, too held back, or too stuck. It was the curse of hiding and I'd done it all my life, especially with Bob. I felt as if I was still breaking away from it. I wanted to be accepted for who I was and to feel free. And it was working. But it wasn't easy.

At Kim's door, my mouth was so dry I felt that I wouldn't be able to talk. I wanted something from this man, and more importantly I wanted him to like me. And our project.

Mel looked at me, took a deep gulp of air, and knocked. I held my breath as the door opened revealing a well-muscled man with a super smile. He was just shy of six feet, and looked to be in his mid-forties. Sandy hair and clear blue eyes all tucked into a very confident-looking package. I let out a sigh of relief when he looked at Mel and grinned. "I thought I'd never have a cup of that great coffee again." Then he turned to me, taking my small hand in his large calloused one, and said, "You must be Sal. I'm Kim, but you can call me Mr. Wonderful." He tilted his head back and gave a deep belly laugh.

"Everyone else does. Isn't that right?"

Mel nodded. "Yes it is," she said as we were swept into the office on Kim's wave of enthusiasm.

Within the warmth of Kim's cigar-smoke-filled workplace, something told me we were at the end of our search. The room was small, but not messy. It held his desk, recliner, small TV, gun rack, computer, and filing cabinets. After a lengthy discussion I knew Kim was the builder we were looking for. But we still hadn't touched on our deal breaker—the small matter of whether or not Kim would agree to let Mel and me working alongside him every day.

"Here's the thing, Kim," Mel said, wringing her fingers in her lap. "We don't have a lot of money, so we need to hire someone who's okay with us working with him."

Kim tilted his head back in another laugh, and I bit my lip. Here it was, the moment when my dreams would be ridiculed. Kim rocked forward in his chair, propped his elbows on his desk and cupped his chin in his hands. "Of course," he said, and for a moment I thought he misunderstood.

"There's no reason why you shouldn't save money by doing some of the work yourselves." He clapped his hand down on the desk top with a resounding thump. "In fact," he looked at Mel, "knowing you, I'd expect it. You already know a lot about construction, and I can teach you how to do the rest."

I was stunned. This man was honest. When we left Kim's office later I felt light and unburdened for the first time since we'd purchased the land. I knew that Kim would not only listen to us and work as a partner, but that he would help us make our dream into a reality. On the drive home, Mel filled me in on everything she knew about him. I learned that Mr. Wonderful was divorced and had three daughters to whom he was devoted. I was divorced and had three children to whom I was devoted. Perhaps we might talk of our life's struggles while building this new house. And this common ground might help me achieve a healthier working relationship with men.

As Mel and I sat together that evening in our old farmhouse, she grabbed some drawing pads and began working on a design, incorporating all of the ideas we discussed with Kim. As an illustrator she easily sketched out a floor plan. Both floors had rooms to size, and she even included where to put the kitty bowls. When she was done, she promised to take them to her studio the next day and put them on her computer so it would be easier for us to make changes as we went along.

A week later in mid-February I was in the field, but this time I had a chair with me. On the ground in front of it I drew an 18" circle and placed an upright stick in the middle of it. For the next three hours, I watched the stick's shadow move through the circle, tracing the sun's movements like a sundial. I wanted my new home to take advantage of the southwest exposure so we might benefit from its warmth during the winter months. Dad showed me this trick and its value years ago.

Sitting for a while longer I scrutinized the woods, taking in each and every tree that I might have to sacrifice in order to put in a driveway and build a house. It pained me to take down even one.

An hour later my phone rang. It was Mel. "Hey. Kim can meet us on the land in an hour if you've got the time." I could hear the excitement in her voice.

"I'm already here," I said, lifting my frozen feet off the ground. "Hurry. I'm freezing."

I went back to the car to warm up a little before Mel and Kim arrived. I felt grateful for Mel, and the land, and our home-to-be, and Kim. It seemed a good time to say thank you. I leaned my head back, closed my eyes, and did exactly that.

Within a half hour Kim arrived in his truck, blowing the horn as he drove up. Mel pulled in right behind him and we all took off on foot through the woods. After a few hundred yards in silence, we arrived at the edge of the clearing.

"This"—Kim's baritone voice echoed off the trees as he held out his arms to encompass the field—"is where I would put my home." He turned to us and grinned. "I love the view."

"Nope," Mel and I said in unison. We laughed, and I let Mel continue. "We've talked about it, and we both want the house to be in the woods.

Kim chuckled and shook his head. "Well, I was sure you were going to have your own opinions, so I might as well adapt right now."

Kim is such an easy guy to be around, I thought as I led him through the woods. After only a brief acquaintance, he had a good relationship with both of us. I felt in a few weeks we would all be working together as one unit.

I showed Kim the places I liked, and he pointed out a few others I hadn't considered. He promised to return within the week to have another look. In the meantime he asked us to get started on the plans for the house so he could begin finding a sub-contractor for the excavation of the driveway and foundation. And he wanted to see the plans so he could give us an estimate on price.

"I'm going to fell the trees myself," I said. "So you don't have to hire anyone for that."

Kim lifted his eyes skyward and smiled. Then looking back at me, he laughed.

"Of course you are, and after all you're only sixty years old. This is going to be one entertaining venture." He turned away, shaking his head, and walked back to his truck. But he'd been laughing, and smiling. He wasn't making fun of me or us; he was enjoying us and we felt it. I looked at Mel and the silly grin on her face perfectly reflected my mood. Pure, utter joy.

"Mel," I said hours later as I dried the dinner plates and put them away. "I was sitting in the field today watching the light, and I had an idea. You could build your studio into the lower level of our home. With that slope, one side of the foundation can be at ground level. With French doors, and lots of windows on two sides of a walk-out foundation, you could have tons of natural light. Best of all," I went on, "it would have its own private entrance."

Mel turned off the faucet and looked at me with eyes that got wider and brighter as a picture formed in her mind. Beaming, she gave me a huge hug. "I never thought of that as an option, but I will now."

Back in the living room I pulled out the house plans. "What's next?"

The Closing

Mel was an Art Director for Rodale's American Woodworker Magazine. Her expertise was exploded views and other illustrations for books and magazines featuring projects that were designed to be built with wood. As the associate art director, she gained a great deal of expertise during those years. Enough so that when the magazine sold and moved to Minneapolis, she declined the offer to relocate. She also built her own art studio. These skills gave her the necessary ability to make architectural drawings for the building inspector.

I drove to her studio. It was time to work on the design of our house.

Hours passed as we labored with her computer drafting program. The final footprint laid out in front of us was twenty-eight feet wide by thirty-two feet long. Small and cozy, perfect for two. Originally I wanted an even smaller home, a cottage actually. Mel was conservative too, but we'd need this size home in order to make the rooms work in our favor. Kitchen, living room with cathedral ceiling, half bath, and my study on the first floor, along with two bedrooms, a full bath and laundry room upstairs. The ceilings on the second floor were roof high, which gave the house an open spacious feel. Small but not tiny. Perfect in comparison to the four-bedroom home I shared with Bob. It, too, was a two story house. Much larger rooms, big living room and dining room combined, two full bathrooms, and a large deck that swept three sides with its enchanting view. We needed space with three kids. That was no longer the case with only Mel and me plus our two large Maine Coon kitties.

We needed three copies of the drawings: a set for us, a set for Kim, and another set for John Marks, the zoning board commissioner. I met John when

I went to the Springfield Township Building the week before, inquiring about building permits. Tall and slim, like Kim, he was serious about his work, but smiled easily. Light brown hair and kind eyes. I liked him. It was his job to inspect the house at various stages of construction, keeping the township informed that we were maintaining the zoning codes. He was a by-the-book kind of guy.

According to John we needed floor plans for the interior of the house and a set of exterior elevation drawings in order for him to grant us a building permit.

Though Mel was confident she could draw up our blueprints without a problem, she was unsure how to accurately draw the land. On a hunch I called Bill, our soon-to-be neighbor. I knew he'd have a set of the sub-division blueprints left over from his project the year before.

He did. Now Mel needed to make sense of them.

It was hard work and it took Mel several weeks to complete the job. Her drawings needed to be accurate, and the house position needed to be accurate. Kim, Mel, and I agreed on the site where the ground faded away to the southeast. Now that the snow was gone, we were all eager to stake it out on the forest floor.

We met Kim at the land on a sunny Sunday morning in early March. He unpacked his surveying equipment and spread it out: tripod and transit level. After much scoping, adjusting, and moving an inch here, a foot there, he finished surveying and hammered thick stakes in the ground at the corners. I tied a string around each, connecting them to one another. Letting the twine cut across the middle to define the rooms, I finished with what looked as intricate as a cat's cradle. When the task was complete, Kim left us admiring our house of string.

I stared at it and said nothing for several minutes, hoping my eyes were deceiving me. Then I looked at Mel in horror. "It's too small!" I yelped. "What have we done wrong?"

It looked tiny. Very tiny. We must have made a gigantic error. Picking up a stick I drew lines in the dirt for the interior walls. Mel saw what I was doing, and picked up another twig to help. "It will never work within those dimensions," I said. "Shit, shit, shit." I pressed my knuckles to my mouth and bit them—hard. The pain steadied me. "Back to the drawing board?"

Mel put her hands in her pockets and looked at the outline. "I'll go back to the drawings and make sure our measurements are correct. I know they are."

"Is there time?" I asked. "We need the final plans for the closing on our construction loan at the end of next month."

"No problem."

My dad loved fooling around with measurements and I wished he was there to help. I remembered one summer day when Dad was asked to travel to a small lake nearby, and I went along. In front of the run-down cabin and falling-to-pieces dock stood a man of great girth wearing shiny black loafers. (With tassels, my dad announced later.) He wanted to purchase lumber to rebuild his dock, but had no idea how to measure the wood correctly. Obviously, he was not a local. It took dad ten minutes and we were back in the jeep headed for the mill. It still makes me smile.

After I calmed down, we returned to Mel's studio and poured over the plans until we came away bleary eyed, but confident that the house size we laid out in string on our land was correct.

In the process, while looking at the blueprints, Mel noticed something we had overlooked earlier. The blueprints were accurate, but we just didn't notice it. "Look at this," she said peering at me over the top of her reading glasses. "Not only does the land slope away toward the southeast, it also has a slight fade toward the west and the field. We only need a five-percent fade to place our septic system out there, and we have at least that much."

Steve had three lots for sale, and to expedite the selling of these he did a perk test on each one. Now the potential buyers already knew the lots had passed that hurdle. On all three lots the tests were done amongst the trees and very close to the road. Bill's lot was the first of those three going up the hill, then ours, and then the last lot next to us on the north side. I knew we would have to clear countless trees for the leach field area if we placed our entire system where the perk test was done. Positioning everything in the field was superior because no trees needed to be removed.

"That sounds great. I'll pay for the new perk test," I said, squinting at the blueprint. "It's another gift. Our woods need to stay in their virgin state. And I want our house in part to be hidden."

Mel nodded. "Yep."

We kept working on our design well into the late afternoon when my cell phone rang. It was Kim. "Who's going to draw up the final floor plans and elevation drawings?" he asked.

"It will be Mel,"

"No architect?" He sounded dubious.

"Nope, it will be Mel."

To make his feelings perfectly clear, Kim said, "Oh my God."

"Nope—just Mel."

I laughed at my little joke, but I'm not sure that Kim saw the humor.

The housing permit would be next; Mel would present the drawings to

John as soon as he was able to fit us into his busy spring schedule. We were hopeful.

———

Next came the closing on our construction loan, it was a nerve-wracking proposition. "Did you bring your check?" I asked for the third time in ten minutes on our way to the real estate attorney's office.

"I think so."

"What do you mean, you think so? Look again in the envelope on the floor in the back." I grumbled, groping around on the mat behind her seat.

"Well, I'm not as together as you are. It's early morning. I never do well at this time of day." She scowled at me sideways as she drove.

"Okay, I found it. I can't believe Kim isn't coming. He should be there."

"Why? He doesn't need to be. I wouldn't be there either if I didn't have to. I'd be asleep, or at least at home having more coffee."

I looked at her in dismay. "I can't believe you two. It's like you're brother and sister or something. You both think alike."

"Stop being nervous, this will be over soon."

I leaned my cheek against the passenger side window and watched the world rush past. Holding back tears, my stomach agitated with what felt like churning stones. I worried about the nagging issue of money, which would soon be disappearing. I felt secure and honest in my life now, more than ever before, but would I have enough money for the future? Whatever that held.

Bob allotted only so much money for the household expenses, mortgage payments, utilities and so on. The rest was sent to a credit union to save for our future and I was given no access to those funds. It was my job to handle the checkbook; Bob wanted no part of it. When it was time to pay the bills each month my hands shook and my heart pounded as I wrote each check. Always. I never had enough funds to meet our expenses and my mind worked overtime trying to figure out how we'd manage. Bob increased the monthly amount only twice in thirty-five years. I worked part time for a printing company to try and make up the difference and although that helped, we were still coming up short. If I mentioned that piece of information to him, he'd become angry, so I kept silent.

Bob was an engineer for AT&T Bell Labs. Even though he didn't get paid a lot of money, as utility companies were known for, there was enough to make paying bills more bearable for me if he wanted. But he didn't. When Bob wanted to purchase something he almost always used a credit card. Then I had that bill to pay as well. After a while the credit card bills were more than I could pay off at the end of each month. I knew I was in trouble. Several times I tried telling him we needed more in order to cover the charges he'd made, but his answer was always anger.

After five years I quit the print shop and went to work for the YMCA. Although it was part time, it paid a little more. I loved that job. I taught swimming and life guarded, getting up at five o'clock each morning to open the building. I made a little extra money by being the one willing to go in early.

Still, it was not enough. I swallowed my shame and asked my mom and dad for five thousand dollars to pay off the credit card bills. It was one of the hardest times of my life. They did give it to me, but my father wanted to have a talk with Bob. I said no. Dad didn't understand the anger issues involved. Four years later the same problem came up again. This time I went to Bob in total anguish. Shaking with fear I told him to increase the monthly expense amount, and he did. Not for a lot more money and not enough to cover all the bills, but more than I'd had. What a surprise and such a relief. But, still, those times were agonizing for me.

"I can't believe I'm going to go into debt for this much money on a home. I always said I wouldn't. I'll be owing money for the rest of my life," I grumbled.

"Most people owe on their homes," Mel said, placing her hand on my shoulder.

"Hmmm."

She had watched me struggle to pay bills over the last three years and knew how traumatized I was each time I sat at my desk. She hated how hard it was on me. "The important thing to remember is we will have the *perfect* home. It has been designed not to cost a lot of money to run. And, we will eat, sleep, and live with nature every day for the rest of our lives."

I nodded. I had made this decision with my heart, and I knew that usually served me well. Still, my stomach felt like a twisted knot and my heart ached as it always did under the stress of money.

———

Within a couple of hours, it was over. The closing was behind us and the land was ours. A new millennium and a fresh beginning. I knew I'd be building a new life now, as well as a new home. The thought of it was electrifying and believe it or not, I wished I might share this excitement with Bob. It didn't seem appropriate, but still, I wanted to. We had always shared the good things in our lives, and at times I still yearned for his company, longing for the beginning of what might eventually become a warm loving friendship. But I knew this wouldn't come for years, if ever.

Mom and Dad were not alive, but I could call my sister, Norma, and tell her about my remarkable day. I'd do that later in the evening when she wasn't working. She always gave me a profound sense of belonging. It was enough. I never wanted to burden my kids; they had their own lives to figure out.

———

We headed home letting the idea of being homeowners sink in. It was exciting. I looked around the rooms we had been living in for the past three years knowing our time there was ending. It was a cute home to rent, and the owners had done a nice job with a renovation. A very large kitchen, huge living room, half-bath along with a giant walk-in closet and entryway on the first floor, two bedrooms, another gigantic walk-in closet and a big sunny bathroom on the second floor. There even was an attic and a basement. We had more storage room than we knew what to do with. Living there for three years gave me plenty of room compared to my first small rental in Richlandtown. The farmhouse was nestled in a tiny valley and helped me feel the privacy I craved.

I felt ready to create different memories. Was it possible?

Yay for Chainsaws

As the morning dawned, I began my new life with our land. It was spring, a pristine spring day, so I drove to our property—our property!—to do a walking meditation through the woods. Toward the end of my stroll I realized that anything was possible now for me. In my opinion, life was all about effort. I gave this gift of effort as a mother, and in this present moment I wanted to make an effort for me. I now had a better understanding of myself, and a deeper awareness of the many limitations that were lifted from my marriage. I was stronger and felt as though I was no longer an embarrassment to my moral fiber, by finally doing work that mattered. Counseling and home-building.

For eight years I'd worked as a counselor, helping people discover answers to life's difficult situations. Our time together helped bring a balance to their world, and also to mine. A perfect harmony between old lives and new. Understanding the value of life's karmas is important to me, and I wanted to pass that on to those who were seeking a more spiritual path. Each and every call I answered hopefully gave strength and purpose to someone's life, and enriched mine as well.

I found a few sectioned tree trunks and turned them on end, took a wide board I'd brought with me and put it between the two. A table appeared. I had my cooler from the car with ice, drinks and food. The chairs and tools came next. In a month it would look cozy under a tarp, but for now it wasn't. Cold seeped into my bones.

With the sun came the warmth, followed by Mel around nine o'clock.

"Look what I've done," I said, waving my arm at the table. "Our home isn't even built yet and already we have furniture."

Mel grinned.

Sitting down, I made a list of what we were going to need first. At the top there were only two things required before we could start clearing trees for the driveway: chainsaws.

Purchasing one chainsaw for our new project was expensive; two seemed out of the question.

I called my younger son, Andy, who lived twenty-five minutes away in Allentown. Of my three kids, he was the one we called Mr. Band-Aid. He always kept our family stuck together, reminding me of my dad in many ways. The glass always half-full, living in happiness, and changing the negative into a positive. They both lived those principles.

"Hey Andy, I have a favor to ask."

"Ask away." I pictured him holding the phone between his ear and his shoulder, a serious expression on his face. He helped anyone who needed him, family or not.

"May I borrow one of your chainsaws for a couple of months? I know you have an older one of Dad's, and I can't afford to buy two."

"Absolutely."

"Okay. Be there in an hour."

While Mel drove to purchase our new chainsaw, I drove to Andy's for his. When I got there he had it ready, complete with a new container of gas/oil mixture. He lifted the chainsaw into my car, then turned and hugged me hard and long.

"Good luck, Mom." I loved him so much, and he was the epitome of effort. I guess some of what I tried to teach did rub off.

When I got back to the woods I took Andy's cover off the saw and reached for the rope, ready to bring it to life. On his chainsaw in large black marker letters were the words, "Go Mom Go!" My eyes stung with fresh tears.

Using a chainsaw was dangerous. You can't have any other focus, and that was tricky for me. For some reason, I always had deep thoughts when I used one. I had to keep telling myself to watch the blade and stay clear. Chainsaw work killed my back and I had to stop often, straightening my spine slowly and then sitting for a few minutes. Sweat poured down my face and I needed a cap to keep it from running into my eyes. Thank God I didn't do this for a living.

I was working hard when Mel pulled in. She took out the new saw, gassed it up and began cutting the smaller trees at the foundation site. There were larger ones also, but we started small. I needed to find peace before I took them down. Prior to cutting any large ones I shut the chainsaw off and sat with my back at their base. Mel joined me. We said a prayer and asked if they would lend themselves to the building of our new home, promising them a place within its walls. I would mill a portion of the wood, and the rest I'd burn for warmth during the winter. I think to this day their answer was "yes."

It was tough going in those early days. Mel joined me when she grabbed a spare minute. Soon piles of brush grew where the trees had been. Each morning I was stiff and sore, groaning every time I sat or stood up. I kept at the work with determination, thinking of my Dad and how physically hard he worked each day of his life. No wonder he wanted to retire to Florida and play golf.

As I worked with the chainsaw, alone with my thoughts in the buzzing of its motor, I realized we needed a tractor, and a cart to pull behind it was required, too, in order to haul brush to the field to burn. I'd already made a little path that wound through the woods and knew the tractor had to be small enough to negotiate it. I loved working hard outdoors each day, and my deepest anxieties from the divorce two years ago were becoming a thing of the past. What a contrast going from no control, to having complete control. When Mel stopped her saw to gas up, I mentioned the tractor and cart.

"That's so funny. I saw Bill as I drove up earlier and he told me about an equipment auction at the Kempton Fairgrounds. They're going; it's on Saturday, the sixth.

"It's kismet," I said. "Let's meet 'em there."

"Okay." We each pulled down our ear guards and got back to work.

When the Kempton auction arrived, I was in even more need of the tractor and cart. Piles of brush mounted around me each day, and I knew we'd never fit our house in the clearing unless we moved the cut brush out. Clearing the debris from the present, as well as the past.

Early that Saturday morning Mel and I drove to Kempton. There were hundreds of farm trucks in line waiting to get on to the grounds. I looked around as Mel drove my white '96 4-Runner, dubbed "Powder" because I loved naming objects, forward inches at a time. She often drove my car in the mornings if we went somewhere. Mel got car sick easily, but if she drove it helped.

"Every farmer in the area must be here," I said, scanning the crowd as we advanced a little.

"I've never seen anything like this," Mel said, gripping the steering wheel tighter.

After forty-five minutes we drove on to the grounds. I couldn't wait to explore the auction. I tried not to look like a wide-eyed tourist as I took it all in, but there was so much to see. The Amish, with their unshaven faces and dark pants, were buying plows, harrowing equipment, and hand tools, while the Mennonites were buying tractors. (Amish did not purchase engines, and Mennonites did.) Most of the men were in their farmer clothing: thick pants, canvas jackets, and boots. Mel and I were in jeans, sweatshirts, and sneakers.

I laughed and nudged Mel with my elbow. "We're an anomaly. Two women. They must think we're sightseers."

In my heart, I felt capable of making sound decisions at my first auction. I was calm and actually looked forward to the experience. As we walked around with the aroma of funnel cake in the air, I was amazed at the multitude of farm tractors, riding lawn mowers, and other equipment. The area was a blaze of color with John Deere green, Kubota orange, and Ford blue. Such a contrast to the black clothing of the Amish.

There were at least eighty tractors, all of them different in varying ways. Some were huge and some were smaller, but all of them seemed in good shape. I had no idea how to choose, so I hung back and watched. Dad always said, "If you don't know what to do, don't fake it. Listen, but do nothing until you're sure."

The farmers were loud, crowding around the auctioneer and his helpers. They appeared to be having fun, even if we were all standing in three inches of mud. I joined the group, Mel close behind. The throng moved from tractor to tractor. A woman, with an outsized name tag, Rebecca, and her helper started every engine as the auctioneer went through the lineup. We needed to hear the motors run before we made decisions on which one to purchase.

Rebecca took a large can of ether, used for its drying effect, and sprayed a healthy squirt directly into each carburetor, while her helper turned on the ignition. We moved down the line, listening to each motor. Spray. For some reason Mel and I always ended up beside her in the mist. Spray. Soon I got dizzy. Spray. Now I wasn't giving a damn if we bought anything or not. Spa—ray. Finally Mel pulled me aside and out of the crowd.

"I bet they spray so people will buy," I said, dissolving into giggles.

"You're stoned," Mel said, laughing so hard she was bent at the waist.

When I sobered up, we again headed to the crowd. I thought back to the smooth hum of my dad's forklift. I had driven it many times to load lumber onto his truck. I knew that sound. Its engine hummed and I compared that memory to these. With that resonance in mind, I managed to select a small blue Ford tractor complete with a mower deck. Outbidding five or six men, I proudly held my number high for the auctioneer to record. When I won, Mel and I jumped around smiling and laughing as if I'd just purchased a Mercedes.

As soon as I finished the last jump and whoop, a Mennonite farmer walked up to us and asked, "Would you like to sell the mower deck from the tractor?"

We didn't need a lawn mower, so I looked at Mel for confirmation and said, "Sure."

"Two hundred fifty enough?"

"You bet."

He reached in his pocket and gave me cash on the spot, slipped under my new tractor with his tools, and took the mower deck off. I stood watching with amazement. It took him all of five minutes. I was still holding his cash in my fist when I turned to Mel. "Yikes, that was fast. What just happened?"

"Not sure I get it either, but we'll use the money later to help pay our final bill. And to buy new sneakers because ours are drenched in mud"

Mel suggested we see what else the auction had for sale. We ended up buying five solid pine interior doors.

Once we paid for our items we met up with Bill and Heidi. They'd purchased some lumber and a few red and yellow ceramic flower pots. We had to get all our purchases home, but Bill had a small pickup truck and we had my SUV. We would figure out a way.

We ended up using a few pieces of the lumber Bill purchased as a ramp, then drove the tractor up and onto the bed of the truck. It barely fit between the wheel wells, but we inched it in.

I made two trips back and forth to Kempton in order to get the doors and lumber home, but by the end of the day it was done. I felt happy even though I was exhausted. When we were finished, I made sure everything was under cover except for the doors, while Mel made a fast trip to Neighbor's Home and Garden in Hellertown, five miles away. She purchased a trailer-cart, lifted it into her Ford SUV and brought it home. By the time she returned, I had everything put away and our clearing looked like a real woodsman's camp. Mel helped me bring the doors back to the farmhouse to store in one of the large closets.

On Sunday, I began to haul the brush from the driveway excavation out to the field. My tractor, which I dubbed 'Bluebie', was delightful and the new dark gray Rubbermaid trailer bouncing along behind looked adorable.

I had no idea how many trips to the field I would make, but it was looking to be hundreds at the very least. The new path was going to be well worn in no time.

Later that morning I stopped the tractor on the way back from the field, searching the area for flat stones. I found two that were large, not rectangular nor smooth and level, but later I wanted to purchase ones that were more compatible with what I had in mind. For now I put each of these stones on top of two very short logs. They were solid and didn't wobble.

Earlier in the week I visited Richland Feed Company, the local feed store. I loved the place. It was old with well-worn wooden floors and counters, smelling of corn and molasses. There was a cat sitting on top of the counter by the aged cash register, and I thought it a perfect setting for a cozy mystery. I bought two fifty-pound bags of cracked corn to use on the stone feeding stations I'd just built for the deer in our woods. I also purchased three bird feeders, stakes to mount them, and a fifty-pound bag of their best mixed bird seed.

I took out a sledge hammer and pounded the stakes into the ground to hold the bird feeders. The spring soil was soft and the stakes went in easily. I hung the feeders and filled them to the brim. Standing back I was proud to have fulfilled my promise to the birds and deer when I first walked this property. Tonight I'd call my daughter, Shelly, in California. She and her family loved hearing about my nature adventures and what I'd done to preserve the space for the animals. It had been a while since we'd talked, and I missed her.

I was getting stronger and my muscle soreness was fading with each new day. Covered with black and blue marks from stabilizing the chainsaw against my legs, I felt proud of the work I was doing.

Changing my life out of all recognition was beginning to be the norm these days.

Parting the Woods

Mel said the final plans were complete. I went with her to the studio, and we went over them one last time before submitting them to John.

"Here," she said, handing me the list of zoning regulations. "Make sure I didn't miss anything."

"Let's see. Distance to the property lines looks good. Septic system requires a five percent grade, so we're more than fine there once we get the perk test done, and we're not living on the land without an occupancy permit. Looks good to me." I handed the list back to her.

"Do we dare turn them in?"

"Guess we have to eventually; we can't start building otherwise. Hope he'll see us without an appointment."

Mel printed three copies; one for John, one for Kim, and one for us. We hopped in her car to deliver them. First stop was John's office.

Raw nerves bit at my fingers as we entered the township building and waited for John to see us. When he invited us into his office I introduced him to Mel. I felt a little intimidated, but Mel seemed fine.

"Let's take a look," John said, spreading the blueprints out on his desk. He was silent for several minutes as he looked them over, then nodded. "Nice work. No one does drawings themselves. You've managed to complete a set of fine-looking architectural drawings that are worthy of any draftsman I've known. Have you ever thought of becoming one?"

Mel just shook her head, her cheeks a little pink, but I knew she deserved the praise, for though we worked together on the floor plans of the interior, everything else was her design. I could only imagine the money Mel had saved us. She had spent hundreds of hours on those drawings. Her design and building experience together allowed us to set aside funds for other construction items. She had no idea how talented she was.

"Thanks, John," Mel said. She seemed uncomfortable in her own skin when other people praised her work, and always changed the subject if possible.

"Looks like you're ready to get started. Here's your permit. I'll stop by the property soon."

That night, after delivering Kim's set of prints, I put our building permit in our new "house folder." There wasn't much in it, but soon it would be overflowing. I spread our copy of the plans out on the living room rug and looked over Mel's handiwork. I loved the look of them and, despite our earlier fears, the house was not too small. Eli, our huge Maine Coon cat, and Toby, a smaller version, curled up on the pages and fell asleep.

"Hopefully you'll feel as comfortable in the house as you do on the blueprints," I said, kissing their soft heads.

We made changes to the plans as we went along with our project, adjusting the placement of the windows and doors while tweaking other small details. Each week we drove over to Kim's office and slipped Mel's new drawings under his door, trying to escape before he teased us.

Later he would call asking if he should throw the old ones out; I always said, "Yes." Then there was the sound of a groan, followed by a laugh. At least I thought it was a laugh.

By the second week of May, most of the trees were down and cut up into logs. Mel and I lifted those sixteen-inch pieces into the cart and dumped them on the north side of the field to split later when I rented a log-splitter. I was thankful I hadn't taken down any more trees—until Kim came to inspect my work.

"These trees are going to be a problem during the building process," Kim said, pointing to several that were close to the marked-off area.

I felt myself go pale, but Mel took it in stride. "No, they'll be fine. You'll need to be more careful."

"Nope," Kim crossed his arms across his chest and I knew he meant it. "You have to take them down." There was no choice but to remove most of them. Picking my battles, I argued for the ones we wanted to keep while promising to remove the others he had marked for death. Kim agreed to my compromise.

I went back to work with my chainsaw, clearing out trees for the driveway. Most of the leaves had not fully opened, which made the cutting much easier. In the midst of my several-day project, Kim hired Charlie Dietz, a local excavator, and brought him to the land. Charlie needed to see the property and the sites we'd chosen for the house and driveway. Kim approached us first, with Charlie a little behind. Turning off my chainsaw, I introduced myself. Mel turned her saw off too, and walked over.

Despite his seventy years, Charlie had a strong frame. His cap sat a little askew, but his height was the same as Kim's. Not heavy, but not thin either. He said little, nodding when I showed him what we'd done so far. He made one request. "It'd help me a lot if you'd leave the tree stumps two or three feet high," he said. "That way I'll be able to see them from my tractor as I dig the driveway."

"Sure," Mel said, her voice loud compared to his.

Finished with us, Charlie and Kim left together. As they walked away, I noticed Charlie scratch the back of his head, glance back at the two women standing with chain saws at their feet, and then speak to Kim. I overheard him say, "those two are some pair. I hope they hold up throughout the entire job."

Mid-May was right around the corner. Charlie was coming soon with his tractor, and the space for the driveway had to be cleared. Thank goodness for longer days. I used every hour, and needed Mel's help as well. Even though the actual tree removal took no time at all I still had to haul the brush to the field.

On weekdays I labored alone while Mel worked in her studio. Evenings I worked part-time with a local chiropractor whom everyone called Dr. Mary. I'd been there more than two years and loved my job. I took patients back to the exam rooms, did blood pressure checks, took history, and wrote what was needed in their chart.

My work with Dr. Mary was a balancing act between house building, versus the money I was bringing home.

———

I was alone on our land early one morning, meditating in the sun. When finished, I took yet another load of brush to the field and heard a truck coming up our road. As the truck's sound grew louder, I looked up and saw Charlie waving out his window. His dump truck was filled with crushed stone and was towing a trailer with his bulldozer on it. He motioned for me to come over. I ran to him, smiling wide as I spoke.

"Are you here to dig the driveway?" I asked. My voice sounded loud in my ears. I'd forgotten to remove my ear protection.

"Yup," he said, blushing as he got out of the truck. I dug deep into my jeans pocket for my cell phone and called Mel.

She answered on the first ring. "Okay, I'll be right over."

I watched Charlie unload the huge dozer and then stood back in the trees. Within minutes he had dug out a quarter of the driveway. I leaned against a low limb to watch, tears gathering in my eyes. At last something definitive was happening on our property— something permanent. This land would never be the same. I felt a little sad. We were destroying part of the past to make way for an exciting future. I prayed that no harm would come to the creatures on this land with the changes we were making.

Charlie stopped his bulldozer and motioned me over. "That tree might be a problem for some of the larger trucks." He pointed at the lovely oak toward the end of the driveway, the one that I said I didn't have the heart to bring down. It was huge, covering the driveway with its branches. Its job was to provide protection and give shade. I couldn't imagine cutting it down. I bit my lip, hoping I could spare its life.

"But I'll be fine." Charlie winked and nodded. *If he could negotiate it with his huge machinery, why take it down?*

Mel walked in from the street as Charlie started up the bulldozer. "He's not thinking of making you take down that old oak, is he?"

"No," I said, brushing away my tears with the sleeve of my sweatshirt. For a woman who professes to be strong both physically and emotionally, I certainly cried easily these days. Mom used to tell me, "No tears, save them for when you're alone." I was never sure why, but I tried to do what I was told. When I was older I realized that tears were an embarrassment for Mom. She wanted no part of being less than the image she portrayed, which was strength and competence.

"Good." Mel crossed her arms over her chest. "You want it to stay, and Charlie can work around it. End of discussion. It stays."

It was good Mel arrived when she did because bulldozing the entire driveway took no time at all. By mid-morning Charlie was finished, and I was happy she didn't miss it. But eventually she had to go back to the studio. Charlie worked the rest of the day trucking in load after load of rock, filling in the foot-deep trench, then grading it to his satisfaction. By the end of the day we had a gravel driveway.

Charlie climbed off the dozer and walked over. "I'll be back tomorrow morning to begin the excavation of your foundation."

"I'll be here, Charlie."

I stood silently watching him leave. The driveway looked like it had always been there, when just a few hours previous it had been filled with trees and brush. So much happened on this one spring day. It looked surreal in the late afternoon sun as I walked back to my car. I wanted to test the new driveway. Driving up it for the first time through the forest took my breath away. I parked, went to the chairs, and drank a cup of water while watching the sun work its way down over the field. Mel joined me after leaving work. She wanted to test it out, too.

Suddenly, a doe came limping up the path toward the feeding stations. She had an injured leg that had healed, and though she hobbled, she didn't look as if she were in pain. Either she had been hit by a car or she'd been shot by a hunter. Still she made the effort to eat and survive. The corn I placed there was cracked and small, and as she ate I could hear her munching from a hundred yards away.

Like the doe, I was pushing forward despite the healed-over injuries of the past. Mom had once said, "You're known by the company you keep." I believed that and I felt great holding hands with nature. It was fine friendship for me.

I turned to Mel. "I want to stay here for the night," I said in a low tone so as not to disturb the doe. "I never want to leave."

Mel shook her head, "You have no sleeping bag and it still gets cold at night. Besides, remember the zoning regulations? No living here without an occupancy permit."

Turning back to the doe, I wished that, like her, I could sleep on the mossy forest floor. I yawned. "I'm too tired anyway. Let's go for Chinese takeout and eat dinner here before we head for the farmhouse."

Mel agreed, and that evening we ate dinner by candlelight at the end of our new driveway. It felt like home.

Digging Down

I drove up the newly excavated driveway early on Friday, still amazed I no longer had to park on the road. With coffee in hand, I sat in my woodsman's camp and enjoyed nature at its best—first thing in the morning. I'll always remember the chill of that early spring day, hazelnut-scented steam warming my face. I felt lifted to a place beyond myself, the feeling of softness, peace, and spiritual love. This property had "soul effect."

"I am going to build a home this summer," I said to the forest. Buds were beginning to open on the trees beside me and the underbrush was filling in. I took my coffee and headed down the driveway. I wanted to look again at the tree that Charlie thought might be an issue. Charlie was our excavator that Kim hired. Older and very kind, I liked him immediately.

Standing away from it, I bent my head back to see the topmost branches as they waved in the breeze. The sky above looked as clear as the lake Mel and I had visited when we were trying to find a builder. I rested my hand on its rough bark, knowing I'd never destroy it. A red-tailed hawk circled, as if to protect. There had to be a way for trucks and other large vehicles to get around. Whatever was necessary, I'd make it happen. If I cleared the bushes and smaller trees surrounding it, more space would open up and I'd spare the oak.

I walked back to grab my chainsaw and there, sitting on the stones, was a golden feather. In my heart I knew it was a keepsake, dropped there by the hawk. It was a memento for leaving the trees here for them to nest in, rest in, and raise their young. *Leave the tree alone.*

While I was widening the driveway, Charlie drove up the street. This time his truck had a backhoe on the trailer. I reached in my pocket for my cell phone and called Mel. "The earth is about to part."

"Be right there."

Mel arrived twenty minutes later as Charlie unloaded the backhoe. We sat at the camp and watched him work his magic. It was thrilling. Again, I wished my Dad was beside me.

I held my breath as the backhoe approached the area we had staked out, hoping nothing would prevent us from placing the house there. I winced as the huge scoop pierced the ground and returned full of dirt and small rocks. The earth smelled rich and I took in a deep breath.

Trees around me stood strong, and I felt as if the land were designed to accommodate our house. Thankfully, no huge boulders turned up within the boundaries of the foundation. I sat transfixed watching Charlie dig the entire ten-foot deep crater, amazed in late afternoon when he left. He promised to return the following week to grade the driveway a little more.

Next step was the masons. They would set the cement footers, lay the block foundation walls, and add openings for the windows and door in Mel's proposed studio walk-out. Things were happening faster now. w

After working that evening at Dr. Mary's, I came back to our land, spending a moment or two in nature before driving over to meet with Mel and Kim. I had a hard time staying away.

This meeting was important. Mel and I had plans to go to a construction auction soon, and we needed the dimensions of every window so we would know what to buy. Kim was not in the loop on our auction plans and we needed to include him.

When I arrived, Mel was still in her car waiting for me. The serenity I gained from our land was gone, so I took in a deep breath to calm myself. I've had that feeling before. When I was a kid I owned a horse. It was an awesome way to grow up. I loved the horse barn my dad built for me, and slept in the hay bin most nights during the summers. It was where I felt at peace. Leaving the gentleness of my horse and the tranquility of the barn to do other things, I always felt a change in my innermost self. I felt that way now. Away from all things safe.

We settled in Kim's office and Mel spoke. "Kim," she said, folding her hands on his desk. "Sal and I decided we're going to a construction auction to save money on our windows and doors. We want to know exactly what you need before we leave."

Kim raised his eyebrows, serious for once rather than amused. He made me think of Bob and my stomach tightened. *Please don't get angry.*

"Why would you do that? Construction auctions are for serious professionals. You might pay entirely too much for an inferior product with no way of recouping your money. I don't even go to them, it's too risky." He shook his head. "I'd recommend using my contractor's discount. Buying from a reputable dealer."

I looked to Mel, suddenly uncertain as I had been so many other times in my life. So far Kim had accepted our ideas every step of the way. If he thought going to building auctions was a bad idea, who were we to disagree? I was a pushover, but apparently Mel felt differently.

"No, we're going," she said, nodding to emphasize the point. "Our church was built with windows, doors, and flooring from construction auctions. They saved a ton of money and the quality was better than what we originally could have afforded."

I held my breath while Kim digested this new information. He frowned. "But the materials were used, right? New products aren't sold there. You might not be as lucky."

"No," I said quickly. "We checked. They sell exterior and interior solid wooden doors, Andersen windows of all sizes and shapes, and wood and tile flooring." I moved to the edge of my chair. "Everything's brand new and in its original box."

"They have an auction every month in Hanover," Mel continued. "There's one this coming weekend and we're going."

Kim looked at us long and hard. "I know where Hanover is, and it's a long way from here." He sighed and shrugged. "Oh what the hell, go take a look at what they are offering. Get back to me with the details." I clapped my hands, but Kim held up a finger in warning. "Do not buy anything until you talk with me," he said, arching a brow as if he were lecturing children about to cross the street for the first time.

The auction was Saturday, but there was a preview on Friday, and I didn't have to work. Perfect. Making two round trips on successive days would be time-consuming, but it might be well worth it. And Kim was right. We did need to check out everything with him before plunking our money down, and this would give us a chance to do so.

———

Rising at dawn the following morning, I raced over to the property. I felt settled once I was there. Sitting by the foundation, I knew this exact space was designed for the porch. I loved screened porches. Dad did too. It was a must in New England if you wanted to be outside on a summer's evening. I didn't have one growing up, but we often dreamed of it.

For now I was more than satisfied that we had a foundation hole, a driveway, four chairs and a cooler. Tools were tucked under a tarp, and our only table was made of tree stumps. But soon a house would be built. Mel and I were going to spend the rest of our lives on this land, growing closer

I went to refill the bird feeders and throw some corn on the feeding stations before Charlie arrived. Walking softly down the path toward the field, I listened to the wildlife around me. There was a lot of bird song. One of the small barberry bushes along the fence row was waving at me. It was quiet, no wind anywhere and none of the trees were moving an inch, but this one little bush was swaying with some unheard music. *Lovely.* My favorite thing about living in nature is the rare sightings I am privileged to view. Small miracles to remind me there is a larger landscape here than the one I see. Perhaps to some they don't seem important, but they ground me, bringing depth and greater quality to my life.

It might have been easy to balk at building a new home with Mel. After all, mom warned me not to make a fool of myself. *Image is everything*, was one of her mantras and I always felt that phrase kept me from being my true self. I never agreed with her. What's in the lesson of never challenging yourself? At sixty years old, I had a lot of longing inside to bring out. I felt this was the perfect time to do that. I found if I let go, things happen in the right way, at the right time. If I allowed them, rather than directed them, that is. Right now, everything in me was moving forward on its own.

Suddenly, I was greeted by the sound of a bulldozer. Waving, I hustled along the path and Charlie turned off the engine.

"Hi," Charlie said climbing down. He walked over to the arm of the nearby chair and picked up a Styrofoam cup. "Here, bought this for you."

He handed the coffee over. "How sweet is that," I said a shyly. Charlie was smoothing out some of the large dirt piles surrounding the house area.

I sipped my drink, watching him. He'd come miles away from the man who scratched his head in surprise at meeting Mel and me. He has warmed up to the idea of working with two women, and I certainly was enjoying my time with him. He reminded me of an uncle on my dad's side, Oliver. He, too, sat on a bulldozer most days. Oliver worked hard, loved nature, and never charged enough money for the work he did. He drove his pickup twenty miles out of the way on many days, just to get six loaves of day-old bread from the store in order to feed the geese at a nearby lake. I loved that about him.

Later that morning I went to look at wood stoves. There were two places within twenty miles, Wood Heat in Pleasant Valley, and Grates & Grills in Dublin. I'd been researching online and was interested in two models of Vermont Castings: the Defiant and the Encore. I liked the Encore a bit better, but needed to physically see them before placing an order.

I went to Wood Heat, but they didn't have any Vermont Castings. Note to self: next time, call before making the drive. I went on to Dublin.

This business must have been here for at least fifty years, I thought as I looked at the aged storefront of Grates & Grills. The plate glass windows were original, and the door appeared decades old. I put my weight against it and walked in. The room closest to the storefront window was filled with propane stoves for outdoor grilling, so I continued to look around. Fireplace screens, andirons, and wood holders filled another space, but there, in the very back room, sat the row of Vermont Castings Wood Stoves. They were striking. Immediately I pictured one in our home, and I flagged down one of the salesmen to ask what size I needed.

"I have two models that will work for you," he said after I gave him the square footage of our house. "The Encore and the Defiant." Satisfaction bubbled up inside me, exactly what my research had shown. It was another validation of my ability to make sound decisions on important matters—and staying warm all winter was important. I'd avoided making big decisions for so long—out of fear of being wrong, fear of Bob's anger, fear of looking bad—that it would take time to regain confidence in this realm, but I was determined to do it. This was the moment that I keenly felt the cost of prior unconscious decisions made earlier in my marriage. Like not choosing to decide on anything anymore, and how the result of that choice had influenced so much of the rest of my life.

My next decision was clear: the Encore would be perfect. It came in a few rich colors, including forest green enamel that was ideal for the southwest corner of the living room. The green cost a bit more than flat black, but it was worth the price.

I let the salesman know it might take several months before picking it up and he promised to hold it for me. "Just give me a week's notice before you want it."

"No problem."

I called Mel from the car as I drove back to the land. I had stopped and picked up an egg sandwich and a coffee for Charlie. As a vegetarian I didn't consume eggs, but I was fine with anyone else's choice of diet. I knew both Charlie and Kim often purchased these sandwiches at a nearby café, and I wanted to surprise him with one.

I had to smile as I drove around the old oak. In defending its beauty I felt as if I'd preserved part of myself as well.

I was surprised how well I was working with Kim and Charlie. It wasn't just Bob's anger and distain that had eroded the trust I'd had in working with men. I had also been brutalized by another man.

When I was in my early forties, I was raped. It happened in our small town, in back of the library parking lot, a place where everyone was supposed to feel safe. My rape was horrific. I exchanged blows and kicks with my attacker, fighting with all my strength against a stronger oppressor, finally losing the battle and falling to the ground like a paper Mache doll. He was vicious and cruel. I battle it still. Dark lonely nights. *Tears.* Hyper vigilance. *Tears.* Guilt and shame. *Tears.* Courage. And *tears.* Spending the rest of my life trying to find myself within this despair, yet yearning to do something that mattered in this world.

I have only one sister; four years older than me. Her love and commitment to me was fierce and there were times that my survival hung on her protection. We are very different as women, but our devotion to one another was infinite. She listened to my rage and helped me to understand my grief. When I phoned, she answered. Always. Being in the depths of despair during this period of my life she held my head above water, even when I wanted it to go under for the last time. An awesome sister.

I had a responsibility to my daughter, and her daughter, as well as to my son's daughters. Perhaps it was time to sit them down and tell them my experience, so they would be more aware of the dangers in life. Rape changed who I was as a woman, never again being fully relaxed, and moving forward took all the guts and strength I had in me. *I will never forget, but I need not always remember.* Five grueling years with a therapist. Weekly sessions, giving me tools to help embrace the woman I longed to be. Strong with a sense of self. The chasm between loneliness and joy is deep. I immersed myself in the natural world to build upon this healing, and that's where I chose to live out the rest of my life. So many see nothing in nature, but it would be a septic existence for me to separate myself from it.

Often a rape victim hides behind walls of silence for years following the incident, sometimes forever. Being heard, even in something as small as saving a tree, gave me back some of the power that was taken away. That ultimate violation can only be repaired by our own selves, and I struggled to keep moving forward with my own voice every day. I felt like a hero.

I walked over to Charlie and handed him the sandwich. He climbed off the dozer and we sat together. He took a bite and a sip of coffee and then turned my way. "You need an outbuilding here on your land. All these tools need to be locked away at night. Putting them under a tarp is risky." He took another bite. "There's been a theft problem in this area lately. People have been stealing equipment and lumber from home building sites. It might help to buy a few 'Keep Out' signs too."

"Good idea," I agreed. "Thanks for the advice."

Now I had another purchase to consider, I hadn't seen this one coming. With the recent wood stove, tools, and chainsaw purchases, I was having budgetary concerns. I didn't want to lose our tools though; they would be expensive to replace. And it wasn't practical to bring them home each night. The concern in Charlie's voice was enough for me. He had worked and lived in this area all his life. I believed him.

Charlie went back to work and I called Mel. I didn't want to discuss finances over the phone so I asked her to come over to the land. She agreed to take a lunch break and said she'd be there in twenty minutes. While I waited for her to arrive, I calculated how much we were spending on gas driving back and forth between the farmhouse and the land. Sometimes it was several times a day just to get the additional tools we needed. An outbuilding would help us cut down on our trips with the extra storage it provided. That idea brought other things to mind, but I wasn't ready to share them yet.

When Mel arrived, we walked around looking at where we might put an outbuilding. "Charlie's right, we need to have this outbuilding."

"I think it should go next to the path."

"Why?"

"I plan to use it for bird seed and corn, along with our tools. It will be between the house and the field, ideal for our needs. We can put the tractor in there too; it's the last thing we want to lose."

Mel nodded. "That sounds like a good plan, but I hate having to spend more money."

"Me, too." I chewed my lip. "Do we have time to build a shed or should we just purchase one already constructed?"

"Let's buy. I don't have time to build anything right now. I'll do an online search. We can look at our options tonight after you get back from work."

"Okay." I called Charlie and left him a message. We were getting a shed.

Mel left for the studio, and I went home to change into my work uniform.

<hr />

When my shift was over, I headed back for an evening of research. We looked over the pamphlets Mel printed out as we ate a late dinner. One shed stood out above the rest. The name of the builder was Stoltzfuss Structures. Amish for sure. They are good carpenters, so I knew we were in good hands. We decided on a custom structure—a rectangular shed twelve-by-eighteen feet, with two windows and a large double door in front. It seemed we would have a building on our land sooner than we anticipated.

Mel and I went to bed. Sleep kept its distance as I recalled the night I told Bob about the rape. I didn't feel like a hero back then. "Bob," I said, walking toward his chair in the living room. "You once asked me what happened to my face when you came home from that business trip to Boston?

I lied when I told you I was hit by a car door that opened as I walked by."

Bob looked up at me. "What was the truth then?"

Scared to death, I answered. "I was hit with a metal weapon of some sort, and then raped. I kicked and punched for all I was worth, but it didn't help. I needed to tell you this because I want you to know everything that happened to me. I'm a victim."

He stood, his face angry and red. "How many times have I told you that you're too friendly? Hugging everyone all the time."

"That is not why men rape. And I don't hug all the time. Only friends of ours."

"Doesn't matter. It's done," he said angrily.

I felt abused all over again, mad as hell, and sad. "Well, I'm going to a therapist to help me get though this. It might be good if you came along with me. I think we both need support."

"Not a chance. I don't believe in shrinks. They're expensive. You better not be spending any of my money on one. I'll get through my part on my own. End of conversation. Let's go to bed, things always feel better in the morning."

"I'm going to NOVA. It's free."

"Whatever."

I hung my head in shame and cried myself to sleep after being emotionally spent from that short conversation. Working at the YMCA was my salvation. When I started having emotional problems associated with my rape, the head of the aquatic department, along with the executive director of the Y, helped me seek assistance from The Network of Victim Assistance. In fact, the aquatic director went along with me for my first appointment. NOVA was located in Doylestown, and was free. There I was counseled for two years, got my feet on the ground, and then was placed with well-known local psychologist, Dr. Barbara Keene. She was extraordinary and brought me back from despair with a gentle and caring love.

For years I had stayed silent, and Dr. Keane helped me understand that there is a fine line between privacy and secrecy. Unhealthy walls are built with secrecy and they eventually isolate you. In order to honor myself, I had to speak the truth. It took constant work, but I've realized it was the key to living a good honest life. Telling Bob what happened to me on that fateful evening helped me to know I was walking my talk.

Growing Into Myself

I woke during the night to the sound of thunder. It was raining, Spring showers, but not hard enough to waken me fully. Dozing, I fell into a thoughtful space and felt comforted as I thought of the injured doe on our land. Both the deer and I were struggling less these days, and we kept going forward.

The next moment my room was filled with light, and I sat up straight in bed. Dawn. Disoriented, I wondered if I was doing the sensible thing for my life. I felt at risk and didn't have much money, yet here I was spending a lot of what I had on a new home. I felt strange this morning and a little stupid. Shaking off the fatigue I forced my eyes to open wider.

Time to hurry back and see if Charlie needed help with anything. When I got there the bulldozer was gone. I found a note from him held on top of the cooler by a rock. *I'm finished. Be back later today with stones for the shed's foundation.*

Standing at the site of the old perk test, I studied the fifteen or twenty trees whose lives would be lost if we put our septic there. The field was a better place for the entire system, even though it might cost up to four hundred dollars more to do another perk. I moved out from the woods onto the street and looked up toward the house excavation. I loved the way the forest stood, shielding our home from passing cars. If we let those twenty trees stand, summer foliage would take care of my privacy concerns. I still felt the need to shelter myself after the rape, even though it was long ago. Remaining silent for all those years kept me trapped inside myself. Fear can be a forever thing.

I drove to Home Depot for heavy plastic rolls, to go under the crushed stone for the shed site. Mel said it would help keep moisture off the wooden floor, making it last longer. *Good for her to know this.*

When I came back I went to work dragging stones and other debris from the shed's foundation area. I raked and filled the cart behind Bluebie many times. It all looked good.

By mid-afternoon Charlie arrived. His smaller truck was filled with crushed stone. I walked over to greet him.

"This is just what you'll need," he said leaning his head out the window. "Where do you want it?" I showed him the site for the shed and he dumped the load close by.

I looked at Charlie's stone, then the area for the shed. The ground was smooth enough after I snipped off any roots that were sticking up, so I unrolled the plastic spreading it carefully to the markers that defined the edges of its foundation. On each corner I put one shovel full of crushed stone to hold the sheet in place.

I wanted to wait for Mel, rather than shovel the stone myself. Together we could do it in half the time, neither of us getting blisters. Or so I hoped.

With an hour or more before Mel was due to arrive, I tackled the remaining brush piles from the shed area and dragged them to the field. The few logs from this project were taken to the wood pile. Standing back, I assessed the mountainous heap. I made a mental note to rent a log splitter so we would not be cold come winter.

Mel was late. I took one of the chairs from my camp and dragged it down to the walk-out end of our dug-out basement and went inside. I sat in the middle and looked up at the dirt walls, noticing the variation of soil color from the rim to its depth of the ground below. I felt small and insignificant. It was quiet in the early evening, and I thought of the quote by John D. Rockefeller. "The poorest man in the world is he who has nothing but money." Personally, I felt rich in my heart. I didn't need much, only enough to pay my bills. As anyone could see, this home was going to be small. But neither Mel nor I felt greedy in our search for this land or our house. This little corner would be enough.

I heard a car coming up the driveway and soon saw Mel's head peeking down at me from above. She was holding a sign that said Private Property and joined me in the basement. I took her picture with the sign as she stood there, then we brought it to the end of the driveway and nailed it to a tree, we didn't want anyone coming up to the house in our absence. I thought of the lame doe again and hoped the sign would help protect her as well.

It only took fifteen minutes to confirm the shed's measurements for the third and final time. As early evening entered our woods, we spread crushed stone on the plastic ground cover. Half the time with Mel, and half the blisters.

We said goodbye to the shed and house foundations, then headed home for the night. Again, I hated to leave and waited anxiously for the day when I could stay on the land. During dinner we looked over our drawings, but really, there was no need. I knew them by heart.

Later, in the shower, I lingered under its spray then went to bed early. Often now it was time to rest, but not time to sleep. I tossed and turned into the wee hours; perhaps it was the upcoming auction or the thrill of the completed foundation. Regardless, my spirit was alive. It was a sign of growth. I had noticed I worried less about what others thought of me and what I did. I took that as a good sign. I was liberated from being told what to do all the time, and now I felt the freedom that comes with that release.

My thirty-five year marriage was tattered and worn out by its end, and I could no longer meet Bob's expectations. He had a rough childhood. His parents were hard on their son, and soft toward their daughter. Bob was required to work after school each day and on Saturdays, never having a chance to compete in high school sports or other activities with his friends. As a result, he never felt the joy or freedom of youth. He carried a lot of baggage with him to our marriage and it left him angry and unhappy a good part of the time. I had anticipated that my married life would be much like my parents. True partners, each devoted to the other. No anger or selfishness, only love. I was wrong to make comparisons. As a young woman it was hard to understand how difficult life could be. This understanding came later.

I imagined our life together as happy, but my joy gradually disappeared. I asked Bob again to consider counseling, but he said no, so I kept going forward regardless of his decisions. I remembered a conversation we had after dinner one evening when Bob was mellow from fine wine and a delicious meal. The discussion was on therapy. He said he'd talked with other men at work and they all agreed that once your wife goes into counseling, your marriage is over. He wanted no part of analysis, and hated that I was doing it. I felt devastated.

I was afraid of Bob's anger. He directed it at me, even though I understand now that I wasn't the cause of it. I didn't know how to help him and I'm afraid I didn't learn how to handle it very well. My parents were never irate at one another; this was all new to me. Bob's anger never turned physical, but it affected me just as much. I found words hurt, sometimes more than fists. And silence was worse. Pretend and smile, cry behind closed doors. That was the message from my mother all the years of my life at home, and now it confused me. I wondered about its significance. What had happened in her life that I was unaware of?

My needs were trivialized, and I felt the fool for asking. I wanted to continue my education, but Bob thought it a waste of time and *his* money. I wanted to continue my skiing and golf enjoyment, but Bob didn't want me away from home. I wanted to start a newsletter for abused women, but Bob would not support it or allow me to take any household funds for the project. I stayed in silence because I didn't have the strength to do battle. And when I tried, I always caved in to his anger.

Many nights I lay awake knowing my life had to change, but lacking the necessary courage to walk away. Finding ways of keeping my own spark alive, I monitored university courses during the day, Psychology and Social Behavior, mostly, never telling Bob or our kids. I didn't have money to take the courses for credit, but I craved knowledge beyond my two-year college degree. I bartered lessons with a golf pro by working at the course for a few hours, and played there as often as possible. I was good at this sport too, and the pro thought I had enough natural talent and ability to take me to the WPGA if I practiced a lot. My dad thought so too, but I never had the chance to find out. You have to have someone to encourage your passion and support it in order to accomplish a skill. Playing golf in women's golf leagues once a week was all I managed. Instead, I felt crushed and too scared to approach Bob again.

Fear can defeat life. It begins in your mind and you can feel yourself weakening a little more each day. Hope and trust slither away like a snake. I fought hard, but didn't know how to win the battle. I became the architect of my own pain.

Thinking back on who I had been just five years ago, and comparing that person to who I had become, I barely recognized myself. I still had sleepless nights, but now they were the result of excitement, not fear. On the one hand, I was my same old self, and on the other, I was unrecognizable.

Preview Day

Mel and I woke with the birds on that Friday morning, and were soon on our way to preview the items for our first construction auction. The day felt memorable. We had a two-hour drive to Hanover, so there was plenty of time to drink coffee and work out our plan for the day. Tomorrow, we would head back to learn how it all worked and do some bidding. It was very exciting. Our cell phones were charged and Kim had promised to turn his on so calls might be exchanged if we needed answers to our questions.

We arrived. The warehouse was aged and vast, surrounded by hundreds of vehicles. Mel and I certainly were not the only ones doing this. We gave each other a quick hug and together we went forward, our drawings in hand. Entering, we stopped dead in our tracks. I stared, Mel stared, and then the crowd pushed us forward. If they hadn't, we'd still be standing there.

Thousands of building materials were stacked everywhere within those walls. Thousands.

"Oh my God," I exclaimed, feeling my knees weaken.

Mel looked toward me with eyes that were huge, but eager. "We can do this, Sal. Come on, it'll be something new and fun."

We began with the right side of the massive building. There were easily fifty exterior double patio doors lining the walls and standing next to them were another fifty single exterior doors. Then I lost count. I started searching for something we might like, but I felt overwhelmed.

"How do we do this?" I asked Mel, giggling nervously.

"Not sure, but it's not rocket science. If these guys can do it, we can too."

Both of us laughed as we walked down the aisles. It was a good thing we had all day, because it was going to take every moment of it. After an hour we began to better understand how the auction would work. First was organization, all like items together; doors, windows, flooring, kitchen cabinets, etc. With everything sectioned out we visualized the auctioneers going first to one section, and then the next and so on. Once we got our bearings, we started with a search for windows and interior doors.

Never had I seen so many different brands and varieties of windows in one place. At least a thousand or more were standing on end, row after row. We walked to the section of Andersen Windows and realized we needed to pick the exterior color we favored. White, Sandtone, or Terratone. We fell in love with the Terratone, a shade darker than the Sandtone.

"Come look in this section, Mel. There are larger windows here in Terratone."

Mel took the tape measure off her belt and measured them, and then looked at our plans.

"Too big. Damn it."

I broadened my gaze and my heart thumped as I looked around for others. I turned back and found Mel sitting back by those same large windows looking at the floor plans with her phone held tight to her ear. I scurried back to listen.

She sounded excited. "Hi Kim, we found plenty of windows, but they're not the same size as on our plans. Let me give you the new measurements." She gave the numbers to Kim and waited a few minutes.

"Wonderful, Kim, that's perfect. Don't worry, I know, only Andersen and Velux." She was grinning widely.

"He can make those windows fit," she said chewing on her bottom lip while scanning our drawings again. "They are slightly larger than the ones we had planned, but they will work. We need to see how many of this size they have for sale. Oh, Kim will only let us buy two brands of skylights if we see any."

"Okay."

Off we went to get a count. We found ten windows of the new dimensions and color, ideal for what we needed. Moments later we found two slightly smaller windows, perfect for the bathrooms. I was settling down now and beginning to have fun.

Our next job was to find kitchen windows. We found one set of casements we liked, so those went on the list. Casements were good as they winded out by a small handle. Not having to lean over the kitchen table and push the windows up would be nice. Then I searched for my study. One of the ten would go on the north side, but I needed a different size to go above my desk. Something that was more shallow and wider. Looking around, I tripped and fell over a box that held the exact ones I had in mind. Picking myself up off the floor, I muttered, "Thank you, God."

Our list for bidding tomorrow was getting longer. We had all the windows we wanted to purchase marked down on paper and now the search was on to see if they had any skylights. An auction employee told us they would be at the rear of the building on the left. We walked to the back wall, turned left and searched until we found them. One was very large and ideal. I loved it, and had to have it for my bedroom. There were a couple others, too, but this one was special. And it was a Velux, one of the two brands that Kim recommended. Kim said that Anderson and Velux were two of the brands that didn't leak. No problem there. No leaks.

Windows accomplished, we set off to the interior door area. We already had five from that first equipment auction. They were gorgeous, but we needed more for the closets, my study, and the pantry. There were so many to choose from that it became fun. Each door was solid pine and stunning. Mel and I made our choices and added them to the list.

By three o'clock, I was freezing. It was only fifty degrees outside and I didn't have the right clothes on for the unheated warehouse.

"Tomorrow I'm going to dress warmer and wear my lined hiking boots," I said rubbing my hands up and down my arms. Time for a break. I sat on some of the boxes around us. It felt good to catch my breath and calm down a little.

I watched the crowd move past. Most of the men looked like contractors, with architectural drawings rolled up under their arms and tape measures in their hands. So far, we hadn't attracted too much attention.

Mel leaned toward me. "Have you noticed that we are almost the only women in this place?"

I looked around and raised my eyebrows. "You're right. I hadn't noticed." Usually I felt intimidated. Not this time.

After a few minutes rest we went to the left side of the warehouse which held the flooring materials. We looked at various hardwoods and agreed on one that would look nice throughout the house because of its golden hue. It went on the list. Tile for the bathrooms was next, and they had a multitude of choices. Despite the variety of colors and sizes, we each picked the terracotta tile. It went on the list.

My dad spent years cutting hardwood flooring from his mill. The random width oak we had in our home gave testimony to his experience. I wished he were still alive so I could use his lumber. I have saved one three-inch thick, twelve-inch wide, three-foot long, slab of thick maple that he gave me years ago. I will use it for a book shelf in my home, Dad, I promise. Dad gave a stack of his pine to Bob and me to finish the basement of our home.

When I left, Bob gave it to his nephew. It was a selfish and mean thing to do to me. I was saddened and angry. I'd love to have had it for my home.

Hours flew by. Once we got to the car and started back I realized how hungry I was. I hadn't eaten all day. Fortunately, I had packed a sandwich for each of us, but before I ate I called Kim.

"Hi," I said a little cautiously. "We're just leaving the warehouse and are on our way home. It should be about two hours until we can get to your office. Hope that's okay?"

He laughed and said, "It's fine. I'll wait. I'm at my desk looking at the sub-contractor list. See ya soon."

"He's waiting for us," I said to Mel.

"Good."

I ate in silence, lost in my own thoughts. I felt exhilarated and compared it to my old self, my old life. Mel had stood behind me for years with her compassion and caring. I loved her. She gave me confidence in myself by supporting any venture I undertook. What a difference life can be with those three gifts. I was filled with joy.

The ride seemed long, but as we pulled into Kim's driveway I felt ready to review everything with him. It took over an hour.

After we'd gone over all the plans and measurements, he looked at us and grimaced. I guess he had an idea of what we had just been through.

"Remember to take Bill's truck and one of your own cars tomorrow," he said. "There will be a lot to bring home. Do you have a place to store everything?"

"Yes," Mel told him. "Our friends, Deb and Marty, have an old barn six miles from our land. They said we could store stuff there."

"You have good friends," Kim said, leaning back in his office chair with his hands clasped behind his head. "I guess you'll find out tomorrow just how difficult this will be."

"You know, I'll need a new set of drawings now that the window sizes have changed. If you win the bid," Kim said chuckling.

Oh boy. It was a good meeting and I left feeling ready to conquer the auction. And some of my fears.

The Auction

Sleep was non-existent. This was getting to be a habit. Many times I went downstairs to the kitchen as I was diligent about packing lunches and filling water bottles. With each trip down I would add another item or two. Advil and energy bars, salty and sweet stuff, fruit. It was important. I didn't want to be distracted by thirst or hunger, knowing it would be a grueling day.

At dawn, I dressed and made a pot of coffee. Soon we were on our way to Hanover, each driving separate vehicles. Mel drove Bill's truck. I followed her in Powder, staying alert by refilling my travel mug from the large thermos. Watching Mel ahead of me, swaying her head to music, I realized I had my way to wake up and she had hers. It made me laugh.

After a half hour I called her on my cell to go over the plan for the auction one last time. I was being annoying.

"We'll both go to the window area first," I said. "Then make our bid on the ten we want."

"And then the doors," Mel said, showing me she had not forgotten the plan. "I'll bid on the windows, you bid on the doors."

"Remember; let someone else start the bidding. Don't forget." My tone begging for understanding. "If no one bids, don't say anything and the auctioneer will come down in price. He needs to get everyone started." I was definitely being annoying.

I had been to many other kinds of auctions, and had learned the hard way. I wanted to pass my wisdom on to Mel.

"I have that down pat," Mel said sounding okay. "You don't have to worry about me."

When we pulled in to the warehouse, the parking area was filled with trailers and trucks. In comparison, Powder seemed small, and I wondered if we would be able to fit everything we purchased in our two vehicles. I brushed my concern aside, confident that if anyone could make it work it was Mel and me. We locked our car doors and then high-fived each other. We were on our way.

I walked in and headed for the windows when Mel grabbed my arm.

"Look," she said throwing her hands in the air. "There's more than one auctioneer."

"Oh no," I yelped. "How are we going to do this?" We looked at each other and I could see my sense of panic mirrored in Mel's face. "How 'bout I bid for the interior doors and you stick with the windows," I said. "We can use our cell phones to keep in touch."

Mel agreed. The workers had announced yesterday that the auctioneers were going to start with the windows first. I decided to stick around for a few moments to see how it all worked. We took our place in the crowd of people holding numbers.

"Oh shit!" Mel shouted. "We forgot to get our numbers." This brought a few laughs from the men standing close by. *Don't laugh at me. I need my confidence.*

We dashed to the table where three women were taking driver's license information. The line now was long and we were scared the windows we wanted would be sold by the time we got back. Once the registration was over, we received our large numbered cards. And then we ran, and I mean that literally, back to the window section.

The auctioneer wasn't in our area yet, but so many men were in front of us we couldn't see a thing. Mel is shorter than me by two inches, so I gave her a leg up and she stood on top of the boxes close by. She was now four feet taller than anyone. Many of the men turned their heads in succession and looked, but she didn't care in the least. She's a Jersey girl, and thank God for it. I found an old chair close by, so I kneeled on that. Now we were in the middle of the action. To reduce my anxiety, I started to giggle. Embarrassing.

We got underway. The auctioneer stood beside the ten windows we wanted. I was confident that Mel knew, after our earlier conversation in the car, that she was not to start the bidding.

I was sweating. Mel had taken her coat off, so I knew she was nervous as well. My heart was pumping so hard that I could feel it knocking against the wall of my chest.

As soon as the auctioneer announced, "Let's begin the bidding," Mel shot her hand in the air. She forgot everything we talked about and was just too excited to hold back. I laughed for no reason at all. What was wrong with me? Nerves were getting the best of both of us, but Mel was not going to let those windows get away. When the dust settled, the windows were ours for one hundred dollars each. If we had purchased them in Home Depot they would have cost at least three hundred and fifty each.

"Okay, now I'm beginning to love this." Mel said climbing down from her high advantage.

"You bid first!" I exclaimed.

"Yep, silly crazy me."

We were hopping around, acting like the amateurs we were. It didn't matter to us one whit. I left and went to the interior doors. Mel followed. Bidding on them seemed easy and it was fun. I let one man start, then I jumped in. Solid wood doors for so little money, how could we go wrong?

As we headed for the skylights I realized that so far we'd stayed together. Even though there was more than one auctioneer, we were still okay. According to the helpers, the skylight windows weren't going to start for thirty minutes. This gave me time to run to my car and grab the sandwiches. We sat and ate while we waited for the group to come our way. Time flew and we still had a lot to purchase. I left for the hardwood flooring and tile area while Mel stayed behind with the skylights. Soon I was back. There was no action there either.

We waited another fifteen minutes and finally the group moved in our direction. The crowd was smaller now, and it seemed there wasn't much interest in skylights. I winked at Mel. "Maybe no one else will opt on the one I want."

"Fat chance."

I waited for the auctioneer to begin. He sold a few of the smaller skylights while I kept my eyes focused on the giant prize.

When he opened the bidding for my skylight I shot my hand into the air. The room was silent. I looked at the auctioneer, waving my arm to get his attention. He was looking back at me with an odd expression. Someone laughed. What was going on?

"Ummmm, are you two bidding against each other?" the auctioneer asked, clearly amused. I turned to my right and saw Mel with her hand in the air. We both forgot not to bid first, and we were bidding against each other. We chuckled, shook our heads, and soon everyone was laughing along with us. The auctioneer knew Mel and I were together in this venture, a good call on his part.

The bidding resumed. I pulled myself together long enough to participate again and ended up with the Velux for my bedroom. I was thrilled. Mine for only three hundred sixty-five dollars. The auctioneer said the skylight had been a custom order. A man from Holland had moved to the United

States over a year ago, ordered it for the home he was building, then had to move back to his country. He never built the house. My gain. The remaining skylights sold for a lot more than at Lowe's or Home Depot, so I let them go. Mel had checked prices for Andersen windows and Velux skylights the week before, and she had the cost written down on our plans. We came prepared.

High on our successes, we followed the crowd to the flooring department. After buying fifty-five boxes of Italian tile for the kitchen, bath, and entryway, we purchased all of the hardwood we needed. Mel was very pleased with the color choices, and I trusted her eye.

We were finished for the day. I did the math for what we had purchased. Tile, hardwood flooring, ten Andersen windows plus two smaller ones, my skylight, and nine interior doors. Then I remembered the kitchen windows we had on our list. Damn it. We were not done after all. I hurried back to see if they had been sold, Mel hot on my heels. Luck was with us again. Our casements were about to go up next. Mel's hand shot up. I kept mine firmly at my side. She purchased them. We were getting exceptional at this auction stuff. One last look around, but I never saw windows for my study. I put those off for next time.

Again I thought we were finished. Again I was wrong. I walked wearily toward the entrance when Mel saw bathroom fixtures. Toilets were selling for only forty-five dollars each. If toilets can be great, these were. I bought two. Gorgeous pedestal sinks were next and selling fast. I purchased two for one hundred and fifty dollars. What a deal!

Outside, Mel called Kim before we loaded our vehicles. Her voice trembled with excitement. "We bought the windows, doors, and one sky-light. We also purchased wood flooring, tile, two sinks and two toilets. All of it new. You'll be amazed when you look at all this stuff, Kim. Sal and I'll be over on Monday to tell you everything."

I almost got to my car before Mel grabbed me by my sweatshirt. "We need to pay for everything."

"Shit, again."

Once more, we stood in a long line and waited our turn. I was tired. My feet ached from standing on concrete for hours, and I couldn't stop yawning. It took an hour and a half to pay. The women who helped us that morning were ready with our bills as we approached the table. We split the amount, each making out a check, and left.

"We saved a lot." I said walking away from the table.

"I still have money left for the next auctions too. How 'bout you?"

"Yep," I said moving toward the door.

Our next test was getting everything into my car and Bill's truck. There was a long line for the flat metal carts. More waiting until one came available. The windows and doors were heavy and bulky. I filled the cart, pushed it to my car, and managed to shove some of the windows in. Only five of the fifteen fit. Darn. Mel loaded the truck next with five more windows, but that was it. We were going to need to make another trip. Or two.

"The auctioneer said we have to have everything out by five p.m. Sunday evening," Mel said. "With the distance we have to travel we're going to need a larger truck."

"Bummer." Still, I couldn't help but grin. We'd done it; we'd finished our first auction.

Hard Long Days

I t was after midnight when we drove into Marty and Deb's driveway. Opening the barn door, I was surprised to see how clean the area was.

"We have such good friends," I said.

"Yep. By the way, I called Penske rentals in Allentown on the way home and ordered a truck for tomorrow"

"Oh my God, that's wonderful."

It took fifteen minutes to unload the vehicles. At last we could go home and rest before we needed to make the return trip.

I went to bed feeling better and better about the day, and fell asleep instantly.

When the alarm rang the following morning I crawled out of our soft nest to look out the window. For a moment, I stared out in disbelief.

"Wake up."

"Why?"

I said nothing, and pointed outside. She joined me at the window. We stood together staring at a driving rain. I dressed and headed downstairs, making sandwiches while Mel made coffee. Lots of it. We packed up, including blankets for padding, and left for the rental lot. Torrential rain and severe thunder storms. Lordy.

The rental was expensive, but as we climbed into the cab I knew it was the right decision. It would make our entire job easier. Mel and I were tired. This would be difficult, but not impossible. We could rest later. The miles faded as we made our way back to Hanover. The two hour ride seemed shorter than yesterday. *Maybe time was an illusion.* Mel drove first and I had the drive home.

I stared out my side window and realized how much I had learned in the last few years. The moments of my life were now filled with new adventures, decisions, and most important; the truth. About everything in my life. I've taken responsibility for myself and own the failings I had during my marriage. It never felt as if I made any decisions, but the truth is I made lots of them. I just didn't make the important ones. I decided not to decide. It was easier. I allowed Bob to choose for me because it served a purpose at the time. It let me stay clear of his anger, yes, but if I never had to make a decision, I'd never be wrong.

I understand myself well enough now to speak of it. My family, Mel, and my friends accept me. There is no judgment and I am not deemed inadequate or lacking in some way. I fit in. It makes me feel calm inside.

"Are you still with me?" Mel asked.

"Yeah. I was thinking about my identity."

"You've done a lot of work on yourself since I've known you. You have purpose now. I've seen it build within you."

"Thanks, but I've had little understanding of myself over the years, and almost no respect. I've allowed others to manipulate me rather than being in control and because of that I've discovered some things about myself that I don't like. But now I'm working on those too."

"I'm happy if you're happy."

"You bet I am."

It took several hours to pack the truck, and we were getting drenched doing it. One auction worker drove our heavier items over with a fork-lift, lifting the hardwood flooring and tile to the top of the ramp where we were standing. We carried everything in. Next were the windows and doors. Carefully we placed them against the walls, padding each with blankets.

It was a good thing I'd noticed there was a custom of tipping, or I never would have thought about it. I gave the man a twenty dollar bill and thanked him profusely.

Back in the warehouse I found one of the flat carts from the previous day, and put our sinks, toilets, and skylight on it. Pushing it to the truck was easy, but hefting them in was a different story.

"Mel," I shouted over all the noise in the building. "Watch your back when you lift. Okay?" I was happy to be working for a chiropractor.

She looked at me and mouthed, "Yep. Got it."

I had grown up knowing the toll of hard labor and sports. Dad's back was strong, but he, too, had pain from time to time. I skied, played softball, tennis, basketball, golf, and swam. I'd sustained many injuries during those days. I've learned from them.

———

The sun set low behind us as we made our way home, happy that the rain had stopped. I sagged against the truck bench seat, realizing my mouth was dry and my stomach rumbled. Reaching behind me I took out the lunches I'd made that morning. As I drove we ate, but it was not enough. I stopped at a gas station and purchased more snacks and drinks. We were burning a lot of calories these days.

Despite the earlier storms, the roads were now dry. We were grateful. A couple of hours later we drove up Deb and Marty's driveway. Again. This time they came out of the house and watched.

"Wow," Marty said with an odd look on her face. "I expected you hours ago. I was getting concerned."

"It took a long time to load the truck, and it's a two-hour trip each way. We didn't think you'd mind if we rolled in late." I said rubbing my hands on my lower back.

"I don't mind." Deb laughed, walking around eyeing everything we'd unloaded. "I'm just happy you're back in one piece. You must be exhausted."

"Damn straight," Mel moaned, tired from the day's work.

By nine o'clock the truck was back at the rental, and we were on our way home. Mel stifled a yawn. "Yeesh!" She said rubbing her hands over her face. "I'm pooped."

We got back to the farmhouse around ten o'clock and our kitties, Eli and Toby, welcomed us home. Each time I had to leave them alone, I felt a little twinge of guilt. Toby was diabetic and needed a shot of insulin each morning. I worried about her when we had to be gone for long periods of time. She looked good though.

I went to bed thinking of how long the day had been. Drained and exhausted from being around so many people for the last three days, I felt my heart lighten at the thought of returning to our land tomorrow. I wanted to fill my bird feeders and give corn to the deer while I immersed myself in nature again. Rain water gives renewed nourishment to new spring buds because it's natural water, and I ached to see this for myself. With the rains we'd had in the past few days, I was sure that new growth was everywhere. I wondered what adventures awaited me.

Mason Woes

On Monday morning I went to the camp for breakfast. Coffee tasted better in the woods and outside. I was never disappointed. I couldn't wait to live in nature.

I left to pick up Kim at his office. We were going to Deb and Marty's barn to show off what we'd purchased. Mel and I spent a few hours Sunday night filling him in about the auction, but this was even more fun.

Mel met us at the barn and we stood together as Kim walked inside. He surveyed everything. Mel and I glanced at each other occasionally. I shifted my weight from one leg to the other praying that our effort paid off, but more than that I wanted Kim to be pleased with all we had accomplished. He looked at the flooring, then the doors and bathroom fixtures, and finally the windows. He turned to us and rolled his eyes, his normal habit coming out again. I took a quick breath and Mel and I started to talk at the same time. He held his hands out in front of him, signaling for us to stop.

Kim smiled, and crossed his arms over his chest. "It's okay," he said, "everything looks very workable." Then he chuckled and added, "No wonder you got those windows for a hundred bucks each. They don't have any flanges on them."

"What?" I asked, instantly dejected. I knew that window flanges were an external rib or rim, used for an attachment to another object for strength. They were necessary.

Mel sagged a bit, but before she could answer Kim said, "It's okay, I don't need them. I can make the windows work." I had a feeling that statement was going to become his mantra from then on.

"Thanks Kim," Mel said, relieved. "I knew you could do it."

"Oh you're welcome. Just call me Mr. Wonderful."

Mel left to go back to the studio and I drove Kim back to his office. "I'm impressed with the money you saved," Kim said. "I plan to purchase an old barn in the coming year, and to re-build it from the bottom up."

He, too, could make use of these auctions. I liked Kim a lot, and loved that he enjoyed working with two women. Divorced with three kids, he knew what he was doing. Perhaps we added something new to his life. Whatever the synergy was, it worked.

"Thanks, Kim. It means a lot to us."

I had more to do before they delivered the shed. It was coming on Thursday and I needed to finish the foundation. Mel had work to complete for her publishers so she couldn't be there. It was up to me now, and I was determined. I shoveled, leveled, sweated, and shoveled some more until my hands were sore. I needed to do it twice, making sure I had it right. Birds sang and their songs urged me on. Every living thing seemed to be giving me extra energy and motivation as I pushed myself beyond what I thought was possible.

By evening, I had made a lot of progress. I looked around for rocks to use around the perimeter of the crushed gravel. Most of the surface stones on the land were about ten to twelve inches round, and perfect for the job. I picked up three carts worth of stones. Between the shoveling and the rock piling I was one tired woman.

Mel came as she always did when she finished work. I was putting my tools away when she joined me at the shed foundation.

"Wow!" Mel said grabbing the level from the trailer cart. "You've worked hard. I'll bet you can't wait to have a hot shower, and something to eat."

I looked at her with drooping eyelids. "As you would say, 'damn straight.'"

We measured the foundation again, and I had leveled earlier. It was finished and ready. I was excited for the shed to arrive.

Overwhelmed with fatigue, I took one more walk through the woods before leaving. Mel came along and we stood at the edge of the field looking at the sunset.

"Is this land really ours?"

"It sure is."

We stood and watched as birds and deer gathered their last bit of food, and everything that had a voice that evening, sang its song. By the time we left, turkeys were roosting in the trees at the back of our woods. I could see their shadows in the fading sunlight. As we walked the path to our cars, I noticed the deer had finished their corn, but they'd be back again later. It seemed everyone was settling in for the night and the universe was as it was intended. *And all shall be well.*

A piece of my heart hurt as we drove down the driveway and headed for the farmhouse. We were building a sacred place and it was hard to leave it behind. Even though I knew I'd be back in a few hours, I wanted to stay in the softness of moonlight.

When I arrived at our land the following morning, the mason and his men were already at work. I had no idea they were coming; Kim hadn't mentioned it either. I felt disappointed and sad not being the first one there. I always wanted to be the first one to step on my land for the day. I felt it kept all things nature in a certain kind of order. It was only an hour after dawn but the foundation walls were already starting to grow. One of the four workers was mixing cement and the others were laying block. *What fun*, I mused—but then, I was not the one carrying the eighty-eight pound blocks.

"Good morning, guys." The workers didn't look like a happy bunch from the way they kept sneaking side-long glances at their boss, and me. No answer. H*mmmm, what did I do wrong?*

"Why are you here?" The boss snarled. "Checking up on us? We're fine so feel free to leave."

"This is my land. I'm here almost all the time. Hostile, are we today?"

"Oh great!" he exclaimed, turning back to his men for a minute.

As I stood and watched the work develop, the head mason finally joined me.

"I can't believe how fast you work," I said when he was close enough to hear.

The mason slowly shook his head. "We'd be closer to done if you had a decent driveway."

I looked at Charlie's handiwork. "What's wrong with it?"

"That damned oak," he said, pointing his arm. "My driver had a hell of a time getting around it."

I cringed, but was surprised by what came out of my mouth next. "Oh. Well, yeah, it's tricky, but the better drivers have no problems getting around that tree." I could tell he was disgusted with me by his side-long glance, and he didn't like being contradicted. He had his cranky pants on that morning and I didn't want to get into a lengthy discussion.

He turned on his heel and returned to work. It was going to be a long day so I made myself scarce, and worked cutting underbrush from the pathway to the field. While I worked I enjoyed the feeling of confidence that came during my discussion with the mason. Even though I shook inside, my voice hadn't quivered.

Lunch came and went as the guys and I worked our way through the day. In the field I stacked the growing pile of branches for burning. When the masons left for the night, I walked to the foundation and looked at the new walls. They were getting taller. Tomorrow they'd be measuring the openings for the windows in Mel's studio. That made me smile and I jumped down into the basement, waving my arms in the air like a lunatic. I was one happy woman.

The next morning I made it a point to be on site before the masons. When they arrived, their angry attitude seemed to continue from the day before. I didn't like the head mason and I don't think the crew did either. When the boss's back was turned one of his guys actually made the well-known finger gesture to him.

The boss assumed I didn't have a clue about construction, and sneered at me every time I got near him. I didn't need his negative energy, so I left him to his work. Grabbing my chainsaw, I set out on the south side to cut up some deadfall from the previous winter.

A few hours later, I noticed Kim heading my way. He wasn't looking too happy so I shut off my saw to let him speak, but he said nothing. Instead he gestured for me to follow him.

We walked back to the foundation. The masons were gone. It was much too early for them to have quit for the day. I looked at Kim for an explanation. He shrugged, threw his arms into the air, said nothing, and left. Kim not talking was reason for concern.

Stunned and confused, I sat down on a cinder block. All the equipment belonging to the masons was gone. Oh my, our first glitch. Not knowing what to do, I called Mel and told her the story.

She was quiet for a moment and then answered, "Let's wait until this evening to call Kim."

"Okay," I agreed, happy to have a plan. I thought Kim and the head mason must have had some issues between the two of them. I was sure they worked other jobs together. "I think it would be better to let him have the day to think about this situation. Hopefully by tonight he'll come up with a plan." I could hardly stand not knowing what was going on.

Evening came and after dinner Mel called Kim. She talked to him for twenty minutes, and hung up.

"He's furious," she said, eyes wide and mouth grimaced. "He fired the head mason. When I asked him why, Kim said it was his attitude and nasty temper toward everyone who got near him. Evidently the man's had a number of personal problems and can't get his life turned around. Kim won't stand for it unless the guy can get the work done harmoniously with us and his crew. Kim also said the mason didn't like us being on the land watching them work. He's hiring a different crew tonight."

We were relieved and satisfied. "I trust Kim," I said, happy to have that nasty guy off our land. "I know he'll make the right choices for his sub-contractors."

"It's not our call," Mel said heading back to the kitchen. "It's his. I'm just content we didn't have to make the choice."

The next day our land was buzzing with masons again. Block was being set by workers that were at ease, laughing and teasing one another as they worked. The new head mason was calm and smiled when he asked his questions. He seemed pleased to accommodate our needs. Kim had asked him earlier for two additional courses of block to add light and height for Mel's studio.

He agree that in a walk-out basement it is always a good idea to go high." More money in his pocket. Nothing was mentioned about the oak near the driveway. A good omen.

I was itching for these men to finish the foundation so Kim could cap it off. It would be full day's work according to Mr. Wonderful, but that effort would be very rewarding because we'd actually be able to stand on the first floor of our new home. *Imagine!*

Last week I asked Kim what *exactly* was involved in capping it off. He answered. "First you have to put the sill plate on."

"Okay."

"I use two-by-six inch pressure-treated lumber, and I lay those pieces horizontally onto the foundation wall with a thin piece of foam between the two. The foam is needed so the wood doesn't come in direct contact with the concrete." He smiled at me, and continued. "Once they're anchored in place with J-bolts, I lay the two-by-ten inch floor joists on edge horizontally, securing them to the sill plate. Over all of that, I put down three-quarter inch plywood and that completes the solid structure base for your home."

"Great explanation." Now I understood the process.

I was anxious to see how large the first floor was going to look once it was capped off. I remembered back to the cat's cradle, and hoped it would look larger.

"Do you think the house will be too small?" I asked.

Kim answered. "No. It's just the two of you. So many people build their homes for someone else to admire, but they don't really live in every inch of the space. That's waste, in my opinion. You and Mel will have all you need, it's perfect."

"I feel that way as well. Thank you."

Butterflies filled my stomach. What would it feel like to stand on the capped off foundation?

Shed Day

Our shed from Stoltzfuss Structures was due to arrive. Mel and I sat together in the damp dawn, hands wrapped around coffee mugs.

Our neighbor, Bill, surprised us by walking up the path to our camp. Mel had called him a few days ago thinking he might like to know when the shed was going to be delivered. I poured him a cup from our thermos, and he sat down to wait with us. After two hours, and an extended conversation about home construction, I heard a truck coming up the road. Could it be?

Mel, Bill and I ran to the end of the driveway in time to see our new, not-quite-finished shed making its way up the road. Black truck doors emblazoned 'Stoltzfuss Structures' in bright red letters. The shed looked a little odd without siding, but Mel and I had plans to use the same shakes for the house and shed. The perfect outbuilding. The driver didn't have to hunt for our address; we waved, he couldn't miss us.

The truck stopped, and I went over to peek at the shed. Ignoring our little group, the driver climbed out and walked part-way up the driveway. Never saying a word he walked back to his vehicle, climbed in, threw it in gear, and turned onto our lane. He stopped after creeping forward a hundred feet and got out again. Without acknowledging us he sauntered toward the house with his hands deep in his pockets. I followed alongside talking a mile a minute. He ignored me. I looked back at Mel and Bill for support, but they had climbed up on the back of the trailer to have a better look at the shed. I kept up with the pace of the driver and again spoke to him of my plans and where I was going to have him place the shed. I even walked him over to the foundation that was ready and waiting. Not a word.

Walking back with me at his side, he jumped into the cab. Backing the truck and trailer out into the street, he pulled forward.

"Okay," I said to Mel and Bill, "He's going to back it up the driveway instead."

"Makes sense," Mel said nodding her head. "The shed door needs to be on the side facing the path. It's the only way we can get in once it's sitting on the foundation."

The driver backed in slowly, but stopped at the big oak. He set the brake, got out, and walked back to the trailer. Without a conversation he unbuckled the straps that held the shed in place. I looked at Mel, she looked at Bill, and we stood there stunned.

"What the heck are you doing?" I asked because I was annoyed.

He ignored me again, so Bill walked over to him. "Are you taking the shed off the trailer?" Bill asked, in a firm voice. Maybe he's mute, I thought.

Barely looking at any of us he shrugged and said, "I'm going to leave the shed right here. I'll never make it around that stupid tree. I'm not even going to try. I'm done."

"No way," I laughed, hoping he was joking.

"Yep!" he exclaimed, letting out a huge sigh. "I'm done."

With that, he unloaded our new shed and it sat there pretty and proud, right at the end of our lane. With his hand outstretched, he walked over to me. "Payment," he said. I looked at him, put my hand in my pocket and pulled out the check I'd written earlier at the farmhouse. I looked down at it, considered my internal battle, and then handed it over to him. He couldn't have cared less. He climbed in the truck with its automatic tip down trailer, and drove away.

"What now?" I asked, stunned and angry.

"Shit," Mel muttered.

After a moment or two, Mel, Bill, and I opened the double doors to the shed and walked in. It was just what we ordered, but I felt irritated and helpless. My heart was filled with disappointment, and my hope for the perfect day disappeared. Now we had an immense problem on our hands.

Closing the doors, I walked back to the camp. Bill and Mel joined me as I poured another mug of coffee. While I drank, we went over our options.

"Neither of us has a tractor large enough to pull the shed up to its place," I said, dejected. "In fact, it's ludicrous to even think about that option. We'd rip the bottom off. If and when we get it to the foundation, how will we pick it up and place it there? How long can it sit at the end of the driveway anyway?" I ran my fingers through my hair, trying to get a handle on this dilemma.

"We have to get our cars down by the end of the day. No other way out, damn it to hell," Mel answered, stomping her foot on the ground. "We should have kept the money. I'm going to call Stoltzfuss Structures later. Jerks."

All of a sudden the entire situation struck me as funny and I began to laugh. The joke was on us. This man, so quiet and maddening, made the shed our problem, not his. Bill and Mel looked at me as if I'd lost the last half of my mind, but before long they were laughing too. It eased the tension of the moment. Together, we walked down to Bill's house to use his bathroom and have something to eat. Heidi had made a pot of vegetable soup, and we ate as we tried to figure out a solution to our predicament.

By the time we finished lunch, we had a resolution. Craig, who lived across the street from Bill, was a contractor. Bill had made friends with him during the last year, so we all walked over to seek his advice. We hoped he'd be home. I spotted Craig's truck in the driveway as the four of us crossed his yard. Bill rang the doorbell and Craig came out and joined us on his porch.

"Hi guys, have a seat." he said sitting down in one of the chairs. "It looks as if you have a problem, how can I help?" Craig listened quietly, saying nothing until we finished our story. Then he looked at each of us and said, "Give me an hour and I'll be over with my tractor." As we walked back up the street toward the shed, I could feel the stress lift from my shoulders. Craig was the answer to our dilemma, and I knew he would make this happen today. I felt blessed to know him.

Craig didn't need the entire hour. He came with his front end-loader while Cody, his thirteen-year-old son, drove his dad's pickup. They had it filled with metal rollers, ropes, straps, and many other assorted tools.

Craig went work and picked up one side of the shed with the bucket loader while Cody crawled under with the rollers. As soon as they were in place, Craig began to push the shed forward. Soon one of the rollers shot out at the back end of the shed. I ran to pick it up and carried it around to the front, and placed it back under again. The shed only moved a couple of inches at a time, but Craig's idea was working. Four hours later, we got the shed to its foundation.

When we reached the base of the stone foundation, I crawled on my elbows under the shed as Craig lifted it gently with the bucket, holding it steady. I gathered the metal rollers and shoved them aside. But I had missed one. Mel dove under to grab it, and I gasped. I never once thought about the shed falling on me, but as soon as I saw Mel under there I became anxious. I needn't have worried. Craig knew what he was doing. He held it secure until she came out.

Another two hours and we finished jockeying the shed into place. Craig worked his front end loader with precision, lifting one corner and then the other, while we shoveled crushed stone underneath until it was level. In the end, it looked charming sitting there.

"You're a miracle man," I said to Craig.

Clearly embarrassed, he smiled at all of us. "I'm happy to help. Always."

"How much do we owe you, Craig, other than our restored sanity?" I laughed.

"How 'bout fifty dollars."

"What?" I squeaked. "Oh Craig, that's not near enough for all you've done. Without you we'd still be scratching our heads at the end of the drive-way." In the end we gave Cody fifty dollars and Craig a hundred and fifty. We would be on the giving end for him some day, I hoped.

After everyone left, Mel and I rearranged some of the larger rocks along the bottom of the shed. It looked landscaped and I couldn't see any of the crushed stone underneath. The only thing visible was the rock wall, setting it off. We had done a good job, but it was our new friend Craig who made it possible.

Mel grabbed one door of the shed while I grabbed the other, and we swung them open at the same time. Entering the twelve-by-eighteen foot structure together, each of us turned in a circle.

Mel turned to me with eyes wide and a large smile. "It's huge," she said, "I could live here."

Tears trickled down my face and landed on my filthy sweatshirt. I had waited and hoped to hear Mel say those words for weeks.

"What did I say?" Mel asked concerned as she laid one hand on my shoulder.

Finally, it was time to share the secret that I had held close to my heart. I looked at her through glistening eyes and answered. "I want to live on this land."

"Of course you do," Mel said, relaxing a little. "That's why we're build-ing here."

I shook my head. "No. I want to live here now, on our land, every day. I'd like to move into this shed with you, Eli, and Toby, sharing every moment of this adventure with the birds and animals while we're building our home."

I watched Mel's face as my idea began to take form, and I could tell she understood. "Yes," she breathed. "It's the ideal place for us."

"I know it is."

We turned and walked out. Early evening had arrived without my knowledge. Quietly, we stood having one last look at our new home. Crick-ets, frogs, and peepers competed for first chair in our nighttime orchestra, while soft shadows settled in around us.

I could see our temporary home in my mind, and was getting it ready for the four of us to move in. I knew the kitties would love it there as well, so much to listen to and see. Letting the farmhouse rental go would save us money each month, and we needed that extra income for the building loan and the other unanticipated expenses that kept us juggling our money.

Tomorrow was going to be filled with fun. I'd bring my pen and paper, measuring tape, and a chair into the shed. I longed to begin transforming our twelve-by-eighteen foot, not quite finished building into a loved space that needed to contain every single one of our homey comforts. Would it all fit?

Making Plans

I walked into the shed with my camp chair and sat. It was dawn. Soon the sun would be rising to its zenith, but for now I could hear the scampering of little feet in the leaves around the outside of the building. What a world I was entering. It was all new territory to me, and the journey ahead seemed like something I'd read in a novel. A yarn about a woman who was about to make remarkable changes in herself, as well as her physical environment. Unquestioned belief that the life ahead was a first-rate choice.

I felt connected to my mother in these quiet moments on my land, wishing we'd had a common ground on which to walk. We were different women, but my inner strength was a gift from her. I'd had always loved immersing myself in nature and it caused many problems in my younger years. I loved being outside, galloping my horse without a care in the world, climbing trees, and swimming in the ponds and lakes. All alone. I knew my mother wanted me to be more cautious. As I aged, I ached to share myself with her. I wanted to live physically closer to her in order to dig around in her thoughts, find out who she really was. Perhaps she had untamed ideas too, but was afraid to carry them out. How would I ever know?

Bob did not care for my mom, but he did enjoy arguing with her. He thought she was too intolerant and too opinionated. They'd go on and on about some trivial subject, both laughing, or not, until one of them gave in to the other. Many times he went with me to Florida where my parents lived in their older years, hating every minute of the trip. I felt trapped between worlds while I was visiting. Bob's: a world of wanting to get away from my parents and do something fun while we were away and near the ocean. Mine: a world of enjoying my mom and dad in the southern state they both treasured.

I planned trips on my own to visit my parents. It was pure fun. Bob hated my being away. I worried every moment while I was gone, knowing that when I returned home I'd have to deal with his anger. Again. It meant more work and he was selfish. In his opinion, my world was supposed to be Bob. But my marriage stunk, and I had been a doormat for most of it. I was young and married someone my parents might like. I've stopped apologizing.

Mom was diagnosed with Alzheimer's disease just before my dad passed. In her lucid moments she told me she wanted to die along with him. Even asked me for help to do that. She asked my son, Chris, to help as well and he was devastated. Mom had made my dad her entire life. Always. She had many transient ischemic strokes, TIA's, or mini strokes, during that last year of her life, and it robbed her of speech. I knew then that we'd never have that conversation I craved. I felt guilty for not going to see her and Dad more often and for not letting go of my fear of Bob's rage when I got home. I carried that fear in my heart the entire time of my visits. My sister and her husband, Myron, lived close to our parents and they cared for them in every way. Every day. I miss my mom. It took her a year after my dad's death to make it out of this world and into the next. I long for her still.

As I wiped tears from my face I looked around the shed, envisioning a mattress, two chairs, and a tiny table. I wanted a rug for the floor as well. If Mel could draw up plans for an entire house, I was determined to make one tiny shed work for a few months.

On my way back to the farmhouse, I thought about when to move us into the shed. The next auction was coming closer, and I wanted to finish packing. Charlie was coming next week to dig holes in the field. The new perk test had to be completed and if it passed he would design the septic system and dig trenches for the drain field. Kim would soon cap off the foundation, beginning the creation of our house.

I had so much to do. Pack up the entire house, and find a storage unit for our furniture, paintings, and other items that needed gentle care. Marty and Deb's barn would hold the rest of our things. My desk and Mel's could stay at the barn along with the kitchen items, bed frames, and anything else that mice wouldn't wreck.

I came to my spiritual life by longing for answers to questions I'd had since childhood. I found a teacher, minister, who had studied for years in the East. She met with me every day for several months, and again for years, until I was able to guide others through meditation and the love of a spiritual practice.

For the next six months I'd have to give up my counseling, and I needed to tell everyone as soon as possible. Not only would it be tough on them, but on me, for I found that by helping others I was ministering to myself. But now I was going to have the time to work on the loss of my marriage and the rebuilding of my new life. I needed to do that alone in nature. I had carried this guilt inside my heart for far too long. It was time to let go of blame.

On my drive back to the farmhouse, lost in thought, I passed Bob's Storage Units in Quakertown. I turned back and drove in. They had a few units of perfect size available, so I rented one. I wanted to pack our belongings, and drop things off as I passed it each day on my way to our land. I'd do most of it myself. Powder and I made quite the team.

When I arrived home, Mel had left for work. I walked through the house measuring furniture, deciding which items to take to the shed. I made a list of what I needed to take to the new storage unit, and what I needed to take to the barn. It made things much easier for me. All I had to do now was mark down which items I would pack first. Stacking our belongings in the barn was going to be hard work. I had to move all the construction items closer to the front and keep our furniture in the back. These possessions wouldn't be needed until the house was complete.

I was eager to move into the shed. Mel said she would build shelves in there within the next week. I had some old black ones from my previous apartment stored in the basement, but Mel hated them. Nonetheless, they would work.

After my measurements were complete, I looked around the kitchen for what might be usable in a small space. It seemed fruitless to imagine having a kitchen there since we had no electricity in the shed, but I was determined to figure out something. I made a few notes on the list and then had an idea. I'd move our two reclining chairs to the shed before Mel got back from the studio.

Feeling sneaky, I loaded one into Powder and drove it to the shed. The floor was sturdy so weight wasn't an issue. I hefted the chair in, and sped back to the farmhouse in thirty minutes for the other one. Good thing it wasn't too far away. I had room for a few extra items, knowing they'd come in handy. When I got there, I chose a spot on the back wall for the ugly black shelves, and nailed them up. I knew Mel would laugh and say this is where they belonged. In a shed.

Next, I decided there was room for my antique dresser. It would fit on the wall next to the shelves and we could share it. Off I went, back to the farmhouse. I could do this with my eyes closed, I thought as I drove. I was having fun so I called Mel and told her about renting a storage unit. I wanted her to have enjoyment too.

"I'm so wound up about living in the shed," I said, driving faster than necessary.

"I'm excited too." Mel laughed. I heard her studio chair scrap the floor, as she stood. "I'm wrapping up my day. I'll meet you at the land in about an hour. I'm going to buy some lumber and make the shelves before dark.

"So soon?" I asked, happy that she wanted to get them finished.

"Why not? I could use a break to do something fun."

By the time our conversation was finished I was home. I had enough time to grab my dresser, a small table, and a rug from our bedroom floor. I wanted to put it under the mattress so it wouldn't be damaged. It might be warmer too, as summer faded into fall.

When I drove up the driveway to the land, I saw Mel's car already there. I hurried into the shed and found her sitting in her chair laughing.

"What are those doing here?" she said, pointing to the ugly black shelves.

"I knew you'd love them." I smirked.

"Finally, you've found the perfect place for them…in a tool shed."

"I'm glad you approve."

"Seriously Sal, promise me we can burn them when we finish the house."

I feigned horror.

Mel worked on the shelves while I sat in the field, tired from lifting and moving heavy objects for most of the day. We took a moment each evening to spray ourselves with bug spray before sitting out there. Mosquitoes and ticks were abundant.

Late afternoon had become a time of reflection for me, and I loved the frame of mind it gave me. The forest was at my back, and the open field and stream below were stretched out in front. I watched the slow dance between the two and felt wrapped in compassion in my new environment. Eyes closed, I settled into an awareness of new truths, now that I was quiet enough to allow them to enter. Allow. Allow.

Prepping the Shed

It was another weekend already, but I was making huge progress packing up the farmhouse. As soon as we decided to move to the shed I wrote to our landlord saying we'd be moving out by the end of May. Only four days remained until the end of the month, and I didn't see any problem meeting that deadline. We could have extra time if we wanted, but with money already getting short it was not an option. The shed held the majority of what we wanted, and I had moved most of the larger items into the storage unit. Things from Mel's bedroom were gone, and my room was looking empty as well. Pictures and paintings were off the walls, and the only signs left of our overstuffed furniture were the imprints left on the carpet.

I started moving some of the kitchen items, including the table and chairs, pots and pans, and glasses and dishware. I packed the smaller items into boxes I picked up at the supermarket. The work was physically hard but the more I moved things to the barn and storage unit, the more I realized I was coming to an end. Not only the end of packing, but the end of my life as a renter and the beginning of a new life with my partner.

I thought about that as I moved toward owning a home once again. This time I would be different. I'd strived for a higher level as I went forward with my life. Jung argued that a conflict can never be resolved on the level at which it arises. It must be raised above the thought that there is only a winner or a loser. In order for a resolution, disagreements must be taken up to the highest level of ourselves. In my mind that means it doesn't matter who is right. You stay in the love of your marriage, and if there isn't enough love there, it won't work. My marriage was over. We never got to that higher place, but I'd learned from it. If a disparity ever happened with Mel or Kim,

I'd stay in my heart until we came to a conclusion. We all wanted it to work.

By midafternoon most of the kitchen was bare and I had taken my last load to the barn. I packed my car full with things that went to the storage unit, and dropped them off on my way to a four o'clock appointment with Mel and Kim at our land.

I got there a little early, and was happy to sit in my chair near the field. My back was weary from packing and lifting, so I stretched out and looked up at the sky. It was a peaceful day. As a cloud skittered past, I noticed a flash of red up in the tree branches. *What was that?* I wondered, and went back to the shed for my binoculars. I sat a while longer. Then I saw the red flash again. Raising the binoculars, I spied its source. A Pileated Woodpecker! Right here in our woods. Crow-sized, they are black with white neck stripes, conspicuous white wing linings, and a prominent red crest. I loved it. Despite their size, this elegant woodpecker was adept at keeping out of sight. Not many people will ever get a close view of one, and yet, here it sat. And it was not just one. There was a pair, and they seemed to be making holes in every large branch around me. Were they nesting or feeding? I couldn't be sure.

Their voices - loud, deep, cuk-cuk-cuk-cuk-cuk, rising and then falling in pitch, were - so different from that of the smaller Red Bellied, Hairy, and Downy woodpeckers I'd been seeing. And their pecking was more like an ax chipping pieces from a small log.

I could have stayed in the field all day watching the bird and animal life, but I could hear cars coming up the driveway. I met Mel and Kim at the foundation and returned to the field with his surveying equipment. He looked with the laser level, and then so did we. We could see that we had a seven-point-two percent slope away from the house, and we only needed five-percent to put the septic system drain-fields out there. We were good to go if we passed the perk test. Charlie was working on the system design because he was sure it would pass. The old site down by the street had no problems perking and he didn't expect any here.

Kim said, "The engineer is coming next week to run the tests. It's okay if you want to watch. It may be boring, but at least you'll get to know a little more about your land."

"Of course I want to be here," I exclaimed. "Nothing is more important to me than keeping those trees at the end of the driveway. They keep our property private, and lovely."

"Calm down;" Kim laughed; "I understand."

After Kim left, Mel went back to the shed. She wanted to finish the shelving. I was still a little weary so I decided to sit for a while longer, watching the sun cast its long shadows into our woods. It seemed like a dappled wonder. Oh, how I loved this property. The longer I sat the more silent it became.

An hour went by and I walked back to the shed. "Wow, Mel, you've finished the shelving. It looks great."

She stepped back and took a look. "Thanks. I feel better about things now that I know our stuff will fit."

We sat together in the two loungers for about five minutes before we heard Heidi and Bill outside. They had concluded their daily nature walk, and stopped by to visit.

I pulled up the two extra chairs I had brought from the patio at the farmhouse and we sat together drinking iced tea from the cooler. What a great night.

"You guys seem quiet," I said, wondering what was going on. Mel and I glanced at one another and I could tell she'd noticed it too. Finally, Bill stood up. Then he sat down again and we waited. He looked at Heidi, smiling, and they both began to talk at the same time.

"We'd like to offer our upstairs bathroom, guest bedroom closet, and anything else you would need for the months you plan on living in the shed," Bill said.

Heidi nodded. "You can have total use of these rooms any time you want, every day in every way."

Another friend of ours had offered her shower, but she lived a distance away. This would be much easier. It was a relief.

I knew Bill and Heidi well enough to know they meant it. Mel had mentioned to Bill that we were going to live in our shed on the land. I never expected such an offer. "Thanks, using your bathroom and shower will be awesome." I said. "We'll be so tired, hot, and sweaty."

"The thought of a nice hot shower at the end of every day is almost too much to hope for." Mel sighed.

Bill turned away from us and pointed to the west wall, "I've been talking to an electrician. You can use an electric line and snake it through the woods from our house to the shed so you have power. He'll bring the line and an electric box tomorrow, if you want. He also said he would tie the other end to our box in the basement. We'd have to bury the line under our driveway until it got to the woods. After that it could stay above ground, but when it got to your path we'd have to bury the line again," Bill continued, his eyes sparkling, Hidden so no one knows you're living here." He winked.

There it was. Bill, too, knew we were not allowed to live on our land until the house was built and we had an occupancy permit. I saw it written in the zoning regs, but had decided ignorance was bliss—if I didn't ask for confirmation then maybe I could delude myself into thinking what we were doing was perfectly legal. Now I had no such excuse. I had done the math.

This outpouring of generosity was beyond anything we hoped for, and we jumped up to hug Bill and Heidi.

"We had no idea you were thinking about any of this for us. We're so thankful," I said, with tears running down my face. "We'll pay you each month for the added electricity on your bill."

Heidi nodded. "We need to be here for one another. It will work out."

I didn't argue. "Thank you guys."

"So," Bill said, clapping his hands together, "Is tomorrow okay for the electrician to come by with the electric line? I know it's Sunday of Memorial Day weekend, but he only has this one day to do it."

"Yes," I said without hesitation. I knew I'd be here waiting. We hugged them again before they left the shed.

There was no way we could afford both the farmhouse rental and the construction loan. No way. Kim knew what we had in mind, but we were confident of his silence in front of the inspectors. We'd act as if we were not living there, keeping everything out of sight and not allowing anyone into the shed. As far as everyone knew, the shed was for the tools and equipment. It wasn't a lie, but it was a long stretch of the truth.

Stunned I said, "Do you believe this is happening?"

"No," Mel said, shaking her head as we re-entered the shed.

I looked around, trying to imagine what it would be like having electricity. With the shelves Mel just finished I could bring the coffee pot, toaster oven, microwave, and the small refrigerator she had in her studio. It was going to work out in ways we never expected.

We made our way back to the farmhouse and its warmth. It was late and we knew we were going to have to do a lot of digging in the morning; there was no other way except to pull out the shovels and get to it. We couldn't hire anyone with a backhoe, it was way too risky.

But we would have electricity. Our temporary home would offer more than shelter, it would positively sing of coziness.

Our Temporary Digs

That Sunday, I shoveled through hard stony ground for five hours. Every inch of my body was screaming, and I gobbled ibuprofen to help the old joints. At this rate, I'd need a whopping jumbo-sized bottle to get me through the next few months. Small price to pay, I thought, as I put the shovels back under the tarp. Of all the things we'd moved into the shed, our tools were not yet among them.

The electrician came and went in short order, and the small refrigerator hummed as if it had been there forever. I couldn't believe it; all of this in a shed. We'd have coffee and toast in the morning, and something heated up in the microwave for lunch. I was more eager than ever for moving day.

I heard someone coming up the driveway so I headed out to see who it was.

"Andy!" I shouted, recognizing my son's car. "Hey Mel, Andy's here." Mel emerged from the shed and was there to greet Andy when he got out of his car.

"Hey, Mom," he said, wrapping his long arms around me. "I only have an hour but would love to help, if you need me."

"We're done for today," I said as he hugged Mel. "But I can give you the grand tour." Andy stopped in occasionally on his way home from Highway Marine, a large full-service boat facility in Quakertown. He loved seeing our progress and wanted to lend a hand as much as he could, but working sixty-five-hour weeks as Sales Manager left little extra time. We were thrilled with whatever support he could lend. Andy had two young daughters and a lovely wife. I hated that he had to work on Sundays during "the season." I knew he wanted to be with them more. His plan was to work with his brother in New York City one day in the near future. Lots of traveling, but still more time at home.

We walked him around. First we showed him the shed with all the new shelves. He smiled and said, "How comfortable this will be for you two. I love it." Then we went out to the field and he laughed at the huge burn pile, and mumbled something about marshmallows and hot dogs. Lastly, we walked him to the foundation and he was amazed at what had been accomplished since his last visit.

"I can't believe you have so much done already. It seems like I only saw the floor plans a few weeks ago. This is all so cool, you guys rock."

"Thanks, Andy," I said feeling proud. "I love it too." Walking him back to his truck I talked about his work, and how tired he was looking. Summers were long in the boating business.

After Andy left, Mel and I went back to the farmhouse to move some of the larger pieces of furniture into storage. I had already moved everything I could do on my own. More ibuprofen.

Mel borrowed Bill's truck and we moved the sofa from the mud room where I had dragged it earlier for easier lifting. The cushions, however, went into Powder so they wouldn't fly out as we drove to the storage unit. There were a few other boxes sitting around so we threw those in, too. When we returned to the farmhouse, only the beds, TV, clothing, and a few kitchen and bathroom items remained. The place was looking bare and it echoed now when we closed the door. The kitties seemed to be okay, even though they knew change was in the air. Soon our farmhouse would be only a memory. For all of us.

I opened the refrigerator to see what we might make for dinner, and found almost nothing. It was going to be a cereal night, but at least we had that. I ate my meal in a folding chair in front of the TV, falling asleep with each bite. Finally I gave in and went to bed. In minutes I was asleep.

Time was flying by while Mel and I worked on the land. The following morning, Mel's absence was notable when I arose. This never happened. Never. I am a morning person. Mel is not. She stays up later at night than I, so it all evens out in the end. Anyway, she was gone. I went downstairs to see if she left a note. There it was by the coffee pot. It was a one liner saying she had given Toby her insulin and was now at the studio. I turned to look at the clock and was astonished to see I had slept until nine. *Guess I needed it,* I thought, as I headed upstairs to shower. These days were grueling and I felt my age for the first time. Didn't matter though, I wasn't about to give up.

After my shower I gathered my clothes for the day and also for work while I thought about Dr. Mary. My employer and friend had been supportive, and I loved her. Every day she asked questions about the project, and we laughed at the craziness of my situation. She gave me chiropractic adjustments each week, and I was grateful to her for the physical relief. She also let me switch my work times; some days I worked afternoons and others in the evening. She was a good soul.

As I stood under the hot water, I wondered what I'd do today at our land. I didn't have to be at the office that evening, so I could plan to do most anything.

I kept noticing the date. There was only one day left in May. Once the few remaining bathroom, kitchen, and living room items were moved, I would clean the farmhouse for the last time. I wanted to leave it squeaky clean in order to get my security deposit back. Two months worth of rent really helps toward construction loan payments.

Suddenly I knew what to do with my day, and it would be a surprise for Mel. No one was scheduled to be at the land, and the rest of this week and the next were going to be crazy busy. Once more I had butterflies in my stomach. "Here I go again, making decisions without Mel," I said to Toby who was curled up by my feet.

I ran up the stairs, yanked the sheets off the beds, and put them in a huge plastic bag with the other dirty clothing. Later I'd stop at the laundromat if I had time. I scooped up the pillows and ran down to my car. Back up again to grab the mattresses. At first I wondered how I was going to do it alone. But I realized if I could drag them down the stairs and through the foyer, I'd have no problem lifting them into the car. Powder was parked very close to the entrance. Easy. Amazingly, they both fit in at the same time. I'd only have to make one mattress trip, dropping the guest mattress from Mel's room off at the storage unit. I stuffed her pillows and blankets in, too. Then with a smug grin, I drove over to the shed.

I drove as close as I could to the door, and wrestled my way in with the mattress. My fingers were sore from it not having handles, and it was so damn heavy and bulky. But just as I had imagined, the mattress fit perfectly. After four more trips I had transformed a shed into a home. The TV on the Lazy-Susan I bought looked entertaining. Why not? Everyone has to have a little distraction. Mel loved to watch her shows, and she never expected to have a television in the shed. The question was, how to hook it up?

My next stop was Radio Shack to get an antenna. I told the salesman what I was doing and he sold me the best one for the job. I drove back to the shed, crossing my fingers as I plugged it into the back of the TV. I sat in my chair to see if it worked with the remote. It did. Four channels and all of them came in clearly.

"Whoooohooooo!" I whooped. What a rush.

Before I left for the laundromat, I stood at the shed door. Everything looked together, and although it was small we had all we needed. Two chairs, a mattress with a rug underneath, a dresser, two lamps, and a small table. The ugly black shelves were stacked with clean clothes, and the ones Mel built held a coffee pot, toaster oven, microwave, and the small refrigerator stood underneath on the floor. The last shelf held our food. We were in good shape.

I locked the door behind me and headed out. I considered taking Bill and Heidi up on their offer of the washer and dryer, but in the end I didn't. Laundromats were faster. We'd use a lot of their electricity in the coming months. Enough was enough.

It took no time at all to wash the sheets, and I ran to the drug store while they were drying. I decided to do the rest of the laundry another day.

When everything was finished, I went back to the farmhouse to see if I had missed anything. As I opened the door Eli and Toby stared up at me. They looked stressed and I wondered how long they had been sitting by the door. "Oh Lordy, Lordy," I said petting them. "Now what should I do with you two?" I knew it would be easier to have Mel with me when I brought them to the shed. That way we could each carry one cat, bringing them in to their new home together.

Everything was finished and I was energized. "I'll be back tonight, my little loves," I promised the kitties, filling their dishes with food. Then I drove back to our land.

As I pulled the shed door open, I had to sit down. Overwhelmed with emotion, I needed a moment to take it all in. For the next hour I sat in meditation, giving thanks. Then I picked up the phone and called Mel.

Snuggled in the Shed

"Hey," Mel said. "Are you at the land?"

Mel sounded tired, and I began to worry. *What's wrong?* I wondered, and then I realized she was probably every bit as exhausted as I was that afternoon.

"Yes," I said, wondering how to tell her what I'd just finished doing.

"Great," she said. "I'll be there soon." She hung up before I could tell her the news.

I walked around, making everything as perfect as possible. What if all she wanted was to go back to the farmhouse to rest? It was warmer there. End of May, of course it was going to be cool some mornings. I was nervous, but walked out toward our camp and sat on one of the tree stumps.

As I sat there waiting, I wondered about living my life without any kind of passion. Before I divorced, I'd gone for counseling, and during the process I discovered my deep desire for autonomy. I'd never known my potential, nor had my deepest desires met or supported. I'd yearned to write an online newsletter for abused women, and also hoped to live my life more simply and away from noise and distraction. I wanted to write books and short stories. I longed for water to be close by my home, or at least having the means to take time each year near a water source. Now I felt I had an opportunity to dig in and search for my life's work beyond motherhood. It was exhilarating.

I came out of that thought as I heard Mel's tires crunching up the driveway. I stood to greet her, then we each took a stump and sat down.

"Hi. Take a look at that gorgeous sight," I exclaimed, and pointed toward the new work around the house.

We looked at the capped-off foundation, jumped onto it and did a little jig, then talked about us applying the tar-like water sealer to the exterior sides of the block base. Charlie wanted to push the excavated earth back against the walls soon, so this would be an important next step. All the while I wondered how to tell Mel what I'd done. I just didn't know when to do it.

Mel sighed, standing up. "Is there anything left to drink in the shed?" she asked, heading in that direction.

"I think so," I said, keeping a straight face even as my heart pumped wildly. "Let's go in and take a look." Walking along beside her I began to feel anxious with excitement, but nonchalantly stooped down pretending to tie my sneaker. I wanted her to walk into the shed alone, seeing what I had done in her absence. The bed was made with clean sheets, and the pillows were stacked on top of the bed.

Mel walked into the shed and didn't come out. I waited. After a few minutes passed, I couldn't stand it, so I knocked. Again I waited, but no answer came. Finally, I pulled the door open and went inside. Mel was lying on the mattress, trying it out. First she stayed flat on her back, then she rolled to her side, and finally on her stomach. She looked at me, squinted her eyes, and made her mouth into a straight line. Then a chuckle erupted from deep in her throat. What fun this was.

"I take it we're sleeping here tonight?" she asked with delight. You have to know Mel to understand that kind of glee. The last time I'd heard it come from deep within was when we rented a cabin on the coast in Maine. We found it online and held our breath as we drove down the driveway to the cottage on the water's edge. It was gorgeous and she ran around the entire outside waving her hands in absolute joy.

"Yes we are," I said bouncing on the mattress. "We actually did it, and here comes the fun part."

It didn't take long for her to realize we needed to go back to the farmhouse for Eli and Toby. We wanted to bring them over while it was still daylight. If we tripped and fell because we couldn't see in the dark, they might get away. That was the last thing we wanted for this first important night.

Driving there I mentioned, "The shed will be very small for the kitties; they won't have much exercise in that small space."

Mel took a piece of paper out of her jeans pocket and handed it to me. "You're not the only one with surprises." I glanced at the drawing and smiled wide, trying to keep the car on the road. It was our shed, with a screened porch attached. Grinning at my obvious delight, she continued. "I'm going to build it this weekend. Actually, we'll all benefit from it. The cats will have a great vantage point to see the woods, and we'll have much better ventilation during the warmer months. We'll store some of Kim's tools there with tarps over them so they don't get wet or damp. It will also provide more inside space for us."

I was biting my lip in thought. "Your plan is brilliant, and we'll need all the space we can get. But, we have to come up with a story for any of the sub-contractors or workers who come on our land. A screened porch will look like someone is permanently living there."

"If we tell everyone that we need to bring the cats over each day because of Toby's diabetes, they might believe us," Mel suggested. "It's probably something we'd need to do even if we weren't living on the land."

We gathered up the kitties, the litter box, toys, bowls, and food, and put them all in the car. Each of us said our goodbyes to the farmhouse, knowing it would be one of the last times we'd ever be there. Of course I would be back to clean, probably the following day. Mel was going to spend tomorrow working on the new porch, so she would be there for the kitties during their initial adjustment. I knew Toby would be fine, but I was a little concerned for Eli. He was still a youngster after all. What did he know of moving to new places?

It was dusk by the time we carried them into their new home. Did I say they needed time to adjust? Ha! As soon as I put Eli down, he headed for the mattress—my side of course. "You've found your new bed," I said to the contented Mr. Eli. "How about me? Where will I sleep?"

Mel snickered. "Maybe he'll share."

I looked over at her and held up my toothbrush, knowing she hadn't thought about that chore. Outside we went, into the woods with a plastic cup of water and a paper towel. We walked to the western side of the shed to brush our teeth. Neither of us wanted to be seen, and anyone coming up the driveway had no chance of seeing us there. About twenty feet back into the woods and brush, there was a small opening. It seemed a good spot to brush and spit. But we were going to have to keep an eye out for ticks.

"This is great," I said as I looked around. "We'll have to get this done early every morning before Kim comes to the house. I don't want anyone watching me brush my teeth."

Mel laughed. "No one will see us here."

Back in the shed I lay on the mattress, Eli at my side. For the first time, Mel spotted the TV. Hopping out of bed, she went to it to have a look, grabbed the remote and scrambled back. When she turned it on she grinned, and pumped her fist in the air.

"We can only bring in four stations," I told her.

"I'm content with that." She watched for a few hours before turning it off for the night. I wondered if her night owl patterns would be a problem in such a small space, but I was always so tired that I doubted it. Time would tell.

It was dark and every sound seemed huge. The lack of insulation in the shed brought the outdoors closer to me, and I reveled in its peace. The scent of damp earth was rich and yet soothing. There would be no sleep for me that night; rest perhaps, but no sleep. As the night wore on I gave thanks and hugged Eli close, feeling his warm fur under my hand. Together we would rest and listen to the animal sounds on this precious first night.

"I love it here. Thank you." I whispered.

Perk Test

I woke to the sound of trucks rumbling up the driveway.

"Yikes," I blurted out, waking Mel. "They're here, and I'm still in my pjs." Pulling on jeans and a sweatshirt, I wandered outside with my loppers—pruning clippers with long handles for better leverage—as if I'd been there for hours waiting for the men to arrive. I saw Kim and Charlie's trucks in the driveway, but they were deep in conversation, so I made a show of cutting some of the surrounding brush.

Oh no, I forgot to comb my hair. No time now, I thought, as I ran my fingers through the unruly white mess. I didn't get to brush my teeth either. Yuck. That would have to wait, too. I hoped Mel would be in better shape when she came out, so I could rush back in and grab my toothbrush. No one would see me on the west side of the shed. Here was the beginning of our new adventure and it was making me giddy even before I had any coffee. I hoped Mel had turned the pot on because I thought I was going to have a slow wake up. "Nope, not today," I mumbled, thinking I didn't know as much as I thought I did.

I glanced up to see Kim, who was walking toward me. Charlie was close behind. "Hey," Kim said grabbing the tape measure from his belt. "We're going to the field because we need to evaluate, one more time, where to place drain fields. Want to come along?"

"Nah, go ahead, I'll catch up with you in a minute," I answered, dying to get back into the shed. Once their backs were turned, I scrambled inside.

"What in the hell are you doing?" I asked, laughing at the frenzy going on. Mel was wildly searching around for her contacts. She didn't want anyone to see her without them, and that left me a giggling mess. She looked so funny scooting around the bed on the floor, less than half awake.

"I can never remember where I put anything when I first wake up," she moaned, flopping back on her pillow. "Especially in a new place like this."

I had to hug myself to control my amusement, "I wish I could make a video of this."

By the time Kim and Charlie returned from the field, I felt presentable.

Charlie looked at me for a moment. "I'm going home to get my backhoe. I'll dig the holes for the perk test as soon as I get back. I have a post-hole digger that attaches to my backhoe. The test is on Saturday, the third. You knew that, right?"

"Good deal. If we need any help. Bill will be here to lend a hand. Hard to believe it will be the beginning of June and we are digging holes for the perk test already."

As an afterthought he said, "I'm going to leave my backhoe here for the next couple days. After the test, I'll dig trenches for the drain fields,"

"Sounds good to me," I said, secretly hoping he'd leave the keys as well. I wanted to drive it around. I always drove my Dad's forklift and bulldozer as a kid, so why not a backhoe when it was parked in my own yard?

"Oh," he said, taking off his cap and running his fingers through his thin hair, "knowing you, I'm not going to leave my keys." With a smile, he turned back to the truck.

"Damn. What are you, a mind reader?" I said, kicking the small stone in front of my sneaker.

Saturday came, and with it the fate of the trees by the road. If we put the septic system there it would take up about a quarter of an acre's worth of trees. I sent up a quick prayer, hoping they would be saved. I couldn't wait to get started. The engineer was supposed to arrive any minute. I made another pot of coffee, thinking we all could use a little help.

I heard a voice from outside so I walked from the shed with a shovel in my hand. Mel and I had put one by the door so if anyone came by we would look normal and not as if we'd just crawled out of bed.

"Hi," I said, looking toward a man of medium height, brown hair and eyes to match.

"Hello, Ms. Paradysz? Or is it Ms. Powell? I'm Ed," he said looking me over. "I'm here for your perk test. Will you show me the holes that have been dug?"

"Sure. I'm Sal. Very happy to have you here, Ed." I took him to the field and pointed to the holes Charlie dug for the test. On our walk out there I said, "I have a deep love for the trees near the street, and for the rest of this land, Ed. My dad was a lumberman and taught me to honor each and every living thing in this world, and I'd like to keep to that. It may sound sappy, but it's how I feel."

He stole a quick look at my eyes, and realized I was sincere. "I like your placement," he said, pointing to the holes. "I'm parked next door so I can bring water to the field for the test."

"Great. I'll be around if you need any questions answered," I said as he walked away. Then I went to find Mel.

As the two of us hurried back down the path, I thought about the simplicity of a perk test. You fill holes of certain depth with water, and then time how long it takes for the water to drain into the soil. Certainly not rocket science, but a needed test to determine what kind of system you'd need.

After Ed filled the holes with water, he went back to his truck for a half hour. With Mel by my side, I waited and watched the holes. Ed came back and took a measurement. He needed to see how much water had drained out. Jotting down his findings, he went back to his truck. We waited again, willing the water to go down. A little later he was back doing the same thing. This went on for about two hours.

On the last trip back, he and his clipboard brought terrible news. "I'm afraid the perk test has failed," Ed said. "You can't have a standard system in this field. It doesn't drain fast enough. You could always have a sand mound though, with an above the ground system."

"Oh no!" I exclaimed, throwing my hands up in the air. "Isn't there anything else we might try? I don't want an above the ground system. I plan to plant fruit trees, blueberry bushes, and raspberries here."

He looked somber, but managed a smile. I'm sure he could tell I was focused on the trees I'd mentioned to him earlier. "There is one more system we might try. It's a more shallow system, and one that will need a pump between the house and field. But, it's not a sand mound, it's a regular system."

"What do we have to do to make it happen?" I asked. "And can we do it today?"

He looked at his watch and frowned. "The new test will take an hour and a half and I only have two more hours to give you."

"Okay," I said thinking fast, "that's enough time."

"You'll need to dig another six holes for the test." Ed said, grimacing. "They'll have to be three feet deep and at least twelve inches wide."

New holes. No Charlie. No keys. Yikes.

I rubbed my hands over my face in frustration and looked at Mel. "Okay, sit down for thirty minutes Ed. We'll get it done." As we ran to the tarps to get shovels and a pick ax, I called Bill and Heidi on my cell. I told them what was happening and within minutes they were running toward us, shovel and picks in hand. I was determined we were going to do this.

By the end of thirty minutes, we'd dug six new holes.

"Oh God, my back!" I exclaimed. "It's killing me." Without the help of a post-hole digger, we'd managed to dig down three feet deep, six times. All of it through stony, hard-packed ground. I was sweaty, tired, and had huge blisters on my hands. So did everyone else. But, we did it.

"I'm pooped." I fell back to the ground.

Ed couldn't believe how determined we all were. He said the depth was fine and began filling the new holes with his bucket of water. He walked back through the woods to his truck. Thirty minutes later he was back. Bill, Heidi, Mel, and I were all still sitting around the holes staring at the water level. We thought if we looked at it long enough, it would drain faster. Ed took the measurement, shook his head, and left us to our vigil.

Sitting there I dared to cup my hands, scoop out some of the water, and throw it on the ground. Mel grinned mischievously and did the same. Then Bill and Heidi joined in. But we each only took out one handful. We looked at one another other smiling, knowing we were taking a chance.

When Ed came back for the next measurement he said, "I can't under-stand why this ground isn't draining better. I was the one who did the earlier perk tests by the street and they were fine. This test should be fine too. I'd bet it's only the top layers of soil that are firm from all the decades of farming." Very quietly he continued, "Keep your fingers crossed. If the water level drains out just a little faster, it will pass." With that said, he walked back to his truck.

I fell back to the ground again. "I'm not sure I can take such grueling work anymore." But I was feeling a perverse sense of satisfaction regardless of the extreme exhaustion.

Mel looked at all of us with a solemn expression, "Let's go ahead and take four scoops of the water out this time." So we did. I asked Heidi if she had a turkey baster thingy and she howled with laughter. We were all veg-etarians. Why would any of us have a turkey baster? We cupped our hands and removed our four scoops of water. This continued each half hour until the test was complete. Our hands were muddy, and the ground around us was soaked and soggy. Each of us plopped our dirty behinds down on the wet patches of earth, so Ed wouldn't notice.

Again, Ed walked toward us with the clipboard. My fear was palpable. This time he looked at us and smiled. "You're lucky ladies. You've passed."

It was going to cost a little more than the standard system, but I didn't care. We had saved the trees. Smiling and laughing, we all hugged. And, guess what? Ed was hugging us too. He was laughing every bit as hard as we were. The five of us left the field together, hand in muddy hand.

As Ed stepped up into his truck to leave, we wiped our grubby hands on our jeans and shook his clean one. "Thank you, Ed." If he noticed the dirt, he never said a word.

"In all my years doing this job, never once have I ever seen people so caring about the trees," he said placing the clipboard on the seat. "It was my pleasure to spend the day with all of you."

"Thanks again." I said as he started his truck. "Come back and visit us anytime. You're always welcome here."

I'm sure he felt our affection. "I'm going to take you up on that."

Mel and I gave our thanks to Heidi and Bill, and headed back through the woods toward the shed. We'd used up every bit of our energy, and I felt whipped. The screened porch would have to wait for another day. I entered our little home, and after changing into clean clothes, I sat in my chair. I was so thankful for Ed and our soon-to-be shallow septic system.

Grabbing my cell phone, I left a message for Charlie. "Come and dig," I said quietly, so as not to disturb Mel who had fallen asleep on her sleeping bag. "The perk test has been completed. It passed for the shallow system."

This day, too, was complex. I'd made an 'on the spot' decision on how to save the trees. Their lives mattered to me. The bizarre events of the day were fading fast, and the only memory left in my heart was gratitude.

Clawfoot Wonder

Yanking the door open for the next to last time, I thought the farm-house looked lonely. It was empty and needed cleaning, so I began the task. It didn't take long; two hours and I was done. I picked up all my cleaning supplies, walked to my car, and closed the door to that chapter of my life. Mel and I still had the keys and we would go back for one last look together. The landlord had given us until today, June 4th, to move out. I thought I wouldn't need the extra time, but I did. I'd send the keys back to him by mail, hoping to get my security deposit back. I didn't anticipate any problems.

"If I drive the keys over," I mumbled driving up the lane, "maybe I'll get the deposit back quicker." I thought about how much the money would help. Two months rent was a considerable amount, especially when nothing on the house project had come in under budget so far. Typical.

When I got back, Mel asked, "Did you remember to grab Eli's porch from the back window?"

"Damn, I forgot. We'll grab it tonight when we go back." Eli's porch was another tribute to Mel's skills. Six months after we brought Eli home from our breeder in Florida, Mel sketched out a design and built him a porch. Eli and his little screened-in porch had become a feature article in "Family Handyman" magazine that year. We never let our kitties go outside to play, but Eli loved sitting at the windows. Mel built a screened-in box, put in on stilts, and moved it to the window on the north side of the house. Then she replaced the bottom half of the window with a kitty door of her own design, so the cats could visit their "porch" any time they chose.

Mel worked for Rodale Press at the time, and when one of her former editors came for a visit, he photographed Eli for his magazine, "Family Handyman." The design became a featured article with a photo of Eli's large Maine Coon self, stretched out in his porch. I didn't want to leave it behind.

Mel was making great progress building her new screened-in structure for the shed, in any spare moments she found. She'd be finished in time for us to go to the next auction. The preview was, again, the Friday before, and I wanted to be ready. We still needed a few items for the bathroom. Mel wanted a tub and I wanted a separate shower stall. We didn't have a lot of space, but it should be enough.

I sat for a moment and perused the newest "Penny Power." It was a small twelve to sixteen page local weekly newspaper, advertising various items for sale. On the fourth page, I found an ad I'd been searching for in the past few issues. Pulling out my phone I dialed the number. A man picked up and after ten minutes he'd answered all my questions.

"I'll be over in thirty minutes." I said grabbing my keys.

Following his directions, I arrived at his house within the half hour. I took one look at the ancient clawfoot tub and said, "I'll take it if you can deliver it to my land."

Shaking my hand, he tipped his head toward the pickup truck close by. "I can bring it by later this afternoon."

"That works for me." I wrote him a check for fifty dollars less than the amount advertised. Actually, I think he was happy to have me take it off his hands.

When I got back to the shed, Mel was taking a work break. "I wondered where you went."

"You'll find out this afternoon." I walked away to hide my amusement.

Raising an eyebrow, she called after me, "I know you are up to something, I can always tell."

I kept busy until the man arrived.

As the pickup came up the driveway, I could see the clawfoot tub peeking over the side of the truck bed. Mel stood there staring with her hands shoved deep in her jeans pockets. I hurried over to help the man take the tub out of his truck. It was so heavy I had to call Mel over to help, and even then the three of us could hardly lift it. It would sit by the driveway until Kim was ready to install it.

As the pickup pulled away, Mel hugged me. "I love it, Sal."

"The man who owned it had it in his cabin up in the Poconos. He replaced it with something newer. I'm going to have it redone for you." The surface of the tub wasn't in great condition, but I had read another ad in the Penny Power for a company that boasted of resurfacing any tub, no matter its age.

Making a picture frame from my fingers, "I was thinking of a cream color for the inside, and a sage green on the outside. I want the plumber to attach a period-piece faucet to it. It will look like something from the nineteenth century."

"Couldn't love it more," she said, her voice catching with emotion.

After Mel finished for the day, we drove back to the farmhouse for the last time. She wanted to shower but I wouldn't let her. "I just finished cleaning it," I said, firmly. "Besides, there are no towels." We went to the basement. Everything looked clean and empty. Back up the stairs to the attic, and it looked good there too. Next we checked the bedrooms. I found a few shirts hanging in a closet, so I tucked them under my arm. Then we walked outside for one last look at the big 'ole pear tree we loved. It was so handsome and abundant that I decided I'd plant one in our field. Finally, we said goodbye and left the farmhouse with Eli's porch in the back of my car.

As I drove, Mel's phone rang. She answered, and mouthed to me that it was Kim.

"I'm waiting at the land to go over some of the items you need to purchase from the upcoming auction."

"Okay, we'll be there in ten," Mel answered.

As we drove in, he was sitting at the camp. Walking toward him, he hooked a thumb toward the shed. "I can't believe you two are living there." He took a long drag on a stinking little cigar. I'm sure he must have known how much we hated it.

"Yep, we are," I said, feeling guilty. "Remember, it's our secret." I sat down next to him, looked at the list he had in his hand, and then raised my eyes to his. Shiny blue eyes stared back as he talked. He went over every item for the auction with us in detail.

As he left to go home, I exclaimed, "Oh my God. I hope he doesn't tell John we're living on this land."

The following morning around ten o'clock, even though it was a Monday, we picked up trash around the foundation of both the shed and the house. There were a lot of odds and ends of wood and brick. It took about three hours to finish. We'd been working diligently for weeks without a break, so we decided to do something fun.

"Let's go to Nockamixen and take a walk along the shore." I said to Mel stretching my back.

"I'm so tired," Mel whimpered. "Can we make it a short walk and then sit in the shade and watch the sailboats?"

"Of course," I said, happy to be doing other things. "That will be restful.

We'll bring our folding chairs."

"Then I want to treat you to Chinese take out. It will be fun and we'll bring it back to the shed to eat while we watch TV tonight."

"Okay." I'd never turn down an offer like that.

Driving to the lake was a pleasure, and fortuitously there was a sailboat race happening. We stayed all afternoon, watching the race and talking about our life in the woods.

Back at the shed that evening, we enjoyed our take-out meal while watching our tv shows. I wasn't quite ready to sleep, so I pulled on a sweatshirt and walked out to the field. Looking up at the sky I found the Big Dipper, the Little Dipper, and Orion's Belt, along with a sky full of fiery stars. I felt as if we were being covered that night with a blanket of softness from the heavens above.

Auction Three

"How could a month go by so quickly?" I asked. Mel turned to look at me as we drove to Hanover. It was another auction preview day.

"Have we really been living in a shed for two weeks?" she asked.

"Yep. And I heard what I thought was a raccoon last night."

"Really."

It felt normal to walk out each morning with a cup and toothbrush in my hands. The natural life agreed with me and Mel had adapted very well. My feet touched the earth and kept me grounded for the work I was doing. I leaned against the trees for support and I swear I felt them lean back. Nature and Sal were becoming one.

By the time we drove into the parking lot of the Southern Sales Auction, it was mid-morning. Knowing how everything worked, we were faster and more efficient. First on our list was flooring. Kim mentioned there wasn't enough hardwood for the entire house and if we wanted continuity, we'd need to purchase more of the same. As we walked toward the flooring area I felt a little concerned. Surely they didn't sell it all.

I searched but didn't see any boxes of the same hardwood we'd purchased last month, but at that moment one of the auctioneers' sons walked by. He was young, but seemed capable so I told him about my problem.

He shifted from one foot to the other. "Stay right here while I go and find my dad. I'll ask him about it and be right back."

I waited and waited until I was sure he wasn't coming. "Let's go find him," I said to Mel. "We can't keep wasting time waiting here." We walked away, but within a few minutes the boy caught up with us.

"Please come back to the flooring area," he said, pointing in that direction. "I have a man with a forklift bringing over more of your flooring. You can purchase as much of it as you need right now." I looked over at Mel. She seemed pleased.

"I didn't realize that was a standard part of auction procedure," I said, looking at the young man.

"Of course if you want to wait until tomorrow," he said, "you can bid on it again. You might get it for less, but it might be more, too. It's your call." He explained that anytime you wanted more of your tile or hardwood, you could buy it for the same price you'd paid before. If they had any left.

Good deal, I thought.

After talking it over we went back to the table at the rear of the building and paid for twenty more boxes. The women at the table said we could take it home now, so we loaded it into Powder. Then went back to look at exterior doors.

I needed one for my study, and I knew what I wanted. It needed to be all glass, so it would bring more sunlight into that room.

As we entered the area, I immediately spotted a front door that was perfect. It was stunning with its leaded glass and side lights.

"This is just the ticket."

Mel was touching the wood. "Love it. It's mahogany."

We measured, and then put it on our list. Looking around, I saw the door that was just the one for my study. All glass. Hopefully, I could win the bid for it. Mel was looking for a French door for her studio, and found it. She felt confident it would be hers. One of us was going to have to cement ourself in the door area during the auction tomorrow. We needed to be up front and ready.

As we drove back late that afternoon, I realized the French doors Mel wanted were too large to fit into Bill's truck. I scratched my head. If we won the bid on the doors we'd have to come up with another way to get them home.

"I've got it," I exclaimed after a few quiet moments. Mel jumped and the car swerved.

"What?" she asked once she recovered control of the vehicle.

"I know how to move the French doors."

She sneaked a peek at me then back at the road. "Great, how?"

"We can use Kim's horse trailer. She can swing that trailer around like nobody's business." It was a little confusing having two close friends having the same name. "We should fix both of them up with each other. How funny. Kim and Kim. But let's call her KW."

"Sal, that's inspired. Call her now about the trailer, and forget about getting them together, they are much too different." I pulled out my cell phone and dialed KW's number. She didn't answer, so I left a message and hoped she would get back to me soon. With a bit of luck we'd have a solution.

When we got home, I called Mr. Wonderful. He asked us to come to his office so we could go over our purchasing plans. I had total confidence that he could make the doors work, but he might not have been as certain. We gave him the measurements as soon as we arrived, and it only took him a few minutes to agree with us.

"I can picture that door for the space, but I'm going to need another set of drawings with the new door measurements." He laid his hands flat on his desk, and then stood. "This will be a record for me—the most revised floor plans for one home. And, I haven't even started building yet."

I worried he was going to ask us to stop changing things, but he didn't. As I looked into his eyes he was dead-on serious and determined to make this all happen.

He slipped one of the slim cigars into his mouth and said, "I've never worked like this before, but it's coming out okay. Most of the time."

"Phew," I mumbled.

It was auction day, again, and I was up and moving by five o'clock. The auctions started at eight and we needed to park, get numbers, and be in the door section. I never had to push Mel; we each knew the importance of our work. And, it was fun. Nice combo.

I was still unsure how we were going to get everything home. I had not yet heard from KW about her trailer, but in my heart, I knew she would help us.

Once we had our numbers, I left Mel with the doors. "Good luck," I whispered. "Remember not to bid first."

She grimaced. "Yeah, you too."

Running over to the window area, I worked my way to the front. I knew I'd have to wing it today, because I forgot to check this section yesterday. I could tell some of the men recognized me, and I smiled. I felt a little better about being around men now and maybe they would help me if I stumbled with the bidding.

As the auction began, I waited for the windows to go up for sale. A quick look around and I'd found the ones for my study. I crossed my fingers as we moved down the line toward the ones I wanted. When the auctioneer began, I stood silently along with everyone else. I was getting the hang of this auction stuff. When one of the contractors put his hand up to begin, I followed suit. We went back and forth. It seemed we were the only two who had any interest in this particular set.

The auctioneer looked at the two of us and scratched his head. "Mike, are you getting this set of windows for the same home you were building last month?"

Mike nodded his head. "Yes I am, Sam."

The auctioneer frowned. "You aware these are the wrong color?"

Mike checked his notes and laughed. "Whoops, good catch, bud." What a memory, I thought, but I reminded myself that this was an auctioneer's job and he did it well. He was the owner, too. "Guess I'll wait and bid on the Sandtone ones. What color are these again?"

"Terratone," Sam said. "That's what this lady needs."

"Well, I guess she can have them," Mike said politely. It was my good fortune that the auctioneer was honest enough to point out the contractor's mistake, rather than just driving up the price.

Sam looked at all of us standing there. "We'll begin the bidding fresh, folks." No one else seemed interested in the windows, but I still didn't want to bid first. Finally the auctioneer asked me what price I wanted to start with.

"Umm," I said, not being exactly sure. Everyone looked at me and laughed. I laughed too. "I'll offer what Mike opened the bidding with when we first started."

"I'd say that's a wise choice," Sam said. "Sold to number 96." The windows were perfect, and they were mine. I couldn't wait to get them home.

Satisfied, I watched the helper scribble my number on the window box. Then I left to go to the door area to see how Mel was making out. "I got the exterior door we wanted," she said, beaming. "I'm now waiting for the French doors to go up." I walked over to look at the large front door again and was sure it would make the face of our home look handsome.

Suddenly everything came to a halt. The bidding stopped, the auctioneer paused, and silence took over. I overheard someone say that one of the auctioneers at the rear of the building needed help. With the action suspended, we took this time to walk back to our cars and eat lunch. I tried calling KW again at her horse barn.

She picked up on the second ring. "I was just going to call you," she said. "I'd be happy to help you tomorrow."

"You're an angel. We'll work the details out later. I'll call you tonight." I snapped my phone shut and followed Mel back to the building. I wanted to get as close as I could to the French doors. They were the ones we needed.

I stood a little behind Mel. People were jammed into one small area, and I wondered why. Maybe everyone wanted to look at the doors, but Mel wanted the one that fit her architectural drawings. I knew she'd do her best to get it. As the bidding began Mel waited. This time neither of her arms shot into the air. She was studying the men around her waiting for her turn to jump in, but it was taking longer than usual.

I whispered into her ear. "Mel, there's a man standing to our right looking to bid on your doors. He looks angry and mean, and the hair on the back of my neck is standing straight up. He doesn't seem in his right mind or something."

Mel looked over at him and flinched. Being the Jersey girl she is, it takes a lot to intimidate her. This man was intent on disrupting what should have been a smooth transaction. He stared down one of the workers and then shoved him aside. Scanning the crowd, he said, "You guys make me sick with all your money."

Mel, fully recovered, said, "What a jerk."

"Shhhhh, I know. He scares me." I looked away and kept my head down for the rest of the bidding. He wanted this door, too, but Mel wasn't about to give up. She won the bid, and as the assistant wrote Mel's number down on the clipboard the auctioneer excused himself for a second. Shortly thereafter, three well-muscled guys surrounded the angry man and escorted him to the door.

Tension eased dramatically with his departure. Our entire section was buzzing about his behavior, but one of the contractors summed it up nicely.

"We're like family here, we watch out for our own." Everyone nodded in agreement.

Our part of the auction was finished. We had purchased everything from our list so I made my way to the back table, knowing I could pay now before the lines got too long. It was still light outside. We were way ahead of last month's auction.

As I wrote the check for our items, Mel went to find a long cart. It only took a minute because the auction hadn't finished yet. Moving quickly, we moved my study windows to my car. The French door for Mel's studio and the stunning exterior door for the house stood side by side. I told the employee at the door we'd be back to pick them up in the morning.

Once we got on the road I turned to Mel. "When we get home, will you go to Kim's office with the measurements? I want to go to the barn and help KW hook up the trailer."

Mel gave a tired sigh, "That's a good idea, love." We were both pooped.

"In the morning we'll all drive back to the auction together in KW's truck. I have plenty of five dollar bills in my pocket for tipping. We're going to need help getting these heavy doors into the trailer."

"It will be a damn tough day," Mel said, yawning. "Once we have the doors loaded we still need to unload them at Deb and Marty's barn."

I sat back and let the miles roll by while I reflected on my inner self. I closed my eyes and sat in meditation for a good thirty minutes. What came to me was love, and how everything I was doing tied me to that one emotion. Love of my land, love for Mel, and love for my new life. I felt committed to the laws of the natural world and believed in my own abilities. The things I needed I already had. Compassion and courage. As Laotse wrote, "A thousand mile journey starts with one step." *I'm on my way,* I thought.

"You certainly know how to drive this rig," I said, as we bounced along in KW's truck the next morning.

"Most horse women know how to handle a truck and horse trailer." KW exhaled with a groan. "I've even driven one through Soho, in New York City. I was lost, but finally found a way out."

Thinking of the narrow, crowded Soho streets, I laughed hard. "I suppose you've got a point there. I had horses growing up, but I never had a trailer. I didn't show in competitions; I rode for fun."

As we made our way to the auction grounds I thought back to those innocent years of my youth. I did work hard with my dad, but summers were also spent playing Cowboys and Indians with my cousin. It was so much fun. We each had a horse then, and spent many endless days in the woods. When she couldn't come with me, I would ride along the streams, my saddlebags packed with peanut butter and jelly sandwiches. It would be dusk when I got home and dark before I finished grooming. After dinner, I'd walk back to read my books in the hay stack, and I'd fall asleep to the soft nickering of my horse, Lindy Lou. I loved that time.

As we neared the site, Kim broke into my thoughts. "I'm thankful I don't have to try to go around that darn oak tree at the end of your driveway when we get home. I know I can manage, but it would be difficult."

I winced. "Most likely I'll be calling on you to bring this huge door over to our house, once our builder is ready for it."

She shrugged her shoulders and chuckled. "Of course. Crazy me to think I'd get out of that one."

We found a parking space close to the entrance and went in. I showed our receipts to the checkers seated at the doors, and walked straight to where our stuff was the previous night. It was gone. Frantically I looked for someone in charge. Finding one of the workers nearby, I explained my problem.

"We thought your doors and windows needed to be put in the back of the building last night," he explained. "Even though one of us stays here overnight, there's always a chance someone might make their way in and steal something. It doesn't happen often, but it has happened. With that nutty guy from yesterday, we didn't want to take a chance." I thanked him, and gave him a generous tip for his effort.

Mel found a worker and asked him to drive our doors to the parking lot with his forklift. They laughed when they saw we had a horse trailer.

"Man, this is great. It's so low to the ground, and much easier to load than most trucks," he said. "I'm going to suggest this trick to other people from now on."

The doors slid in without a hitch. We tipped the man and headed for home. The trip back was an easy one as KW's truck was more than powerful. Hearing a funny noise beside me, I peeked at Mel. She had fallen asleep to the hum of the diesel engine.

At Deb and Marty's barn, I realized I'd forgotten that we needed help. I had thought of asking Andy to meet us here. He would have, I'm sure. This was going to be interesting. Deb and Marty both had weak backs, but they were still willing to lend a hand. The five of us grabbed onto the French door and managed to push it down the ramp and onto the cement floor. It was all we could do to get it back far enough to be able to get close to the barn door, but when we did—that's where it stayed. We followed suit with the front exterior door. I was concerned about the leaded glass as we shoved it down the ramp, but even though it bumped hard on the cement it stayed in one piece. The rest of the stuff was easy by comparison.

I handed money to KW for gas. "Thanks sweetie, this couldn't have happened without that trailer. You saved us."

"Not a problem." She sighed. "Will you follow me to the barn and help with the trailer? It is hard to take off by myself."

"Of course," I answered, but I was one tired woman. "Mel, I can handle this. Go back to the land and I'll meet you there in a little while. KW will drop me off."

I couldn't get back to the shed fast enough. I was worn out. Toby and Eli greeted me with bright eyes and kitty purrs. We'd been gone off and on for the last three days, and they needed play time with us. Mel turned on the TV, and for the next hour we gave most of our attention to them.

As I rubbed and petted, I said, "You were very quiet today. Are you okay?"

"Just tired. Maybe even beyond tired."

As I walked out into the woods to brush my teeth, crickets welcomed my presence with their songs and I smelled the faint odor of wild cherry blossoms.

I must be in heaven.

A Summertime Jig

It was hot for the 20th of June, and summer was here with a vengeance. Charlie was coming tomorrow to push the topsoil back against the building. My job was to apply a sub-surface water sealer before then. This sealer stuff was a thick, tar-like material applied to footing and foundation to seal out any moisture. It was an important job to get right if I wanted a dry basement. And I did.

The ten five-gallon containers, each weighing thirty pounds or so, thumped like base drums as I dropped them on the ground from the back of my car. I was as close to the block foundation wall as I could get. There was a two-and-a-half foot wide trench between the building and the excavation walls. I wouldn't be able to see over the dirt on the high side, but the land faded away from the house on the other walls. Easier there, I thought. With so little room to maneuver, this was going to be a challenge. Knowing the day would only get hotter; I decided to start with the most difficult surface first. The north side.

I was on our land alone today with all of nature surrounding and grounding me. Earlier, as I filled the bird feeders, I saw a flock of American goldfinch settling into the woods. Within the past three weeks, the color of the males had gone from a green-gold to screaming intense yellow. Even brighter than in April, I thought. Spring and early summer brought in various birds from their winter habitats. Already I had seen rose-breasted grosbeaks, purple finches, and rufous-sided towhees. I was waiting for my favorite of all to show up: the wood thrush. The songs from that bird always made me stop whatever I was doing. It was so eloquent that listening to it made me feel privileged to be in nature's surroundings.

Why, I wondered, was it difficult for me to feel equal, especially with men? If I had to guess, I'd say it was because I had not felt that equality since childhood. Even getting married in the Catholic Church, and I was not Catholic, Bob and I had to kneel behind the rail that stood at the alter. The priest made the announcement that the rules were solid on this, non-Catholics had to be kept back. Being raped made me feel even worse about men. There is no equality in rape.

As I worked on the land, I began to understand the difference between being alone and loneliness. Of being weak internally, or strong. On this land, I was not lonely or weak. It was an opportunity to become myself, to find out who I truly was. At sixty! I was experiencing new feelings of worthiness every day, working hard physically and intellectually while I made my way through these new emotions. I was learning more than how to build a house. Entering my seventh decade I was learning who I was as a woman.

I shook myself out of my reverie and opened a can of sealer. Brushing it on was difficult, so I grabbed the nearby roller and started again. This is easier, I thought, making my way around one side of the building. By late morning, I was so hot and tired that I doubted I'd finish it all in one day. But later, I found my strength and kept going. Toward late afternoon, I was done.

I climbed out of the trench to have a better look, and as I walked around the side of the foundation, I saw Kim standing there looking at me. I had black tar splotches all over my clothes, my head dripped with sweat, and my face was streaked with dirt, but I had finished the job.

"Charlie's coming over in the morning to move the dirt back around the foundation," he said.

"I know that," I said a little snarkily.

He looked down at his feet for a minute. "You have to apply a second coat of sealer before he gets here."

"Ha ha, very funny." I hoped he was teasing me, and waited to see if he meant it.

"I meant it," he said, and walked back to his truck. No wonder he had purchased so many containers.

Suddenly my buoyant mood vanished. I waited two hours making sure everything was dry, and began again. It was eighty-eight degrees so it had dried quickly. Climbing down into the trenches I opened another five-gallon can and got started, but this coat went on a little easier.

After an hour, Mel came from the studio and picked up the other roller. Having someone to talk and laugh with made the job go much faster. We finished just as the sun was setting.

I hurried to the field to watch the sunset, and Mel was right behind me.

Sitting together in silence brought me peace. It felt remarkable to watch each day's end by viewing the colorful show take place just beyond the woods. I may have been sweaty and weary, but I was filled with bliss from a good day's work.

An hour later, I dragged my tired, dirty body down to Heidi and Bill's for a well-earned shower. I needed it more than ever that evening, mostly because I had used paint thinner to remove the tar from my arms and legs.

My life was different these days, but it was working out just fine for me.

I woke the next day to the sound of a bulldozer coming up the driveway, and grabbed my watch to check the time. Six fifteen in the morning, and Charlie was already here. "How early does this man get up?"

Climbing out of bed, I scrambled into jeans, tee-shirt, and sneakers, and walked out holding on to the shovel we used as a prop. Charlie waved his hat at me, and I wondered if he was on to us. As far as I knew, Kim was the only person who shared in our secret. I realized both of our cars were parked in the driveway, so of course he knew we were somewhere on the land.

Later, Kim drove up and opened the back of his truck. He took out a shiny red piece of equipment. It was about two and a half feet tall, a foot and a half wide, sitting on wheels. It looked brand new.

"What's that?" I asked, bending over to get a better look.

He planted his feet wide apart and placed his hands on his hips. "I have wanted a generator for years. You don't have electric service to the house yet, so it gave me an excuse to purchase one. So, thanks." He thumped my shoulder with his strong hand. "Bringing electricity in and having a temporary pole set up for this project would cost you a lot of money. I don't see the need for that."

"We should be thanking you then," I said. "If you want we can keep the generator on the screened porch every night. We'll throw a tarp over it to keep it dry, and hidden." I started feeling a little guilty knowing we already had electricity, but then I realized the extension cord we had for the shed was not enough muscle for Kim. He needed to use power tools and those took a lot of amps.

"That'd be great." he said. "Oh, and keep an eye out. I should be getting a lumber delivery within the next hour, so let me know if you see them coming. I need to help the guy."

Mel left for the studio and I got out my brush cutters and went to work around the shed and paths we walked every day. There was only a little work left to do. I cleared branches along with underbrush, and stepped back to take a look at my progress when I heard a truck coming up the driveway.

It was the load of lumber. I said a quick prayer of thanks when he made it around the ol' oak.

"Kim," I called. "Lumber's here." He came out from the back of the foundation to greet the truck, letting them know where he wanted the wood to be stacked. I noticed that Charlie had already left.

"I never heard Charlie go down the driveway," I said.

"He finished about an hour ago."

I watched as Kim and the driver stacked the lumber. The pungent smell and the sound of board against board, took me back to happy sawmill days—days filled with good hard work—days like today.

I went back to clearing brush until later when I noticed Kim was having lunch. I made a quick pb&j and joined him. He eyed my sandwich and laughed. "Peanut butter? What are you, four?"

I laughed, too. "Are you going to tease me throughout this entire project?"

"Probably," he said as we ate. I didn't much care because he and I were becoming good friends.

"I know this question is personal, Kim, but we seem to have a lot in common. Did you have a lot of expectations when you entered your marriage?"

"I didn't think so at the time. But reflecting back now I believe I did. Maybe too many."

"Me too." I was quiet for a while and so was Kim. Later, I made fresh coffee for each of us, and we sat there for ten more minutes watching the turkeys luxuriate in their dust baths.

Kim gestured with his head, "That's what you and Mel are going to have to do now to keep clean." I ignored his silly statement.

After lunch, I went back to work with Bluebie, picking up rocks to place around the new clearing I'd made. I was going to call this a park from now on. Hours later I looked at the time. Four o'clock. How'd that happen, I wondered.

It was nice to walk up to the foundation without the ditch being there; it felt more permanent. Charlie did a good job. For the two and a half-foot height difference from floor to ground, Kim had thrown a couple of two-by-six inch boards together for a ramp. I walked up, and stood on the floor of my new house.

Kim had started framing three hours before, and now two walls were nailed in place already with openings for the windows. Kim had a reputation of being a swift, hard working, and dedicated contractor. Now I knew why. He had worked in the basement putting support bracing in place, and a few other jobs down there as well.

Around four-thirty, I walked over to say good-bye to Kim as he sauntered to his truck. He had finished all four walls. "I'll be back at seven o'clock tomorrow morning, and every morning until the job is complete. I'm bringing my daughter Stephanie along too. She's just graduated from high school and needs a job before college in the fall. She's a good worker and is becoming quite the builder. I've had her help me many times in the past, so you're in good hands." He looked so proud.

"No wonder you were willing to work with women," I said. This was exciting. Our land was honored again, this time with Stephanie's presence.

Kim left. I started a fire in the little fire pit I'd made early that morning, and called Mel. I described what had been accomplished in her absence. She said she'd be home in an hour. I used that time to go into the woods for long sticks, and brought them back to the park area. Then I went into the shed and pulled out a package of veggie dogs and four potatoes. When Mel drove in later, I covered the potatoes with foil and threw them into the fire. Mel got out of her car without taking her eyes off the new walls. She walked up the ramp with me following, and whirled around. We felt like we were playing house and tried to place ourselves in the kitchen, living room, and my study. At last, we each knew for sure that our house plans were going to work. Our house was not too small after all. What a relief.

We finished being a little crazy and walked down the ramp and out to the fire pit. Sticks in hand, we roasted our dogs. After grabbing plates from the shed, I took the potatoes out of the fire and put butter, salt, and pepper on them. It was all delicious.

Once Mel and I cleaned up the mess, we went back to the fire pit and sat down, looking at our new walls in the soft light of our left-over coals. I loved this small park area I'd made. It was a twenty-yard oval, outlined in stones. The fire pit was in the middle with four chairs placed nearby. It was hard to go in for the night. I wanted to bring my sleeping bag out and sleep by the fire, but I didn't want to be seen early in the morning in case I overslept.

John, the zoning inspector, was due to have a look at the foundation. He needed to make sure everything was being done according to code. And the bank inspector would be here soon as well. He, too, needed to approve the foundation so Kim could be paid.

I wish we knew when John was due to arrive. I was a little concerned we might not hear him coming up the driveway, and he would catch us living here. It kept me on edge.

After another hour we walked back to the shed. I grabbed my only sweater and headed to the field while Mel stayed back and watched TV. With the woods at my back, I opened my arms to the sky and danced a little summertime jig, hoping the night animals weren't laughing. *I'm so happy.*

Moving Along

I was tiptoeing around the shed at daybreak in an effort to let Mel sleep when I heard a noise. An instant later Kim was singing reveille; tah—dat—dah-da-dah, tah—dat—dah-da dah! Mel started to giggle, got up, and threw on a sweatshirt.

"I guess we're going to have a wake-up call every morning, from now on," I said to Mel.

Mel shouted, "Stop the racket, you're making me nuts."

I no longer cared how I looked when Kim came to the shed. I even walked out in my pajamas occasionally. I was used to the remarks that followed.

"What's the matter, aren't you morning people?" Kim shouted back. "Come and see me before you leave for the day."

"Okay, Mr. Wonderful," I crooned.

Kim loved waking Mel. In fact, most days he'd turn his CD player in the direction of the shed, then turn up the volume. He left it that way, too, until one of us came out and yelled at him to turn it down.

The year 2000 was an election year. Kim was a staunch Republican. Mel was a Democrat. It was fun listening to the two of them go at it together. One night, after we were already in the shed, Kim walked in from the street and put a Republican bumper sticker on Mel's car. It took almost a week before she spotted it. She was so embarrassed to have been driving around with it on her car. We retaliated by borrowing some Democrat signs from a neighbor. Mel placed them all around his office one morning on her way to the studio. What fun.

After coffee, Mel and I walked to the house. Mel teased Kim about his singing reveille, while I admired his handiwork. He and Stephanie had already finished framing in the first floor. We had met Steph a few days earlier when she came to ask her dad for some money. Like all kids, I thought at the time. She worked hard and brought a beautiful presence with her to our land. Although she was quiet, she stood tall and confident. Most of the time she held her opinions to herself, but occasionally she'd grin at the banter.

I tuned back in to the conversation just as Kim asked, "Would one of you go to Home Depot or Lowe's for more nails for the nail gun this morning? I don't want to take the time away from working on the house, and Steph's busy, too."

"I'll go, Dad," Steph said quietly. "I'll take your truck."

"Nope. Sal can do it; she has less to do than us."

"Whatever you say, Mr. Wonderful." She laughed and used her dad's gesture of an eye roll.

"Fine," I said. "Mel has to work at the studio, but I don't have to go to work until late afternoon so I'll go for the nails." Steph was going to be a lot of fun, I thought as I went for my keys.

While I was gone, the lumber company delivered two glulams, and OSB board. By the time I returned, Kim and Steph were putting them up for the first floor ceiling. This thirty-five-foot-long solid beam, made up of laminated wood measuring eight inches wide and twenty-one inches high, was a daunting sight. Kim had installed one for the basement ceiling, too, and there would be a third for the ceiling of the second floor. I couldn't believe that the two of them managed to get it in place by themselves. It was gigantic and looked heavy.

"Kim," I said staring at the massive beam. "How did you get that monster up there?" The one for the basement ceiling was heavy, too, but they didn't have to lift it over their heads.

"Ropes." Kim looked at me and winked.

Kim and Steph were amazing workers, so capable and strong. Their arms were ropy and muscled. I knew the look. My dad and I both had the same arms when we worked side by side.

Kim came down the ramp. "We'll have to get a crane in to lift the last one up to the top of the second floor, but that won't be for a few weeks yet." Again I thought about the oak tree at the end of the driveway. A crane. Lordy.

Kim dusted his hands on his thighs as he came toward me. "Charlie finished with the drain fields. He'll be back soon to dig a trench from the field to the house. It's a long stretch and will take him most of a day to dig it out."

"Will Charlie have time to do more grading?" We had mountains of topsoil everywhere. "It would be easier walking around the house if the piles were gone."

Kim shrugged. "I'll ask him."

My phone rang. It was Mel asking me to come over to the studio. "I'm trying to pick out some shakes for the siding," she said, "and I want your opinion."

"Sure thing," I said, and waved goodbye to Kim and Steph as I drove over to have a look.

"I like these shakes," she said pointing to her monitor. "They're southern long-leaf pine, and are going to last longer than cedar. They'll look like cedar, but will be slightly thicker. And this siding is impervious to bugs and is guaranteed for fifty years."

I shrugged, and lifted my eyebrows. "Fifty years? I doubt either one of us will have to worry about replacing them then. They look good to me, too, let's go for it."

Mel called the company to place the order and request a sample. We'd have it to show Kim in a few days.

I said goodbye and got back in my car. It was going to take a month before they'd deliver the shakes. It worked well with Kim's schedule. I was anxious to see the sample.

By the time I got back to our land, Kim and Steph were gone. They had accomplished so much in one day. The framing was moving faster than I had expected. Most of the first-floor rooms were studded out.

I brought Bluebie out from under the tarp, and picked up the stray pieces of lumber that had fallen around the base of the foundation. At the beginning of this project, I had promised Kim I'd keep everything clean. On the coming weekend I planned to set a match to the burn pile, getting rid of the burnable refuse. The pile was huge, and it was more than a little scary to think about setting it on fire. I wouldn't wait so long the next time, I vowed.

It took four trips with Bluebie and trailer to clean everything up around the foundation. Next, on the first floor, I picked up the pieces of extra wood and separated good from bad. Kim asked me to save the unusable pieces for his campfire when he went fishing with his friends in upstate New York. Mel and I used the smaller ones for our own little fire pit. There was deadfall everywhere in the woods; when I had time I'd collect that, too. We'd never be at a loss for firewood.

It was almost time for me to go to work, but I took a quick walk to the field anyway. I realized that I never should have sold the mower deck from Bluebie. Most of the field was either dug up because of the drain fields, or covered in piles of wood. But in the clear spots, the grass was getting high. I still had the self-propelled mower I used at the farmhouse, so I'd have to go to Deb's barn and bring it back. If I could find it. The barn was packed full. I'd have to find another storage place for the remaining windows and doors we needed from the next auction.

I felt like a scavenger scurrying around from friend to friend, asking if they had extra space available for us in their garages or barns.

How would I ever repay all of this kindness?

Mice on the Loose

Another tiny rodent scurried across my shoe. "Mice. I hate mice." I was in the barn searching for my lawn mower. So far I'd seen two mice, and where there are two, there are more. It was silly of me, I knew. I could pick them up by their tails and throw them across a field, but still I was frightened of the little creatures. They startle me. Their beady black eyes, and the speed at which they scampered around, coming at me out of nowhere with no warning, made me shudder. I took a deep breath and soldiered on.

Finally, I spotted the mower. Of course, it was way in the back. Working my way toward it I saw yet another mouse making a dash toward the new windows, as if to mock me.

The mower was heavy and awkward, and it was all I could do to lift it over the construction items and out of the barn. As I was putting it into my car, I noticed a cozy mouse nest near the gas tank. Struggling to remain calm, I lifted the mower out again while baby mice fell to the ground. Grabbing my gloves from the back seat, I shook off my revulsion and forced myself to pick them up. I didn't know where to put them. Finally, I opened one of the drawers from Mel's dresser and placed two of them inside along with some of the nesting material. Then I hunted for the others making sure I had them all, including the mother. I didn't want to take her along with me, not because I was a little fearful, but because she needed to be there for her babies. I left the drawer open so they could come and go until they were grown, but I wondered how many more we were going to find along the way.

When I got back to the land, I told Kim about the mice. He laughed.

"It isn't funny," I protested.

"How many have you found in the shed so far?"

This time it was my turn to laugh, "We have two kitties. How's that for planning?"

"Good point," he said. "Good point."

___

Later that day as I headed to Lowe's, I rolled my windows down and turned my music up. It was gorgeous outside. I passed a dump truck in the next lane, the driver turned toward me and waved. He must like my music, I thought. I glanced in his truck bed and it was filled with wood chips. He was headed in my direction, so I followed him until he stopped at a small vacant lot near Quakertown. I jumped out of my car before the driver had a chance to dump his load. He rolled down his window looking a little puzzled.

"Are those wood chips designated for someone else," I blurted out, "or may I buy them?"

He looked more relaxed and said, "You can have them and a lot more if you want."

"This load plus another would be great." We agreed on a price and he followed me home. I asked him to dump them in the cleared out space near the bottom of the driveway. I knew they'd be perfect for the area around my fire pit, and the paths as well.

I looked up from the driveway toward the house and saw Kim standing on the first floor with his hands on his hips. "Nails?" he yelled.

"I'm leaving right now." I shouted, running back to my car. "Sorry." Even his impatience couldn't spoil my glee at getting the wood chips.

When I got back with Kim's nails, I set to work with my tractor and cart shoveling the entire pile of wood chips before I went to work. I filled in the park area and path, using every single chip. Realizing I needed more, I gave the guy a call on my cell.

"Hi, this is Sal over on Deer Trail Road. I was wondering if you'd bring me another load of woodchips."

"Sure, not a problem," he said. "I'll bring more by the end of the week." Perfect.

As I walked to my car to go to work, I realized I'd forgotten to take the lawn mower out. I opened the hatch to get it and spotted another baby mouse, running around in circles looking for its mother. I picked it up with the same gloves, found an empty nail box to put it in, and drove back to the barn with the box in my lap. I called work to tell them I'd be a little late. When I got to the barn I put the baby mouse in the drawer with the others. The mother had already built a new nest, and it was much larger. As I drove to work, I wondered what material that mouse used. Hope it wasn't from something important. I called Mel to let her know about the mice in her dresser drawer. To my relief, she didn't mind at all.

Life Adjustments

Dawn. Late June. I sat at the creek's edge and witnessed first light from a new perspective. I'd hiked down through the field and had been there for most of an hour, occasionally raising the coffee mug to my lips. None of the small birds minded my presence, nor did the geese. Cows in the next field were eyeing me and so was the large red-tailed hawk in the dead tree close by. Hunting for breakfast, he wasn't disturbed enough to fly off, but he did keep guard.

I didn't want to leave just yet. I thought I heard Kim hammering at the house, but couldn't be sure. I did hear music. More than likely he was waking Mel.

Sensing something approaching, I stayed silent. Before long I heard footsteps behind me, and thought it might be the small herd of deer that often bedded down near the creek. Bit by bit I turned my head.

Yes, it was the deer. They walked within fifteen feet of me before catching my scent, and then ran off to drink from the creek. They put their black noses close to the water, giving it a sniff first before swallowing. Then the small herd made their way through the field grazing as they went. They felt safe here, even though I was close by. I liked that sentiment but worried about hunting season in the fall. I hoped they might be protected and safe. I made a mental note to ask the farmer who sold us our property if he allowed hunting in his fields.

The longer I sat on the dead log, the stiffer I became. Still, I didn't want to move. I was filled with anticipation of some other animals that might yet come my way. I stayed another half-hour and just as I was about to get up, I heard quiet feet and the snap of a twig. A bunny, I thought, or raccoon, opossum, or skunk? Time seemed to stop and I waited, holding my breath. Turning my head to the left, I spotted a dark red fox. He was stunning, full-grown, and had a long bushy tail tipped in white. I must have been downwind because he never noticed me, not even from ten yards away. I froze and watched him. He stopped, too, and then ambled over to drink from the enticing creek.

This guy was handsome. The curve of his neck and alert eyes made me want to pick up a palette and brush, even if I didn't paint. He was striking. There were baby geese at the wider expanse of the creek, and instantly I knew what he had in mind for his breakfast. Not on my watch. I stood up slowly and he ran away, unafraid.

At the top of the field near our woods, I stopped dead in my tracks. Music was coming from my house, but it was not the music Kim usually played to wake up Mel. It was Kim and his daughter Steph, singing to Bocelli's arias. Their music was clear and loud, as if it were right beside me and it was the first time I'd heard them sing together. The acoustics must be remarkable in these woods. I made out every word of Andrea Bocelli's Romanza. Kim loved opera, and so did I. He had played this aria many times, and his great baritone voice did it justice. He and Steph sang the lyrics skillfully, and it was clear they loved being together.

As the song finished, I walked up the path and into the shed. Mel had gone to work, but she'd left a message saying she had already given Toby her shot. I stayed inside and enjoyed another cup of coffee, not wanting Kim and Steph to know I had been listening. It was all too sweet; our incredible wooded setting, and glorious music. My dad used to sing as well. He sang tenor and the fullness of his voice used to carry around the lumber yard. He sang in an all men's chorus, and with a barbershop quartet. And yodeled. Such memories.

I felt my heart lift and thought of my sixty years. The pages of the calendar were flying past, but I knew I was filling them now with the passion of my own efforts. Building my new home. Counseling. Both gave me an extraordinary lift.

Last week I talked to my daughter, Shelly. After we chatted for a while about my grandkids, we talked about understanding her problem of expectation. She had expectations of everyone, from her kids to her husband and friends. One example was she felt the kids needed to do more to help out, without her asking. Others were expectations of phone calls from friends so she wasn't always the one who did the calling. Together, we worked on recognizing it, along with the anxiety that expectation brought to her life. In our search on how to let that emotion go, I, too, learned something. From this point forward, I'd appreciate what the sub-contractors accomplished on my house, rather than expecting them to finish on my time schedule. Letting go of expectation lessens stress. Shelly was happy to talk to me and she said it had felt good. Listen and grow together, mother and daughter.

Today I was going to help Kim with the framing. Because of the cost, and our begging, he decided to use OSB board rather than plywood. Oriented Strand Board, better known as OSB, is actually sheets of composite made up of many strands of wood all oriented the same direction to make it strong. Kim explained that to me and said it would also save us a lot of money. That was important.

Moving the sheets of OSB from the first to the second floor was challenging. "Yikes, these are heavy."

"I'm used to their heft," he said walking up the ladder. "I've lifted them for so many years that I never think of the weight issues anymore. It's just something that comes with my line of work."

"I'll hold the sheets in place while you nail them in," I offered. I noticed I was feeling less shy with Kim these days.

"Sounds good to me. That way Steph can stay with what she's doing." She was focused on framing windows in the bedrooms.

The work went swiftly and by four o'clock we had finished. My next job was to move the remaining cement blocks from the foundation to an area nearer the shed. There they would be out of the way and not quite as noticeable. I went to get Bluebie.

"Hey Sal," Kim hollered out from deep inside the house. "Box up those smaller end pieces of wood for me and put them in my truck. I'd like to take them home."

"Sure, no problem." I answered finding a box to put them in. It was great working alongside Kim, but at times, it made me think back to my marriage.

I longed to work like this with Bob, but it wasn't always comfortable. Regardless, we accomplished a lot together at a cottage we helped build on Watson Pond in Otis, Massachusetts. After we purchased the land, my uncle came with his excavating equipment and dug the hole for the foundation. Then my cousin erected the cement foundation walls, and finally another of my uncles helped Bob and me build the house. My dad supplied the lumber, but he and mom had just sold the business and retired to Florida.

That was bad timing on my part. I always wanted to live closer to mom and dad in a way that held no stress. I thought this town about eight miles away from my childhood home might be perfect. A cottage we came to on weekends and vacations and one where they were welcome to watch their grandchildren grow and thrive. It wasn't to be. But Bob's parents came from

Westfield, which was fifteen miles away. They came often. In fact, all the time. It never was much of a vacation for me, really, as I had to make meals for all of us. I'd work outside, come in and make lunch and dinner, and go back out to work. I did love the work part though, and being right on the water was a joy. We had a canoe along with a small boat and motor. I loved that my kids were having the opportunity to discover nature. The lake provided both fun and a venue for learning.

Later, I glanced at my watch. I would soon be leaving. What I wanted to do was stay here and work some more with Kim.

Mel and I made sure that our home expenses were equal, and we each paid our half of whatever new cost came along. I promised myself that in the next few days I'd sit down with my bills and checkbook to see if there was a way to stop working for Dr. Mary. I wanted to focus on building the house. I knew I'd be entitled to collect Social Security in two years, so I began thinking about the interim. Hmmm....

I did sit down and study my budget. It took several days before I was satisfied with my plan, but now I was sure it would work. Late one afternoon, I showered and headed for the chiropractic office. I'd finally made the decision to give Dr. Mary my two weeks' notice. She'd been dear to me over these past few years, so I was hesitant. I didn't want to let her down. I loved being her aide, and enjoyed taking patients back to the examination rooms where I wrote down the history of their current symptoms. I helped them feel comfortable while they waited for Dr. Mary. Patient interaction was critical to their care. Lately I'd been so worn out from all my work that I was afraid I might not be giving enough to the practice. She deserved better from me.

As I walked into the office, I saw Dr. Mary and her husband, Gordon, sitting at their desks.

"Hi, guys."

Gordon gave me a wave as Dr. Mary looked up from her work. "Hey Sal, how are you doing today? Any new stories?" She laughed.

"I'll tell you the mouse tale later. Right now I'd like to talk to you before the patients start coming in, and before I lose my nerve. It's something difficult for me to say."

It did not come as a surprise, and both Dr. Mary and Gordon were supportive of my new adventure. Dr. Mary invited me to come back in the future, and said I could work as a substitute. It was a good meeting. I knew they would soon find a replacement for me. Her office was a great place to work.

Driving home after my shift, I felt good about my choice and wanted to tell Mel. I'd spent hours pouring over my finances before reaching this resolution. When I got back at eight o'clock, Mel was already at the land. I'd expected her to work until midnight tonight, but she had come home early. Mel's most creative hours were during the evening, and I was used to her working late.

Hoping and yet knowing Mel wouldn't be upset, I gathered my courage and stood in front of her. "This morning I made a decision and a commitment to our project. I gave Dr. Mary my two-weeks' notice tonight before work. It was an act of self-determination for me, sweetie." I said. "I needed to make this decision on my own without input from anyone. If it's a mistake, I'll correct it."

"You were only working part time." She shrugged. "You'll do fine. In a heartbeat you'd go back to work if you needed to." She knew how dedicated I was to building our home.

"Yep, I'd do that," I said. Finding part-time work was never a problem. It's my new life that challenged me now. I was confident in my choice, because I was physically exhausted at the end of each day. Working on the land, and then going to Dr. Mary's at night had been hard.

As Mel and I made our way to the field in the dark, she said, "You mowed the grass. It looks really nice.

I was surprised she could see it that well at night. "Actually, I did it yesterday." Mowing the grass quieted me. "Thanks for being so understanding about my quitting work."

"That decision was not mine to make. It was yours."

"Thanks anyway for not making it a big deal."

Our kitties adjusted faster than us as they lazed around the shed. At times, Mel and I were stressed. Paying for this project added new challenges to our world, but the cats took it in stride.

With hands deep in her pockets, Mel grimaced as she looked at me. "How about the mice situation in the barn? It's a good thing we didn't put all of our furniture in there. The mice would have loved our overstuffed sofa and ottoman." We had a good laugh with that thought.

Back in the shed for the night, I was on my mattress ready for sleep when I heard voices outside. Mel heard it too. We sat up and looked at each other. Quietly, I dressed, picked up my flashlight, and went out. Mel followed. As we tiptoed through the woods I started to giggle. Perhaps I wasn't a good sleuth after all. We heard the voices again, and stopped to listen.

Soon my eyes adjusted to the moonlight, so I turned off the flashlight.

Someone was walking our way.

Mel's words interrupted the quiet night. "What are you doing on our land?" She belted out to the figure on our right.

A middle-aged heavy-set woman jumped, and pressed her heaving chest with a hand. "I've lost my pet deer, and I'm looking for them. You scared me half to death! Have you seen them?"

"Pet deer?" I asked, holding back another chuckle. Mel elbowed me in the ribs.

"I adopted two deer from a man who couldn't care for them any longer," she said. "I brought them home and have been taking care of them now for a year. Every once in awhile they get out of their fenced-in yard."

"No, we haven't seen them." I said staring at her face in the semi-dark.

Just then, I heard more voices. Men's.

"Who is that?" Mel asked her.

"I don't know," she answered fearfully. "I came alone."

Mel was on it. As far as she was concerned no one was allowed on our land since we'd put up the "No Trespassing" sign. Mel took off like a shot through the woods, and I followed along behind.

When she reached the men she stopped. "What in the hell are you doing here? This is private land and you're not allowed on it."

"We're off duty police officers," one of the men said.

"So what?" Mel shot back.

The tall thin man with dark hair frowned as he answered, "We happened to be at the station earlier when a call came in about pet deer being lost in these woods. We came to help find them."

"Don't you have anything better to do for God's sake? Let me see your identification," Mel insisted. Satisfied, she told them about the woman we talked to earlier.

The other officer, heavy-set and wearing a Philadelphia Eagles cap said, "We didn't want to scare anyone, but did want to check it out. We know about those deer; they've been loose before."

Mel held her exasperation, but I thanked the officers. As they walked away they laughed. Bad mistake, Mel started after them again, but I grabbed her shirt from behind.

"Mel, calm down." I giggled again.

I pointed at my dirty "Life Is Good" tee-shirt and my ancient sweatpants. Then I turned my flashlight on Mel, and she was wearing her snowman pajamas. "No wonder those men walked away laughing. It's a good thing they didn't shoot us." I'm sure they wondered where in the world we came from, and I'm equally sure we were an amusing item for them to take back to the office.

Walking back to the shed we passed the woman who was hunting for her deer.

"My son called. The deer are back, safe and sound. I'm on my way home," she said.

After she walked away, I said, "What an adventure."

"Oh yeah."

Back in my sleeping bag I laughed one last time. What a picture, Mel in her snowman pajamas, and me in filthy clothes. It was a classic.

I kept an eye out for the next week or two, being a bit more watchful for anyone I didn't know. The police didn't return.

Hopefully, no one spoke to John.

Swinging Glulams

I grumbled, waking to the sound of Kim's reveille. "Whatever he wants he could have asked us about it last night."

"It's not like we could sleep through the racket he makes anyway." Mel groaned.

Crawling out of my sleeping bag, I stumbled to the porch in my pajamas. "What the heck do you...?" I snapped feeling extra tired today.

"The crane is coming today." Kim interrupted with great pleasure. "Steph and I are going to put in the topmost glulam. I thought you'd like to know."

"I don't want to watch," I said leaning against the door jam. "Frankly, the thought of it scares me. Do we need to move our cars to the street?" The idea of watching the remaining glulam swinging in the air with Kim and Steph so high above the ground, made me a bit wary. I had come to love them and I didn't want them injured.

"No, not at all." Kim said dryly. "Unless, of course, you want to go somewhere."

"Funny, Kim. Mel has to go to work," I explained. "And I want to leave before the crane gets here." I looked around the porch before going back into the shed to change.

After moving the cars, I started back toward the shed. Kim stopped me. Leaning his head to one side he stared at me a minute before he began to speak. "Guess what. You have to stay on the land and help us today. Like it or not you are going to be the one guiding the crane." I looked at him with such a huge sense of fear that he threw his head back in mock reaction, and Steph, standing close by, tried to cover her laughter. "I'm only kidding," he huffed, "I know you want to leave while we are doing this job."

Kim and Steph went back to work, and I headed to the shed to get our bags of laundry. I could get a few loads of wash done, and do some food shopping while I was out and about. Grabbing the grocery list from the shelf, I took off for the day. Mel did too, each of us in different directions.

I didn't even get to the bottom of the hill before I spotted the crane. Coming around the corner, it looked gargantuan and took up most of the road. I pulled to the side and let it pass. Yikes!

My day was planned. First I'd go to the laundromat, then the market. It would take three hours to complete the laundry, as I had at least five loads in my bags. While all loads were washing, I'd go to Tractor Supply and purchase jeans. They actually had Levi's there of all sizes and shapes. My old ones were either covered with dirt, sealer, or holes. Andy had a picnic scheduled for the 4th of July, and I wanted to save out one decent pair.

I'd been wearing Levi's since I was eight. My mom used to purchase them at Peebles's Store in our town. That small general store carried everything you'd need. Food, clothing and boots, magazines, and best of all ice cream and penny candy. I stopped in every day when I was young to get a coke to sip, a new comic book, or an ice cream cone to have on the walk home from school. The selection of penny candy was grand to the eyes of a child. One of the women working there would stand behind the counter patiently with a tiny bag in her hand. As we kids selected a small Tootsie Roll or a Mary Jane, she'd place it in the bag and then stand there until we made our next choice. I loved that store.

Once, at age nine, I stole a candy bar from there and ate it on my way home. I was so filled with guilt that I finally told my mother. She made me go back and pay for it, along with the instructions to tell Mr. Peebles, the owner, that I stole it. What an ordeal. Once I got back to the store it took me over an hour to work up the courage to tell. I never did it again.

In no time I was back from buying jeans, and switched the wash over to the dryer. Sitting and staring at the spinning clothes gave me time to think about the shed I was living in, and the home I was building.

For a while I thought I'd used up all my courage when I made my decision to leave my marriage. It was by far the most difficult and heartbreaking thing I'd ever done. After years of redoubling my efforts to make right what was dying between us, I realized I couldn't fix it alone. I asked Bob to help us modify our life together. He said no. He did not want to go to therapy to try and understand his anger, he was unwilling to give me money for my own business choices, and he said, "I'm unwilling to transform myself to suit you." My image of marriage haunted me. Fear kept me from change.

Bob's anger was like a hurricane let loose, a lunatic banshee. Only in front of me, though. Not often did he allow others to witness this. Not every day, but often enough. I told him on a boating trip that we took on our 35th anniversary that I was leaving the following day. I asked if we might become friends, helping one another throughout the rest of our lives. He said no.

That was the end of the rope for me. With him unwilling to change at all, I finally left, holding freedom in one hand, and guilt in the other. But I marched forward.

The drier buzzed and snapped me out of my reverie. It was time to fold. When I finished, I headed for the food store.

When that job was over I went home. I couldn't wait to see how it all worked out with the crane. A small part of me was nervous, but the rest was eager. Driving up the driveway I saw the glulam nestled in place at the top of the second floor. The house looked lofty. Kim and Steph had laid sub-flooring on the second story, and had already studded it out. Then they set the huge beam on top of the framing, and nailed it in place. The glulam would hold the weight of the roof rafters, so the load would be distributed evenly.

The house stood proudly in the afternoon sun. Kim was leaving for the day, and Steph had already gone home. I could tell he was happy with the way it looked.

"It all looks so solid," I said walking toward him from my car.

"The wild-ass crane operator almost hit me with the damn glulam. Jesus; I just about fell off the second floor. I shouted and ducked while the glulam flew over my head. I made Steph stay in the truck. After I nailed it down I got off the ladder, smoked a cigar, and drank coffee until my hands stopped shaking. What an ass!"

"Oh my God," I said, voice quivering. "I'm so sorry. Go home and relax." I was happy not to have witnessed it, but I felt a bit guilty for not being there.

"Seeing it's Friday," he said talking with the cigar in the side of his mouth, "you and Mel need to bring the first floor windows over sometime this weekend. I want to start on them first thing next week. I'm also going to start working on the roof, so there will be another plywood delivery on Monday morning."

After he was gone, I called Mel, and gasped. "I want to tell you what happened today."

"Wait," she said quickly. "I'm coming home."

Walking to the shed with our clean clothing and food, I saw Eli and Toby scampering around the screened porch. "Soon you'll be able to have a larger place to play." I scooped Eli up and twirled him around.

Hearing a car pull up the driveway, I ran out to see Mel. Her eyes were glued to the house, and she missed hitting a tree by inches. I couldn't blame her. Our home seemed to have grown twice its size since morning. She got out grinning, and we walked around together, staring at the flooring and siding. My eyes were open wide, and my lips held onto a grin. A huge old ladder was placed against the upstairs hallway, from the first floor to the second, and up we went. Once on the second floor we each had our hands on our hearts. The roof wasn't on, of course, but all the walls were framed in and it was gorgeous. The glulam was nestled in place above us and looked faultless.

"Kim is an artist," Mel whispered turning to look at every new thing. "Seeing all of this in our drawings, and then creating it. Can you imagine figuring out how to distribute all of this weight evenly, and then build it accordingly? It's really a testament to Kim's talent."

"No, it's a testimony to both of you," I said patting her on the back. "You made it work on paper, and he built the physical form."

We sat between the studded walls letting our legs swing over the edge, while I told Mel the 'Kim story.'

After an hour of talking and looking around, I said, "Kim says we have to bring the windows here by Monday morning. I want to go to Andy's picnic on Sunday, and we have the auction on Saturday. I'm so thankful we don't have to go to the preview this time. We know what we want."

"Wow," Mel said, "it's all happening so fast."

I ordered a pizza, and we ate it on the second floor, my legs swaying off the side of the house. Contentment filled my heart. When we finally tore ourselves away, there were two hours left of daylight. We had more than enough time to bring the windows over from the barn.

Once there, Mel went straight to her dresser. She looked in the drawer and crossed her arms. "They're still here," she said closing the drawer a little. "How cute."

We carefully placed most of the windows into our cars and drove back.

"If we borrow Bill's truck tomorrow, we can finish this job on our way home from the auction," I said, while we unloaded.

"Great idea," Mel said, nodding. "Let's save time where we can."

Walking down the path for my shower, I took note of the lovely twilight. Birdsong, crickets, and dusk. It was like a benediction.

A Day Off and a Picnic

With the help of Bill's truck, our third auction was a great success. We got the windows and the last of the doors we wanted, and brought them all home the same day.

After a fitful night of sleep, I crawled out of bed at dawn the next morning. At three o'clock I had bolted upright in bed listening to the sounds of night. My pulse raced, but I hadn't heard anything alarming. Sometimes at that hour my demons or emotions took over: feeling trapped, or sensing flashbacks, vulnerability, claustrophobia, or the feeling of being naked. They kept me awake until I confronted them. I closed my eyes and let my awareness wander through my mind until it rested on a particular area of stress. And there I went to work. I still held on to a small amount of guilt I suffered from divorce. And these sensations always came at the most inconvenient times.

It had been five years since I left home, and two years since my divorce. But once in a while when I spent time with my kids and grandbabies, guilt still held me in its grip. Especially at a picnic or some other family function. It was only awkward for me though; my kids seemed adjusted. I had to be persistent and keep doing the work it required, working with all the passion I had to accept the role I had chosen. My choice of divorce was the right decision; I just didn't want to waste the opportunity. I allowed myself time to deep breathe until I felt the tension leave my body, then I slept.

It was Sunday and I didn't have to go back to the auction. No workers were scheduled to arrive. Mel slept in.

I fed the kitties, and headed out to the field with a peanut butter sandwich, coffee, and binoculars. Daybreak in the woods and first light in the field always brought something special to look at. I hoped today would be no exception. It was chilly on this early July morning, so I threw on a sweatshirt. Shade always gave me the chills at this hour, but the morning was stunning and I sighed with contentment. The only thing on my to-do list today was Andy's picnic. He didn't have one on Memorial Day so he scheduled one for today instead. It wasn't until late afternoon, so I could savor the morning as long as I wanted. I wished that Shelly didn't live in California so she could be there. Chris too, from Long Island, but they both had a lot to do with their families. When Chris walked the land with me back in the winter months, he thought he'd have more time to visit, but his work kept him away most of the time. Still, when he did come he loved the project.

I stared at the piles of cut logs, knowing I needed to rent a log splitter to prepare for the coming winter. Perhaps I could do that sometime in the next week, now that Mel was caught up with her work. I'd make it a point to ask her this morning. Split wood needs to season, and our field was the perfect place for drying. One of our neighbors had offered two large oaks that he cut down last winter, and I had cut them up in early spring. They'd been dead for years, he said, perfect for splitting. Left to dry in the field all summer, the chunks of oak were ideal for cold weather. The trees we took down when we cleared the land would be the next ones in line. I expected all the wood to dry nicely by winter.

Not everyone understands wood, and the seasoning process, I thought. Dad would be proud that I remembered the basics of what he told me. Standing dead, storm-damaged, and felled trees don't season at the same rate as wood that's been split where sun and air can get to it. Seasoned wood can be recognized by its loose bark, lighter color, and checked or cracked ends. It takes at least six months for wood to season, but one year exposed to the air and sun is better.

Picking up the binoculars, I noticed hawks soaring overhead, and I watched them fly the air currents. Looking at the large electric stanchion toward the back of the field, I saw twigs coming out of the side of a connecting plate. Wondering if it could be a hawk's nest I ran back to the screened porch, retrieved my spotting scope and set it up on the table between the two chairs out in the field. Kneeling down, I looked through the eyepiece. It took a moment to zero in on the twigs. Imagine my surprise when I saw a red-tailed hawk sitting on a ragged looking nest made of brushwood, sticks, and moss. The nest looked massive—roughly three feet in diameter. We were going to see hawk babies. I couldn't wait to tell Mel.

Feeling content, I sat down and ate my sandwich. Just then, a red fox careened around the corner of the field and disappeared into the tree line. Wow. It was like watching a nature film. I wondered what I would see next, and kneeled down to look through the spotting scope again. Such a difference between seasons. The area was alive with wildlife of all kinds during this summer.

Mommy hawk was still sitting there looking proud. I wondered if she felt hot in the morning sun. She'd be there in a thunderstorm too. It was her job to keep predators away from the nest and to keep her babies warm.

Mel came out to the field to join me, coffee mug in hand. She had her favorite snowman pajamas on and seemed eager to look through the binoculars.

"Look at the red-tailed hawk's nest," I said as I shot up out of my kneeling position. I moved away from the scope, and Mel got down on her knees and looked through the eyepiece.

"How beautiful is this?" she said, putting a hand over her heart.

"Would you like to go to the picnic with me this afternoon?" I asked.

"No, but thanks for asking." she answered. "I haven't had much alone time on our land, and I want to wander around in the woods."

I completely understood. "In that case, I'll bring back a plate of food for you."

"Thanks. Much better than all the cereal I've been eating," she said.

We sat quietly for awhile before I broke the silence.

"I need to rent a log splitter, and get some of this wood split and dry before winter."

"Good idea. We have a lot to do. How long do you think it'll take us to split it all?"

"A couple of days, most likely," I answered. "I know that money is tight, but having four or five cords stacked for winter will make it all worthwhile. It will also pay for the stove in two years."

"How large is a cord?"

"Four feet high, four feet wide, and eight foot long."

"We're going to have some massive piles in this field when we're finished."

I decided to rent a splitter for two days during the coming week. Hard work for sure, but doing it together would make it easier. Both of us had some experience with log splitters, so despite the potential dangers I didn't anticipate any problems.

I walked back to the shed through the woods, coming in from the north side. It gave me a different view of the house.

"Let's get as many pictures of our house as possible during the building process."

"Great idea. I'll take some this afternoon while you're gone, and I'll take a video too. Then we can relive these days in years to come."

We worked for the rest of the morning. I cut and moved more brush to the field, getting the burn pile ready. No burning on Sundays, the township wouldn't allow it. I hoped when we did set the fire it wouldn't disturb the hawk. The pile was huge, so I split it in two. One to set aflame and one for transferring pieces to the fire as it died down. I didn't want to risk setting the woods on fire.

To be extra safe, I wanted to stop on my way home from Andy's and get two long hoses to attach to the ones Bill had on his side of the field. It would be safer than just having our five-gallon water containers nearby. I looked forward to the day we would have our own well. I was surprised how much water we went through for coffee, drinking, and washing up. No wonder the early settlers always found land near a stream.

My work done, I went to the shed to change clothes for the picnic. I pulled out my new jeans and looked at them. Too hot, I thought, and changed into shorts and a tee-shirt. I felt so light. When I put on sandals and walked out, I felt exposed. One leg was covered in black and blue marks, and scratches ran down the right side of the other leg. Lordy.

Sitting in Andy's yard, I felt quieted and sat with my head back, and my eyes half-closed. Abby and Amy, my granddaughters, aged four and seven, were playing ball with their dad while I sat with Kathy, my daughter-in-law. We talked for an hour about Andy's work, Kathy's work, and my home building, and then Andy fired up the grill and cooked dinner, complete with veggie burgers for me and extras for Mel, even though she wasn't there. Kathy had made salads, and a dessert. It was a normal event for them, yet so much different from the life I was living.

"I've been living in a shed and existing on a diet of take out, cereal, and microwaved Indian dinners." I said to all of them.

"Can I live with you?" Amy asked, laughing.

"I'm sure you'd love the food, but not the work."

"Look at your legs," Abby said, pointing with her finger an inch away from one of the larger bruises.

"Don't laugh at me, you little stinker," I said, jumping up and chasing her around the yard.

Tired, but happy, we sat down together. Abby crawled onto my lap and put her head back against my chest. It felt cozy and comfortable, and I drew her closer.

"Are you still satisfied with working at Highway Marine?" I asked Andy, still holding on to Abby.

"I am for now. I'd love to work with Chris in the future though, and as soon as I have more experience in management, we'll have a talk."

"Great," I said. "List management and marketing would be perfect for you. Selling is your specialty."

"Thanks, Mom."

Kathy came out from the kitchen with a huge serving dish in front of her.

"I could certainly get used to this," I said, taking a homemade cookie from the platter.

Later, as I kissed and hugged Amy and Abby goodbye, I promised they could come over soon to drive Bluebie. Amy squealed in delight at the thought of driving the tractor. She was so cute.

After making a fast stop for two fifty-foot rubber hoses, I headed home. In the shed with Mel's burgers and salad I noticed she, too, had a look of contentment on her face.

"I've had a quiet day walking through the woods, taking pictures, and enjoying myself," she said, nabbing the cookies first.

While Mel ate, I went to the house and walked around.

Soon we'll be living in this space, I thought. I am the richest woman in the world.

Wounded and Stitched

Feeling refreshed from my day of leisure, I was ready to get back to work. I had called to reserve a log splitter, and I was on my way to pick it up. Mel stayed on the land to collect our gloves, eyewear, and ear plugs. It was all stored in the shed. I wanted to be safe because this was dangerous work.

When I got back from ORE Rental, I transferred the splitter from Powder to the back of Bluebie, and then moved it to the field. It was filled with oil and gas, and I had an extra five-gallon gas tank ready to refill as needed. We worked hard all morning, but did take two breaks for cold drinks. After each break we'd change positions. One of us would carry logs over to the splitter while the other worked the controls. The sun was hot and I knew it would be a long, tiring day. After four scorching hours, we stopped for lunch. Kim joined us by the fire pit where we had placed our new Adirondack chairs. "This is like a little family," I said.

Kim's response was a roll of the eyes.

Half an hour passed with easy conversation, but I realized that if I sat in the cool shade any longer, I'd never go back to the field. It was far too enjoyable. Mel went back to the log splitter, too, while Kim worked in the house. Finding a rhythm, we kept at it all afternoon. Immense piles of firewood were beginning to grow. In fact, they were so massive I couldn't see over the top.

Late in the day, Mel yelled over the noisy engine, "I'm going over to Bill's to get a different pair of gloves. The ones I'm wearing have holes in them and are hurting my hands."

"Okay. I'll keep on working for a while," I shouted back.

I split five or six more logs and then came to one exceptionally large piece. As I hefted it onto the splitter and grabbed the controls, something took my eye. I looked up for one split second, wondering if it was the mommy hawk. Big mistake. Huge mistake. I felt the wedge strike my finger and I jumped back from the machine. When I did this, it released the dead man's switch. The splitter came to a stop and I stood there a moment, stunned.

I looked at my glove and saw blood dripping onto the ground. Ugh! I was hurt and knew it immediately. Incredibly the pain hadn't set in yet. Probably I was protected by shock, but not for long I'd guess. I didn't want to see how terrible it was, but I needed to take in several deep breaths in order to keep standing. My hand hung by my side until nausea subsided, but when I did sneak another peek, blood pooled by my foot.

"Mel!" I shouted at the top of my lungs. She was on her way back to the field and came running over. By the time she reached me I was leaning over, hands on my knees.

I told her what happened, and we slowly walked back to the shed. Kim had gone for the day, so we sat on the porch together. I took my bloody glove off, looked at my middle finger, and winced. Mel grabbed a towel, soaked it in water, and dabbed at the wound. The cut was worse than I'd imagined. It was about an inch long, bloody and ugly. As I looked closer, I could see the wedge on the log splitter had just missed my fingernail. The gash was deep and I think I saw bone because something looked white and glossy. It ran from the top of my finger to beyond the first knuckle.

After a few minutes Mel turned pale, and started to sweat, I worried she might faint so we sat quiet for a while. Holding the water soaked towel tight on my finger, Mel decided I needed stitches. I was sweat soaked, filthy, and in pain, but there was no time to shower and change because we couldn't stop the bleeding. When Mel recovered she drove me to the Quakertown Hospital emergency room, eleven miles south.

Along the way I remembered back to when Dad used to get hurt at the mill. I hated to see his jeep in the driveway at the house anytime during the day. He never came home unless he got hurt. Often it was something stuck in his eye, like a sliver of wood. He couldn't get it out so mom would go after it. Having him hurt scared me, and I felt incompetent.

Mel let me out at the entrance, and went to park the car. After giving my personal information at the desk and filling out papers, I sat in the waiting room. Mel came in a minute later, and then a nurse walked us back to a small curtained room. I sat on a gurney waiting to see a doctor, while a nurse cleaned my injury. By now, the pain had kicked up a notch and it hurt like hell. I was fortunate that it hadn't sliced through the nail.

I looked over at Mel, and she was as white as the paper lining on the table beneath me. She put her head between her legs, and it kept her from fainting. The nurse kept an eye on her, and I was grateful.

The doctor entered fifteen minutes later and looked at my hand. "You're going to need stitches and a tetanus shot," she said, readying the instruments. "You'll also need pain medication, and an antibiotic. This is a nasty cut you've got here. How'd this happen?"

"Log splitter." I answered.

I winced when she stuck the needle directly into the wound administering a local anesthetic, but after that it was less painful.

"I need to stitch through the fingernail," she said picking up some thick thread. Mel groaned. She stuck the needle through the nail and out through the skin on the side of my finger. I was watching the entire episode as if I were a spectator. At the moment it didn't hurt as the doctor kept on, but I knew the wound was going to pound like crazy later on. She repeated the process six times and then stopped. "That should do it."

She gave me cleaning instructions, told me what to expect for the next few days, and handed me the prescriptions. My finger was heavily bandaged, and I was thankful it wasn't anything worse. "Thank you, Doc," I said climbing off the gurney.

Mel stopped at the drug store and ran in to get the prescriptions filled. I couldn't wait to get back on my land where I felt safe and secure.

My work day was over, but I intended to get back to splitting again in the morning. I would wear a glove over the bandage, and Mel could move the logs into the splitter while I managed the controls. I was confident in my ability to finish the job.

After showers, we walked back to the shed. My sleeping bag looked like an oasis.

The next morning I pulled my glove on over my bandaged finger. It hurt a bit, but I felt I could work with the logs as well as the controls.

"No way," Mel said when I suggested it. "Being injured is a huge shock to your system. You need to take it easy, and probably shouldn't be doing any work at all." I knew she was right. I loved splitting logs though, and hated that this accident happened.

Mel pulled the rope and the wood splitter jumped to life. I wiped blood off the wedge and manned the controls while Mel did the hard work. I hated it. I wanted to share the burden, but knew Mel was right. Despite my wound, we made good progress and kept at it until we broke for lunch.

As I walked toward the shed, the cool sweet shade was a welcome change from the searing heat of the field. I was pleased anew that we decided to build in the forest. Mel volunteered to make us lunch, and I agreed to let her. As she walked into the shed, I pulled Ibuprofen from my pocket. My hands were sweaty, but I pulled my gloves off anyway. My finger was throbbing, but I didn't want to take prescription pain medication while working with heavy equipment.

We sat in the park eating and listening to Kim. He was working on the other side of house, and I didn't want to interrupt him. I hadn't told him about my accident yet, but I would when the time was right. The rhythm of his pounding matched the throbbing of my finger. I would have loved to stay in the shade all afternoon listening to my house being built, but I only had the log splitter until the end of the day.

We finished splitting wood around four o'clock. The huge piles of logs were gone, replaced by mounds of split pieces about eighteen inches long. I was anxious to stack it, as it would give us more space in the field.

Mel went to get Powder while I brought the log splitter to the edge of the woods with Bluebie. Once we hooked it up we'd take it back to the rental place. We'd easily be there by five, and wouldn't be charged for another day. I was hot, and the glove made me uncomfortable. I didn't want to take it off until we were finished because of possible infection. I was sure my finger had bled again, but the day was almost over. I could wait another hour.

The rental facility was filled with activity when we arrived. Everyone who had rented equipment needed to return it by five o'clock. No one wanted to be charged for an extra day. Mel stood in line to pay our bill, while I drove the splitter around back. The workers removed it from my car and checked for damage. I noticed the handle had blood on it, but they never said a word.

We drove back to our land and as soon as the car stopped I ran into the shed. Mel came in a rush behind me. "Are you okay?"

"I need to get my glove off right now," I said, my face contorted. I was ready to cut it off, not giving a damn that the gloves were expensive. Then I took a calming breath, peeled it off my hand, and stared at the bloody viscous mess. Mel peeked at it and once again got clammy and white; even a Jersey girl has her limits. I poured water into a container and took it outside on the porch, then removed the bandage. There was too much blood to see if the stitches held or not, but I did what I could.

"How is it?" Mel asked coming out a few minutes later. Her face was still pale, and a thin sheen of sweat remained over her upper lip and forehead.

"Pretty good, actually, but I'm going down for a shower in a few minutes. I've put a clean bandage on it for now."

Later, in the bathroom at Heidi and Bill's, I washed it out and was surprised to see that the stitches hadn't ripped apart. The doctor said going through the nail would make them hold, and I saw she was right.

The warmth of the shower felt amazingly good, and I began to relax.

On the walk back, the path looked stunning in the long shadows of late afternoon. Exhausted from the day, I went inside and laid down on top of my sleeping bag. My hand was throbbing. I thought about my pain meds, but decided to wait.

I stayed quiet for a couple of hours, and that helped. When the pain was more manageable, I felt ready to go outside again.

Walking to the field in twilight, I felt a sense of accomplishment. I could barely see the stacks of wood, but could tell they were huge. We had done a lot of work in two days.

From the field I went directly into the house to see how much Kim had accomplished. He had almost finished the plywood on the roof on the east side. The road side. I knew he'd complete all of it by the end of the week.

When it was fully dark, I went back to the shed. Mel had finished making our dinner, packaged lasagna, and I was thankful for her effort. We sat and ate in front of the TV, and soon I was yawning, longing to be in my sleeping bag. I went outside to brush my teeth and get ready for bed. A gold sliver of the moon was coming up over the field, and I could see it through the leaves of the trees. Almost as if I were being pulled by its force, I headed in that direction. Mel came out and followed me.

The peepers from the creek below sang their evening song. "I still can't believe all this is ours, Mel."

"Me either, baby girl. Me either."

Sal, sitting on scaffolding nailing shakes on to the north side. A waiting pile of shakes lay below on the ground.

Mounds of earth from our newly dug trench for the electric and cable. The east side of the house still needs shakes. Mels' studio windows sit at ground level.

Sal, sitting in our "new" clawfoot tub just delivered amidst the sand from the masons.

Mel, finishing the temporary screened in porch to our shed home. The porch roof was a sheet of heavy plastic over reclaimed sheets of osb. Kim's generator sits near the entrance.

Mr. Wonsidler starting his dowsing while Sal watches. A saved sapling is in the background.

Kim at the peak lifting a bundle of shingles off the conveyor.

Mel, up on a ladder by the top glulam that almost knocked Kim off the second story.

Eli (left) and Toby getting ready for a nap in our shed during the warmer days.

Feeling Grateful

I expected John, the building inspector, to visit again. Soon. When a truck rumbled up the drive I grabbed our shovel, our thin cover story, and ran out to see who was there. As the vehicle moved deftly around the oak, I recognized the driver as Kim's delivery guy. No wonder he drove effortlessly up the driveway; he'd done it many times before.

"I want to get John's visit behind us," I mumbled, shaking my head. Each time he came, my body tensed, and it didn't relax until he left. Still, John's visit was important and could not be avoided. He had to inspect and approve the framing before Kim could call in the plumbers and electricians. All decisions rested with John, so he was "the man."

Kim and the driver unloaded plywood and two-by-fours. As soon as the delivery guy left, John drove up. I glanced around. Everything looked normal, and all was in its place.

John got out of his truck, "Hi, Sal. I'm here to inspect the framing."

"Great," I said, trying to act nonchalant as he went about his assessment.

As Kim carried plywood to the roof it distracted me, and I marveled at his strength. The OSB board we were using for sheathing was heavy, but the plywood seemed even heavier. He grabbed two pieces at a time, holding the ladder with one hand while balancing plywood against his shoulder. It had taken Mel's and my combined effort to move the last pile into the house. Even with the two of us, it was not easy.

Once on the roof, Kim dropped the plywood in place, and Steph nailed it down. They were moving quickly, and I was sure they'd be done by evening.

"Wow, our roof will soon be finished," I shouted up to Kim. "This is so exciting, I have to call Mel." I pulled out my cell.

Mel answered, "I'll be back a little earlier than usual this afternoon. I'm still sore from splitting the wood and sitting in this desk chair isn't doing my body any good."

"Why don't you stop for takeout on your way home? Surprise me with something new. It will be my treat for you're taking such good care of me after my accident."

"Sounds good to me." Mel and I fit together so well. Both of us on the same path, working toward the same goal. The synergy worked and it felt good to have her in my life. Bob and I had worked toward the same goal for our kids, but for each of us personally there was no easy goal. Bob hated his job at Bell Labs and Lucent. Straight out of college he started working for AT&T, but never seemed to enjoy it or its benefits. He liked the people there, but not the politics. I hoped whatever he chose next for work was a better fit.

Snapping my phone shut, I noticed John and Kim deep in conversation, and moved closer to listen.

"I'm sorry, Kim," John said, shaking his head. "I can't pass it like that."

I gasped. "What can't you pass, John?"

Seeing the horrified look on my face, they both laughed.

"Not the house, Sal. The ramp," Kim said. "By the way, why is your hand bandaged?"

"Did you have to ask while John is here?" I mumbled, looking down at my shoes. "I cut my finger on the log splitter, and got it stitched up at the hospital. Hurts a bit, but I'll be okay."

"Splitters are dangerous. I'm sorry you're hurt."

John cleared his throat. "Me, too. By the way, the house passed with flying colors. The ramp is only a foot wide though, and it has to be widened. It would be dangerous for sub-contractors trying to carry items into the house." As John spoke, Kim took another two-by-six off the pile and nailed it to the existing ramp. John, clearly pleased said, "That will do it."

He handed Kim a sheet of paper and got back in his truck. As he drove away, my sense of relief surprised me. Not once had he ever made a suggestion we were doing anything wrong. It was my guilt about living there in violation of township rules that had me holding my breath. I felt like an outlaw.

Feeling my tension drain away, I grabbed the spotting scope and headed for the field. I wanted to see if the hawk was still sitting on her nest. We had made a lot of noise earlier in the week with the log splitter. I wouldn't have been surprised if she took off, but I hoped she stayed here.

Adjusting the scope I squinted through the eyepiece, and there she was perched on the edge of her nest. Fussing and pecking she took out pieces of shell, dropping them on the ground below. The babies had hatched. Soon there would be little heads popping up to watch, but I couldn't see any yet.

"How fun is this?" I asked. As I sat there a little longer, I thought back to my life with Bob again. One of the times when we went to Florida to visit with my parents, we stopped in a small town on the East Coast, south of Jacksonville by sixty miles. Palm Coast was its name. We'd spent time in previous years boating in that area on the Intercostals Waterway. A small boatyard kept drawing us back. The boatyard was for sale. On this small lot there were eight house trailers and many stored boats. Folks that owned them paid monthly rent to the owner. Also, you could motor your boat right up to the dock in the back that sat at the edge of the building. The owner had an area where he did small engine repair. The entire operation was not large, but we felt it was solid, and thought about buying it.

I had told Bob I would open a part of the building as a snack bar, serving breakfast and lunch to the fishermen. I also wanted to sell boxed lunches that folks could throw into their coolers as they headed out for a day of boating fun. I was excited about the entire idea. Bob was great at repairing small engines and I thought he could make that part of the business work well. Together we might make a go of it and live in Florida. It was not my favorite state to live, but my parents and sister lived there. I thought I might get more support. The boats and trailers on the lot could stay, and that would be steady income as well.

We visited there many times. The business didn't sell fast. I know Bob wanted to invest in this venture and quit his job, but he never could make that decision. It was his to make; I didn't need to be a part of it. And because of his anger, I didn't want to encourage or discourage. That was how I felt at the time, and to this day I still agree with my choice to remain silent. I wasn't the one working at Bell Labs; Bob was. He just couldn't make the change. Too scary.

I wasn't sad about his choice, but I did feel a little resentment that I wasn't able to see how I'd do with the snack bar business. I wondered how different our marriage might have been if we had tried to own and run the boat yard. But, I knew from day one that my marriage was wrong. My dad knew, too, as he asked me at the door of the church on my wedding day if this was something I really wanted to complete. He said it would be okay to walk away right that moment. A big mistake. I knew inwardly now that things between us wouldn't change unless Bob got personal help. Perhaps Bob might have been happier, but I still felt it had to be his option to leave the Labs. Otherwise, I'd feel responsible if things didn't work out. And at that time of my life, I might have crumbled from the pressure.

I decided to work on stacking wood, and soon realized how much easier it was than splitting it. And my finger was healing well. The throbbing had stopped, and each time I changed my bandage, it looked better than the time before.

Mel came out to the field as soon as she got back from work. "Wow, the piles are huge. Good job, Sal."

I stood back and looked at my progress. "I must be getting into shape." I said, running my fingers through my sweaty hair.

Mel went back to get her gloves, and together we worked until dusk. Finishing up, I stood back looking at what we'd accomplished in the last two hours. It was amazing how striking the wood looked, all stacked in symmetrical rows.

Walking toward the chairs at the edge of the field, Mel took one last look at the hawk's nest. "No movement," she said, as she packed the scope in its case. "Maybe tomorrow there will be tiny heads peeking out."

As we approached the house I was stunned to see that the roof was finished, and Kim was gone. All the plywood was in place, and our home was now under cover. It was beautiful.

Going into the house, Mel did a little dance step. "Is this ramp a little wider?"

I nodded. "John came by." She whipped her head around to look at me. "It's all okay. Everything passed inspection after Kim fixed this access ramp."

I climbed the old ladder to the second floor, and for the first time I saw how the upstairs bedrooms and bathroom would look. The ceilings were so high I felt I was in a cathedral. Looking down into the living room below was pure ecstasy. This was my home, my very own home. I felt dizzy from the thought, and stepped back from the edge. It was almost too much to grasp, but I was actually building my own home with my own hands. The skylight from the first auction was set to go in my bedroom, and one day the bed would go beneath it. It was darker now that it was going to be. I couldn't wait to sleep under the stars.

I went back downstairs at the sound of a car coming up the driveway. "Oh no," I said. "I hope it's not John." I peeked around the corner of the house, and it was Andy.

"I've come bringing dinner." he yelled to us. "I knew you were in here, I heard you laughing." He climbed up to see how it looked from the second floor. Andy is six-feet-five-inches tall, and even with his height, the roof towered over his head. "I admire everything about this new house," he said, as he came back down the ladder.

"Are you giving your mom a personal stamp of approval?"

"I am. Great job, you two. I've got to run, but I wanted to bring something by for you to eat. It must be a challenge each night having to worry about dinner. I brought Italian. A variety of pasta dishes."

"Whohoooo," Mel exclaimed. "Can't go wrong there. Thanks."

He laughed and said, "I left it outside in the tub!"

"You nut," I said. "Thanks, sweetie." I wrapped my arms around him in a bear hug and squeezed.

"You're welcome. Have a good night, guys, and enjoy your meal."

After Andy left, I climbed the ladder again to my room. Mel brought Andy's food into the shed and placed it in the refrigerator alongside her takeout of Chinese spring rolls, Udon noodles with tofu, and veggie dumplings. We were set for tonight and tomorrow night's dinner.

Sitting down where I wanted to place my bed, I leaned back against the wall and closed my eyes. "I am so grateful for my life, God." I said.

New melodies greeted my ears as I crawled from my sleeping bag the following morning. Their voices sounded different today. A new bird perhaps? Still in my pajamas, I tiptoed into the woods to listen. I hoped my toothpaste's minty odor would not turn any of the birds away.

Searching for the one that stole my morning sleep, I found a wood thrush. My favorite songbird. They have a vast song repertoire, and I'd hoped for months I would hear one here. Stooping beneath low-hanging branches, I made my way through the underbrush and lowered myself onto an old log. He now had my full attention. Lifting his head, he sang for me. His song was so magnificent that it brought goose bumps to my arms and tears to my eyes. I sat there wondering how this bird made such a difference in my heart. Its songs drew out the very best in me, and I wanted to give back to this nature-filled spot. My promise was to provide for all its creatures, keeping my land revered for as long as I lived on it.

Thoreau wrote of the wood thrush: "Whenever a man hears it he is young, and Nature is in her spring; wherever he hears it, it is a new world and a free country, and the gates of heaven are not shut against him." My heart opens wide every time I think of that quote. I marveled at the bird's speckled breast in the early morning sun, and closed my eyes.

In my early twenties, I thought I knew how my life would turn out. Being a mom was wonderful, and I loved giving my three children the best of me. It was my sacrifice, and one of which I was most proud. As a mom you sacrifice your own personal time, and give it to your children for those important years. As a wife, I worked hard to bring harmony to our home. It was difficult trying to keep Bob from showing his anger in front of them. Moms are always important, balancing heated outbursts, arguments, and strong opinions within each person. But with more than enough love to go around, I found my own methods. My children grew up happy and secure, found lives of their own and went their separate ways.

As I grew into my own self over the years, the old way between Bob and me became unacceptable. Now I moved forward toward my goal, listening to my own life's song, and I felt akin to the thrush. It moved from one song to another all spring, as I moved from one part of my life to the next. I said goodbye to my conventional existence and moved forward toward a more spiritual, solitary self. I shared a partnership and a home with Mel, but my life was my own. For the first time since college, I lived as the real me. Now I wanted to use what I'd learned for the rest of my life. I would never again forget what it feels like to own courage. It was liberating and just as therapeutic as learning I had bad feelings residing in me too, like anger and hate. Anger at myself for all the ways I felt I was misleading the kids. Hate for not feeling free enough to let the world know this marriage wasn't working for me. Hate for the lack of communication that I never seemed to be able to make happen. I HATED that part of me.

Walking down my spiritual Path helped me understand. Also, I freely discussed them with my therapist. I wanted to be authentic. It was a slow process, but I was making progress.

Hearing a truck come up the driveway, I dove into the shed and changed into jeans and a tee. A minute later I calmly walked out, shovel in hand. Backing up the drive was a huge truck, complete with a conveyer belt attachment. I ran over to watch the action. Kim was already on the roof of the house, yelling orders to the driver. Once the truck was in place, the man got out.

"Hey Kim, I have your order in full," he shouted.

Unlocking the conveyer, the driver worked with hand controls directing and lifting the long belt to our roof. He placed the heavy bags of roofing shingles on it, and sent them up to Kim.

What a slick way of doing this, I thought. This is so much safer than ladders. Kim secured small pieces of two-by-fours here and there, so the packages stayed on the roof. When the truck left, he and Steph nailed the shingles in place over the tar paper they'd put down earlier. The shingles were light brown and I was satisfied with our selection. Originally Steph and I wanted green, but Mel and Kim thought brown looked nicer. At the beginning of our housing project I'd decided to leave all color options up to Mel. She was the artist, and I knew her choices would be right for our house. Everyone thought two women would never agree on most things, but they were wrong. Our personal choices were very similar.

As everyone worked, I walked to the field. Pulling on my gloves was easier now. I only had a large band-aid covering the stitches on my finger. The pain was often there, deep down, always a reminder to be careful and stay safe. I stacked wood, hoping to finish by noon. I was done by eleven o'clock and looked for the next thing to do. I was exhausted, but needed to push on. I got the lawn mower from under the tarp and went back to the field. When I finished mowing, it looked orderly with stacks of wood drying in the sun, and freshly mown grass. The only blemish was where Charlie had disturbed the ground to dig the drain fields. It was graded, but needed seed. Everything smelled fresh and alive here in this vast openness.

I drove to Neighbors Home and Garden Center in Hellertown, and looked for grass seed and tomato plants. I found three plants, plus a large bag of seed. I wanted to surprise Mel and plant tomatoes near the end of our field. Tomatoes loved sun, and they would get plenty of it there. It was a bit late, but I felt just fine about it.

Once I was home, I planted them. I filled the holes with water while my mind went back to the perk test. That time I took water out, this time I poured it in. Funny that. I used the two hoses I had connected to Bill's, It was easier than filling buckets. I couldn't wait till we had our own well. Hoses would be used from the house to the field, and every job out there would be easier.

I had to wait a little longer before the well drillers arrived. Learning patience was becoming my new world and I had never, ever, been good at it. Tired and hot I went back to the shed and sat in meditation. It calmed me. Always.

Picnic Fun

On the Saturday before the 4th of July, Mel and I decided to celebrate our accomplishments so far by having a picnic in the field. Since we weren't celebrating together on the actual holiday this would be fun. I asked Heidi, Bill, and Heidi's mom, Christel, to join us. I felt clever as I prepared a potato salad using only a microwave for the potatoes. I'd never before thought to nuke the potatoes in their skins. Living in the shed required ingenuity, and I was pleased not to need Heidi's stove.

Mel made a fire ring at the topmost part of the field, surrounding it with stones. At two o'clock, I piled the food I'd made along with the paper plates and eating utensils in the cart and hauled it out with Bluebie. It was a crazy joy that came to me as I listened to the rattle of bowls and dishes bouncing around on the floor of the cart, and the deafening clatter made me giggle. Even Christel remarked that she heard me coming long before she saw me. Mel started the fire and I cooked veggie burgers on a little grate, and veggie hot dogs on sticks. Along with the burgers and dogs, we had potato salad, macaroni salad, chips, and a cake decorated by Christel. She made it look like the United States flag using strawberries, blueberries, and white icing.

We sat there until dark, eating, laughing, and having fun. Stories of house construction, auctions, and life in a shed kept us cheerful.

"Remember the night we jumped up in our sleeping bags because the rain was so loud?" Mel said, while acting it out.

"I do." I said. "Not much separates us from the rain." I answered, laying my head back against the chair. "Now we love hearing rain on the roof."

We all quieted down and let the sounds of nature fill our hearts; while we watched birds fly over us heading for their evening roost. Deer ran past in the lower field. Fawns were running on the inside of the herd, moms being protective as always. I loved listening to the deer snort when they sensed danger. That and stamping their front feet on the ground. But they were beginning to trust me now, and feeding them at dusk was something I felt honored to do.

When the evening was over, crickets and peepers sang to Mel and me as we made our way down the path to our little home. Tucked into the shed for the night, we relaxed, and played for hours with Eli and Toby.

All too soon, sleepy and content, I crawled into bed. What a grand day. After a moment, I realized I had not gone back to the house before I went to the shed. I looked over at Mel in her sleeping bag. She was already asleep, so I carefully tiptoed out onto the porch, pushed into my sneakers and walked over for a look.

There my home stood in the light of the moon. It was tall, sturdy, and elegant. Inside, I climbed the ladder and looked out of the windows toward the north. This was Mel's room, the one she'd use for her clothes and personal items. It felt different because it was darker than mine, and lacked light from the east. Once the skylight was installed, it might have moon shadows. The woods were hard to see from this vantage point, even with the moonlight. But what I did see looked mysterious and exciting and deep. Because of the denseness, the scene took on a wild and glossy darkness. And as I stared out, I felt a mystical bond with these acres. Winter's limiting palette had the compensating loveliness of allowing me to view the lay of the land. But summer's foliage gave way to the lush thick denseness of underbrush and low hanging branches. It beckoned to me.

I watched the moon's movement for about an hour, and then made my way back to the shed. Eli was waiting for me, and we snuggled into the night together. I think we were both purring.

Driving to Andy's for yet another picnic on Sunday I studied my hand on the steering wheel and noticed how well my finger was healing. I had chosen not to baby it while working each day. Maybe that's the answer to healthy healing, I thought.

I felt like a kid playing hooky from school as I drove into Andy's driveway, loving how many picnics they had each summer. I walked into the house and with no one in the kitchen, I put my potato salad in their refrigerator and then walked out to the back yard. Everyone was out there and the girls were anxious to show me something. Andy had made a tree house, and they wanted me to climb up and see it.

"How adorable," I said to Amy and Abby once I squeezed inside. "You even have bean bag chairs in here. You'll have so much pleasure with this hide-a-way for the rest of the summer." They were proud of their little space.

"It's just like your shed, Grandma White," Abby said, her blue-green eyes wide with excitement. She always called me by that name, mostly because her other grandmother had brown hair and it was a good way to distinguish between the two grandmothers.

"You're right, Abby," I said trying not to chuckle. "It's a little smaller, but every bit as nice."

I climbed out of the tree house. "Great idea, Andy," I said, looking down at him leaning against the tree.

"Thanks, Mom." Andy answered looking satisfied. "It was a lot of fun."

I felt proud of him for this effort. Bob, too, had worked hard for the kids as they grew up. Andy learned a lot from him with building projects, car repair, and other things that had to do with saving money by doing it yourself.

After an hour, most of their neighbors and friends had arrived. Everyone brought something special for the picnic. It was a nice mix of people, and the food was yummy. We even had homemade strawberry ice cream. It was so delicious I kept eating it. Three bowls. Good thing I was working hard physically.

"Hey, Dr. Grant," I said to Andy's neighbor, who was standing by the barbeque grill. "Would you please take these stitches out of my finger?" I was so eager to get rid of them that I'd planned to take them out myself. Perhaps he would help me out if I told him that truth about my doing it. He and his family had purchased a home close by while he was studying under a surgical practice at the Lehigh Valley Hospital Center. He was already an excellent plastic surgeon, but learning more was part of his plan.

"Let me take a look," Grant answered. He inspected the wound before going across the street to his home for tweezers, antiseptic, and Band-Aids. A few snips and few tugs later, and the stitches were out.

"Your finger looks really good. Have you had a tetanus shot recently?" Dr. Grant asked with obvious concern.

"They gave me one at the hospital." I answered, nodding my head.

"Great. Be careful with that log splitter. You were lucky this time. I have stories to tell that would curl your toes."

I nodded, knowing he was right. "Thank you. I'll be more careful next time." I flexed my finger to see how it felt. Not too bad, I thought. A little stiff and painful, but it had healed well.

I wanted to be home before dark so I could take a peek at the hawk's nest. I hoped I might see the babies. After a while, I said my goodbyes and headed home. I was grateful to have Andy living close to me. My older two kids lived too far away. At least I got to see two of my grandchildren fairly often.

When I got home, I looked for Mel in the house and the shed, but she wasn't in either place. Going out to the field I found her on her knees, looking through the scope. She jumped when she saw me coming.

"You have to look in the scope," she said with obvious delight. I thought it might be too dark to see anything, but I got down on my knees and peered through the lens. Sitting there on the side of the nest was the mommy hawk, and in front of her were two small heads covered in pale yellow down. I saw the look in the mother's eye as she stared at them. It was softer than usual.

"How absolutely breathtaking," I said.

This was a first for me. I'd seen a lot of birds in the past, but nothing compared to this. Nothing. I felt as if I'd been allowed into a very special moment with Mother Nature.

Mel and I were excited to discover we could see fireworks from the surrounding towns from the top of the field. With all of it happening at the same time, the sky was filled with beauty. I had no doubt that this was to become an annual affair. The mommy hawk never moved away from her nest during the fireworks display. She knew her job, and it made me content.

When everything quieted down, we walked back to the shed.

Mel came home from work at noon the next day, having picked up our remaining skylights from Home Depot. Kim, Steph, and I were there waiting for her. We had purchased all but three skylights at the auctions. Two of these would go in the upstairs bathroom, and one in Mel's bedroom.

Kim said, "I'll take these up to the second floor."

"I don't want to go back to work. I'd rather be here all afternoon with you guys," Mel said, her longing obvious.

"Let's see how the skylights look after Kim leaves for the day," I said, knowing her discontent. "I'll wait for you to come home, and we'll look at them together."

"Okay, I can live with that," she said as she walked toward her car.

"Wait and see," Kim said to me, "they'll fit perfectly in their framing. Then I'll cut the holes in the roof and drop them in, while Stephanie works on the shingles."

Later, Kim asked me to run to Home Depot for nails. When I got back, I noticed three strangers in the driveway. They were neighbors from several houses away.

"We heard singing," one of them said, "so we walked up."

I guess Kim and Stephanie had been singing arias again, this time from the roof. Their sound must have traveled nicely down the street. Everyone wanted to hear it better, so they came up to listen.

Shaking my hand, the one man among them said, "I'm Dick, and this is my wife, Dot. We live on the other side of Bill and Heidi."

"Hello," I answered. "Thanks for walking up. Our contractor, Kim, and his daughter, Stephanie, love to sing together. Their voices carry quite a distance. I'm happy you heard them. It's so nice having this much joy being put into the building of our home."

"And I'm Irene," the third neighbor said, taking my hand in hers. "I live up the street in the gold house. Come up anytime, we'd love to have you. I've been listening to them sing for the last few weeks. It always makes me smile."

"Thanks for coming over to share in the music magic," I said.

"Our pleasure."

Kim had no idea they were standing there because he and Steph were working on the opposite side of the roof.

I spent the rest of the afternoon cleaning up around the foundation. There were bits of tar paper and pieces of plywood everywhere. I saved the remainder of the tar paper rolls and put them under tarps for future use. We would need them when we put the shakes on the sides of the shed. That seemed far off, but I saved everything.

Kim finished for the day. He picked up his tools, and laid them carefully in a pile inside the house. We didn't have to worry much about them anymore. They were dry, and strangers wouldn't be as likely to steal them if they were inside. Still, we kept an eye out for anyone driving around that we hadn't seen before.

Mel came home an hour after Kim left and joined me in the field. I was watching the babies in their nest. What fun it was to see them grow. We walked back up the path, returned the scope to the shed, and went to the house. When I entered, I instantly saw how the light within had changed. With skylights in the roof, it was much brighter on the second floor. I scampered up the ladder to look around, and Mel was right behind me. We were stunned.

"Wow," I said to Mel. "Look at the difference in the lighting. We won't need to turn the electricity on, unless it's very dark."

"We planned this really well," she said looking around.

The skylights were extraordinary. The two in the bathroom faced east, and gave us morning sun. In the shower area the sun glistened. Mel would see the stars at night from the tub.

Mel's bedroom faced west. She would experience the late afternoon sun, and each evening's sunset. We loved her room; maybe we'd switch and we'd both sleep in there once in a while just to feel the difference. I was joyous with the way our home was turning out. All of our hard work was indeed paying off.

My bedroom skylight also faced east. The thought of waking at dawn to sunshine on my face was awesome. An early riser, I was excited to experience this.

A memory pushed into my thoughts from when I was young. My dad built my horse barn in the lower lot and most mornings I cranked open the window to hear the soft knickers of my horse, Lindy Lou. As soon as she heard the window opening, she knew I'd soon be there to give feed and hay. I can still hear that sound to this day. She trotted along the fence waiting for me to appear. I spoke to her softly and stroked her forehead. I loved tucking my face into her warm neck, feeling her strength.

Lindy Lou frightened easily. She was afraid of most everything alive, birds and squirrels and anything that wriggled along in our path. I learned a very important lesson one summer's day. We had taken a long ride together and had come up alongside a stream. I got off and tried to lead her to the swiftly moving water for a drink. She stopped dead in her tracks. Eyes wild. I had a tight grip and urged her forward, but she bucked and backed away. Thinking she must be as thirsty as me, I took my yellow rain hat out of my saddlebag and filled it with water at the stream's edge. As I walked toward her with my hands extended, she took one look at the yellow hat and bolted. The reins that I had tied to a small sapling were strong, but the tree easily gave way to her tugs.

Off she went up the middle of the main road that ran from Otis to Bland-ford. Route 23, in western Massachusetts. It was hilly and the cars and trucks would be coming down quickly. I thought she was going to be run over. I ran up the hill as fast as my legs allowed, knowing I'd never catch her until she stopped to rest. Or get hit. I was panicked. And crying. I kept running, walking, running, until I got close to the top of this one hill. There, a man had stopped his pickup and was holding Lindy Lou's reins. The two of them were off the road and in a small clearing. My horse was calm now and eating grass. I was embarrassed by my mistake, but thanked the man and took the reins.

As we rode home I learned never to get off a horse that spooked at most things. If she needed water ever again on a ride, I'd ride her to the stream and let her lower her head to the water. And I brought a canteen with me that tied on to the saddle. Lesson learned. I was a lucky girl.

Tucked away in the shed for the rest of the night, I realized that within a week our shakes for the outside of the house were being delivered.

"The shakes will be here soon," I said, nudging Mel.

"I know. I got a message the other day. The driver will call when he's leaving the shipping area to let us know the projected time of arrival."

"It could be any minute," I said, getting more excited at the thought.

"Yeah, but then the really hard work starts."

I knew Mel was right. Kim would get us started, teaching us how to place shakes and properly nail them in, but after that, we'd be on our own.

Shake Delivery Gone Bad

Afew days later, I was shocked when an hour after she left for work, Mel returned to the shed.

"Is everything okay?" I asked, surprised and a little worried to see her back so soon.

"Yes. The shakes are being delivered in a few minutes." She looked frantic. I wasn't sure if I was excited or stressed from the heat, but whatever it was I felt a bit keyed up as well.

"Hey, Kim," I shouted, bounding toward the house. "The shakes will be here any minute!"

"Great," Kim said. "I have to finish the flashing around the skylights. You guys can handle it, can't you?"

I looked at Mel. "Why not?"

Quickly we searched for the best place to store the shakes. Finally, we decided on a level spot next to the driveway on the north side of the house.

"Just in time," I said to Mel. "Here comes the truck."

As it started up the driveway, I held my breath. The driver stopped and then backed away from the oak. He tried again, and didn't make it. This went on for twenty minutes before he finally got out, and walked to where we were standing mid-way up the drive.

"That's it. I'm going to drop them at the bottom of the driveway," he said. "You'll have to come down and get them because I can't make it around that tree. I have other deliveries to make." As he spoke, Kim watched from the roof. He was leaning into the roof with one leg bent against the shingles, and the other leg stretched out for balance. Clearly, by the look on his face, he was amused.

"We'll come down with the tractor," Mel said. "Hold on a minute."

"Oh, Lordy. Does everything have to be dropped at the end of our driveway?" I said, as we stared into the truck at the foot of our lane. I was astonished at the number of shakes we needed for this job.

"Looks like it," Mel groaned. "Damn these men anyway, they all seem to want us working harder than them for some reason."

Stacks and stacks of shakes, tied with heavy twine, filled the truck. The driver handed them down to us. Each bundle weighed about forty pounds, and was approximately two and a half foot wide by two foot long. As we handled them, the shakes kept slipping out from under the cord, making the job unwieldy and frustrating. The bundles broke loose again and again, and the driver was getting angry.

"I'll run over to Bill's and borrow his pickup truck," Mel said, throwing her arms into the air. "This is taking too long."

When she returned I saw that Heidi had come to help. Together, we all moved shakes into the back of Bluebie and Bill's truck, and then we drove them to the house. We unloaded, and did it over again. And again. We worked for over an hour, and still we were not close to being done. The driver was getting increasingly annoyed with us.

"I'm going to throw the rest of these on the ground," he said, "so I can complete my other deliveries."

I looked at him. "No, you're not," I said, wiping sweat from my face with my sleeve. "I don't want to have to bend over for each of these bundles. You're going to stay until we're finished." I had learned my lesson when the shed was delivered. No one was going to do that to me again.

It was at least ninety-five degrees, and we were all dying of thirst. I ran to the shed for drinks. I had been thinking that the driver was going to have a heart attack at any moment, because his face was apple red and he was overweight. Panting, even. Lordy!

"Are you okay?" I asked, handing him a Coke. "I think you should sit, and let us do the rest."

He didn't respond, but he did take the soda and sat, leaning his back against the wall of the truck. Within a few minutes he looked better, but we urged him to stay seated. Mel climbed up, stood in his place in the truck, and handed the remaining bundles down to Heidi and me. We threw them into the truck and Bluebie, and we drove them up to the house. In another hour we were finished.

The driver pulled his truck the hell out of there, and tore down the street. Fast. Mel, Heidi, and I, took off our gloves for a minute while we rested, and looked at our hands. They were filled with slivers from the shakes. As I sat in the shade, I pulled them out of my aching fingers, one splinter at a time.

It was hot, and my hands were sweaty. It was difficult to believe Kim was still on the roof. I didn't know how he managed it in this heat.

"It must be well over a hundred degrees up there," Mel mused, echoing my thoughts.

"Dinner will be my treat," I said to Heidi and Mel. "I'll go and get pizza, salad, and garlic knots, and we can eat together after Bill comes home from work."

"I love that idea. We'll see you soon." Heidi said, leaving to go home and shower.

Soon Kim came down the ladder from the roof. He was done for the day.

"You had everything under control with the shakes," he said with a self-satisfied chuckle. "There was no need for me to work on them, too. As it was, you were getting in each other's way. I saw the driver's red face all the way up on the roof." His shoulders shook with amusement, as he left to go home.

Mel and I went next door for showers, and then I called to order dinner. It was a beautiful evening to watch the hawks, and I could smell the heat rising off the corn each time I went to the field. When Heidi and Bill came over to look into the scope, I left to get the pizza. When I returned, we ate as if it were our last meal. We were starving. One of these days I'd be cooking in my own kitchen again. I loved to cook and bake.

Night came, so we said our goodnights and left the field together. Heidi and Bill went down their path, and Mel and I went down ours. The forest floor felt soft under my sneakers.

"What a day," I said. As I thought about the delivery, I got the giggles. "Can you believe that driver?"

Soon Mel was laughing too. But when I approached the huge ungainly pile of shakes, a sobering thought stopped me. We would have to hammer every one of them onto our home. I looked at my splinter-scarred hands, and my finger that had just healed. It was a daunting prospect. I also wondered whether or not we'd finish with the shakes before the cold weather. Now the house looked huge as I looked from the pile of shakes to the amount of surface to be covered.

I woke with butterflies. Kim was going to teach us how to nail shakes today. Reaching for my tool belt, I wondered how I would do. I liked Kim, and trusted him as a teacher. I wasn't sure why, but I felt shy and intimidated. I squared my shoulders and knew I'd get through it. By the end of the day, I would know how to put shakes on a home. What an accomplishment.

By the time Mel woke I had already brushed my teeth, and listened to the wood thrush. This morning he sang a different song, and I felt it was just for me.

My tools were hanging on my hips, and Kim smirked as he stepped from his truck. He rolled his eyes again, staying within his character. I scurried back into the shed like a mouse to the field. What was wrong with me? I was so afraid I was going to make a mistake and ruin the beauty of the house.

"That's ridiculous," Mel said, when I told her my concern. "You are a quick study."

"Thanks," I said. "Your confidence in me makes me feel stronger. I feel a little inhibited, but I've accomplished a lot of work here so far. I can do this too."

"You'll have no problem with the shakes, and after an hour I'm sure you'll love it." Her buoyancy steadied me, and off we went to learn about shakes.

"Most builders put on shakes with nail guns," Kim said, "But not me. They will stay in place better if you hammer each one in by hand. A lot of shakes are ruined by too much pressure and some of the nails will go completely through the board if you aren't careful. Then you have to pull the nail out and start over, leaving a hole that needs to be filled. Most likely that shake would be thrown aside."

"Can't you adjust the pressure on the gun?" Mel asked.

"There's the wrong way, and the Ziegler way," Kim answered, in a manner that ended the conversation. I'd heard this mantra enough times to know we'd be using our hammers.

Kim started us on the north side—the side that would show from the driveway. "Why are we starting on this side?" I asked.

"It's a good clean place to start. You can work there for a while from ground level. Now listen up. Each bottom row will have two layers of shakes, as you work your way around the house," Kim said. "Take each shake separately and line it up like this." He showed us how to use a chalk line, first measuring and then holding it tight on both ends, snapping it against the house.

"You'll put the next layer of shakes right on that blue line. The measuring needs to be exact, or it will look crooked when you get to the other end." Mel nodded. She had done this before, and was confident in her ability.

"Why didn't you tell Kim you've done this before?" I asked Mel after Kim left us alone.

"Everyone has their own way of doing things. I needed to see how he wanted it done. It's his way now."

Grabbing a shake I thought about what we were nailing them into. First, there was the OSB board covering the studs on the outside of the house. Then a layer of Homasote, a one-inch foil covered insulation, and then the shakes. I hoped the OSB was the right choice to hold all the nails, but Kim was sure.

We began hammering. Mel was on the first layer, working her way to the end of the house. I started the second row right behind her. When we got to the corner, we started again repeating the process. Mel set a quick pace, but I was keeping up with her. She was right; I was a quick study. And I loved it so much I couldn't keep the smile from my lips. I was laying a covering on the outside of the house to keep it safe and dry, just as I had for the outside of my own self. I knew how to do this work. I actually knew how to do this work! I was proud of what I learned, and wished again that my dad were alive to witness it. I wasn't sure about Bob, but perhaps he might have been pleased too.

By noon I began to see how our home was going to look at the finish line. The rows were nailed perfectly, and I felt good as I sat eating lunch with Kim and Mel in the park. The shakes were about the same color as cedar. If we let them weather, they would surely look like the cottages on Cape Cod.

After lunch I returned to work, hammering to the arias of Bocelli. I wore light shorts, a tee-shirt, and work gloves. I still felt hot. Despite the July heat, Kim worked in long pants. He never worked in anything else because it was too risky. He was always on his knees, or working with tools. I felt fortunate to begin this job in shorts. Despite the pace Mel set, I knew from the pile in the driveway that it was likely to be late fall by the time we finished. By then, I'd be in jeans and sweatshirts, and who knew what else. Maybe a straight jacket. I didn't want to think that far ahead.

Instead, I had to think about the upcoming auction. It would be our fourth. We still needed an interior door and some kitchen cabinets. Oh Lordy, I hadn't even thought about the kitchen.

Tired of Auctions

Early the next morning Kim told me the electricians and plumbers were scheduled to arrive.

"They'll all be working here at once for the next few weeks, so it will be a fun-filled time. It's late July now, but it won't take long for them to finish. You should know up front that they'll pull in early each day." He looked toward Mel.

Mel grimaced. "Well, thanks for letting us know ahead of time, it will save us a lot of anxiety. Damn it, I hate getting up early."

"By the way," I said, "we know you don't want us to get our kitchen cabinets at auction because they might not fit or look nice when you're finished. However, because of our money situation, we'll probably have to."

"We'll see," I looked for the smile in the creases of his eyes, but wasn't sure it was there. We were daring to not do things the Ziegler way.

After many months of ignoring the kitchen, I was beginning to get a little anxious. It was an important room, and I wanted it to be in perfect blending with the rest of the house. I needed to give it more attention.

We'd made trips to Home Depot and Just Cabinets. Both were doing a kitchen work-up for us. I knew the dimensions and that, along with Mel's drawing, was all they needed.

We went to the auction preview after lunch, and I marveled at the selections.

"There must be fifteen or twenty sets of cabinets here," I said to Mel. Some were in oak or pine, and others were in darker wood grains. All of them were just okay. It was hard to get excited. We walked around taking measurements while we looked at each set.

Mel spotted a good-looking bisque-colored kitchen sink lying on the floor by the cabinets. We made a note of its number on our list of things yet to purchase. It was a large single sink, deep enough to handle pots and pans.

"Hopefully no one else will be focused on this one," I said bending down to have a look.

"I know. It's great." Mel said, hitting the return button of the tape measure.

Finally, with our hands on our hips, we turned and looked at each other.

"I'm not seeing anything that really takes my head," Mel said, giving voice to my thoughts.

"I'd rather go without; I'm not seeing anything I like either."

"I don't want something in my home that isn't what I want. We've worked so hard to get everything just right." Mel jammed her hands into her jeans pockets.

"Let's stop looking," I said with finality. "It's time to rethink all of this kitchen stuff." We'd be back the next day, but only to get the sink.

It was dusk by the time we got home. I drove and Mel slept, curled up in the seat beside me. I woke her when I shut off the car, and she went to bed to rest and watch TV. I wanted to go to the field, so I said goodnight and went out.

I sat and thought over our kitchen situation. It had been a long day and neither of us was happy with the result. I trusted that in time the answer would show itself to me, but when I looked down at my hands they were shaking.

I had to walk with confidence throughout this venture, regardless of my fears. I just had to. Suddenly I bent over the side of the chair and vomited. Oh yuck. Guess I am nervous. I went over the numbers in my head. What if we couldn't afford the rest of the project? Our plan had been to purchase all of our doors, windows, and flooring at auctions from money in our savings accounts. Even credit cards if we had to. We didn't want any of those items on our mortgage. That way, even if I had to work at a fast food restaurant, I'd still make my half of the mortgage payment. I didn't want to pay retail prices for kitchen cabinets or for any other item in the house if I could avoid it. We wanted to keep our mortgage as low as possible. Part of me wanted to discuss the costs with my kids, but I knew innately that this was something I needed to do on my own. Even though Chris was good in business I was his mom and he gave much to me already. He loved the land though and felt good on it after he'd walked around. Even in the snow.

I fell asleep in the field, and when I woke it was after midnight. I tiptoed into the shed, and slipped into my sleeping bag. The minute its silky fabric hit my legs, I felt something change. I knew we would be okay, and tomorrow would bring answers.

⁓

Forcing myself out of bed at five-thirty was painful, but it was even worse for Mel. After dressing, I ran to the house for a second while Mel grabbed our sandwiches, drinks, and wallets. I wanted to look out of the skylights.

I climbed the ladder to the second floor, and went into my future bedroom. Even filled with building materials, it felt like home. I stood where the closet was going to be built, and looked down at the floor. A small postcard lay there, so I picked it up and stuffed it in my pocket. I'd throw it away later. The light from my skylight covered my upturned face, and with the sun rising over the trees I could see the pink sky of dawn. Talk about a room with a view.

Realizing I was holding up our trip I climbed back down the ladder, ran out of the house, and jumped into Mel's car. She was waiting, and handed me a cup of coffee before we set off.

About halfway to the auction, I stuck my hand in my pocket to make sure I'd brought along my credit card and cash. I knew by now I didn't want to carry anything in my hands, or have a wallet I might set down by mistake. I needed to be free of clutter in order to heft doors, windows, or anything else we'd purchased.

Reaching into my pocket, I felt the scrunched-up post card, my credit card and cash. I looked for a trash bag, but smoothed the card open against my leg in the process. It was an advertisement for the Peak Auction in Baltimore, and I noticed some of the items for sale. One of them was kitchen cabinets. Lucky us, I sang with my inner voice.

"I'm going to the Peak Auction in Baltimore in three weeks," I said waving the card in the air. Of course, Mel had no idea what I was talking about.

"Just to take a peek?" she said with more humor than the early hour warranted.

"No, funny girl. Listen to this." I read the postcard to her.

"It seems like an answer to our prayer," Mel said at last. "But let's check it out before we drive all the way down there."

When we got to Hanover, Mel asked a few contractors that were milling around the building if they knew anything about the Peak Auctions in Baltimore.

"They have great prices, especially for kitchen cabinets," one older guy told her. "I'm going to head there myself." We looked at each other with hope.

"Another auction in three weeks," I muttered, letting my chin fall to my chest. "I'm getting exhausted from all of this driving."

We were lucky that day. We got our sink for sixty-five dollars, which was far below the retail price of $150. We paid our bill, loaded the cast iron sink in the car, and started home. It wasn't even three o'clock yet, and we were finished.

"Let's stop at my studio." Mel said. "We can go online, and see what the Peak Auction has to offer."

"Great idea." I said grabbing the postcard to take another look. "It will be late August already when we go, but we have to think about our kitchen. Like it or not. Time is getting short."

We sat together in front of the monitor in Mel's studio, and my eyes were opened wide. The kitchen cabinets looked extraordinary. They also had stoves, refrigerators, and dishwashers. I rubbed my hands over my face and through my hair, excited at all the possibilities.

Back at our land, we spent the last two hours of daylight working on the shakes. "Good thing Kim put up this scaffolding," Mel said. "It's much easier than ladders, and safer, too."

"It is safer, but I'm not used to it yet. We're fifteen feet off the ground now, but he needs to raise it even higher in a day or two."

"We'll be so focused on the work that the height won't matter. Shit, we can do this." Mel said.

It was getting dark. I walked to Bill's house and went inside for my shower, and then told them about our day. "There's an auction in Baltimore on the 25th of the month," I said. "We can't get enough of them, it seems. May we borrow your truck again?"

"Sure. I love driving your car instead of mine." He laughed and so did I.

Walking back up the path, I decided not to preview the auction. We'd save money on a hotel by going down very early Saturday morning. I knew they'd have kitchen stuff, so why not go on the actual day trusting we'd find something that would work for us?

———————

The next several weeks we worked on the shakes. Kim raised the scaffolding again, and we were moving right along.

"I'm happy you're making such good progress," Kim said, late one afternoon.

"Thanks." The praise boosted my confidence enough that I was comfortable working alone the next day while Mel went to her studio.

When I finished for the day I stepped back and realized we still had a long way to go. And this was only one side of the house. We needed to be done by winter, and didn't want to pay Kim to do it. Laying shingles was slow work, and I knew the labor cost would be enormous. Mel was going to take time off in order to get the whole project completed. I tried not to be overwhelmed.

That evening I went to the field yet again. The baby hawks were growing larger each day, as they, too, were gaining more confidence. Fledging time was almost here and I was going to miss them. I read online that the fledglings stayed around for the rest of the summer, while the mothers kept close, and then they moved on. It was not going to be the same without them. The experience reminded me of watching my three children grow, knowing that leaving their home was a sure thing. A painful occurrence, but it was reality.

Nature can be heartbreaking, at times, but there is an order to it. Overall, I hoped for no more than that in this project.

Our Kitchen

Heading toward Baltimore weeks later it felt, again, like a miniature convoy. Mel was driving Bill's truck, and I was in Powder. It was still dark, yet I was wide awake. I hardly believed that it was August already, and the twenty-fifth of the month to boot. Before you know it Eastern Standard Time will kick in and it will be getting dark earlier in the evenings. We still had so much work remaining on the house. I was becoming fearful that the move-in date of October was not realistic anymore.

We all had our fears, but my personal ones were drying up and blowing away like the bugs in the field at summer's end. I was working well with men, building my house, and feeling my life change all at the same time. Forgiving myself and rebuilding my future felt grand. Just last week when one of the electricians told me I looked good in my tool belt, I grinned and said, "You betcha. I may be old as dirt, but that isn't stopping me anymore."

Following my Mapquest directions, I left the interstate and traveled along back roads, leaving civilization behind. I drove for miles without seeing any indication of an auction house.

"How was an auction this large in the middle of Podunk?" I asked myself, as I pulled into an old gas station and repair shop. I looked into my rearview mirror to make sure Mel was following. She was.

Inside, I showed the ancient man behind the counter my directions, and he said, "Of course I know where that is. Just keep on driving for another four miles and it will be on your right."

I walked back to Mel who rolled down the window, and told her what the man said.

"He's probably putting us on and has no idea whatsoever," Mel said with a cynical tone. Getting up early was wearing on her.

"Well, we'll soon find out."

Mel pulled up a little and yelled out the window. "I can't wait to get there. Our kitchen cabinets await us." She smiled, then laughed, and sped out in front of me. Guess she's okay after all, I thought.

"Four miles went by a long time ago" I said with disgust. "I bet the guy from the gas station is having a good laugh."

As soon as I said that, I spotted some activity going on up the road. As I drove closer, I saw a large parking area with lots of trucks and trailers.

"We've arrived," I said, shutting off the ignition.

Mel ran in to pick up our numbers, while I high-tailed it over to the kitchen cabinet area.

I walked around the sets of cabinets getting more excited each time I opened a drawer or door. The selection was much larger than I had seen anywhere else. By the time Mel came over to look, I had picked out two that were absolutely amazing. One maple set was striking—light in color, and the design of the doors was finished in a mission style. The other set, cherry, was gorgeous. It was darker, but it would work for us if we used track lighting.

"What a difference between this auction and the other one."

"So many to pick from," Mel said, her eyes wide with anticipation. I showed her my two favorites. "Either one," she said. "They're both attractive. I knew we were going to be lucky at this auction. You'll be spending more time in the kitchen, because you love to cook. I'll be fine with whatever choice you make."

Mel got to work with her tape measure, and I called Kim to tell him what we'd found.

"I can make either of them work. Go ahead and bid," Kim said. The decision was ours as to whether we wanted the lighter set or the darker color. We sat down on one of the boxes and considered our options.

"We need to have a back-up plan," I said, "just in case we don't win the bid on our first choice."

"Okay. What is our first choice?"

I shrugged. "I'm not sure yet. How much time do we have before the auctioneer comes to this area?"

"Our kitchen has the fewest windows. We need the wood to be light in color, if at all possible." Mel said. "If not, we'll make sure we have great lighting. This area needs to follow the rest of the house. Lots of illumination."

"When a house is dark, it looks smaller," I said. "And neither of us wants a dark home. The kitchen has an eastern exposure. Either set of cabinets will be stunning in early morning. During the afternoon and evening though, we'll want the kitchen to look radiant."

"Perhaps the maple set, then?" Mel asked. "Its light wood and clear finish will keep the area glowing. We won't need to use another source of lighting."

"And the cherry set will be our backup," I agreed. "We'll have to spend more on lighting, but it will be worth the cost. But what if the cherry ones go up for auction first?"

"We'll cross that bridge when we come to it," Mel said, furrowing her brow.

"Maybe we ought to look for a third set, just in case we lose the bid on the first two." I said walking up and down the aisles. The third kitchen set we found had fewer cabinets, but the wood was oak. Not my favorite, but I could live with it.

"We can order extra cabinets of this style from Lowe's if we need them," Mel said. She had opened one of the drawers, and looked at the brand name on its side. "These are the same ones they sell in their stores."

Walking back to look at our first two choices, Mel, once again, opened the drawers. "The brand name on these is the same as Home Depot's." I was happy she had done the research.

I felt settled. Knowing we could order more to match any of these sets, helped me feel more confident of our decision. I was ready and waiting for the auctioneer to begin. Finally, around one o'clock, he made his way over.

This auctioneer was drastically different than the ones we were used to at Southern Sales in Hanover. He was more professionally dressed and a little intimidating to me, but still he had a twinkle in his eye. It must be a trait of all auctioneers, I thought.

"You need to do the bidding. I'm too nervous."

"I'm on it."

Mel was ready, but looked a little confused with what was happening around us. I was standing close by and was all excited and eager to get started. Everything seemed to be moving in slow motion.

The bidding started slowly, very slowly, and we didn't have a clue why. People were everywhere, standing in rows three feet deep, but no one was saying anything.

"This must be a mind game," I whispered. "Hold on tight, and jump in when it gets hot and heavy."

She looked back and mouthed, "I'm thinking the same thing."

All of a sudden the action took off. People were yelling and bidding and Mel was trying to keep up, but she was having trouble.

The auctioneer was speaking in a voice that neither of us understood. His mouth was moving, but what was coming out was nothing but gobble-dygook. Mel shot her hand in the air when she thought it was her turn, and then she looked at me for help.

At that moment the bidding stopped abruptly. Everyone was looking at us, and one other guy. I didn't know what to do. I stood there stunned, waiting for something else to happen. Anything, to happen.

Finally, the auctioneer looked at the man who was bidding against Mel. He said, "Pick your set."

Damn it. I knew he was going to pick the maple set, because I saw him looking at it earlier. We waited quietly because we didn't know what else to do.

Mel turned to me and whispered, "I have no clue what is going on." The auctioneer looked at us, and I didn't know why.

Finally, the man who won the bid said, "I'll take the cherry set."

Then the auctioneer looked at Mel. "What?" Mel said. He started laughing, and soon all of us joined in.

"At this auction, everyone bids at the same time. When the bid is won by someone other than yourself, the next bidder has the chance to take any kitchen set for the same price. If they want. Otherwise, you'll have to do the bidding all over again. You take a chance either way. The bid could be higher or lower the next time."

Mel said, "I'll take the maple set." And that was that. We got our first choice after all.

The scary thing, however, was we had no earthly idea of how much we just paid for it. I never understood a word the auctioneer said when the bidding got wild, so I walked over to the set of cherry cabinets to find the man who had won them.

Without hesitation, I walked up to him and asked what we were paying for these kitchen sets.

"You won't believe it," he said, and then he told us the good news. "I only paid two thousand dollars for mine. Some of them have divided drawers, and others have sliding shelves. At the other auctions, sets like these are selling for thirty-five hundred to four thousand dollars. In the Home Stores, they sell for up to ten grand."

We looked at each other and jumped in the air laughing, yelling, and high-fiving each other. Everyone close by looked at us, knowing that we finally understood the enormity of what had just happened. They cheered us on.

Mel called Kim, and I listened in. "I'm ecstatic," he said, "but you have more cabinets than you can use. Maybe you could sell some down there?"

"I don't want to," Mel said quickly. We'll use two in the laundry room to hold our cleaning supplies, and I want to save the others in case we find another need for them. Perhaps in the bathroom, if there's room."

Kim agreed, "We'll decide what to do with the other ones another time. Good job guys!" I was still stunned with what had happened. People around us were in total concentration on what they had yet to do for their own selves, and I knew why. You needed to pay attention every minute at this auction.

I moved away and looked around to find where we needed to pay for our purchases. Then we'd start packing.

After settling our bill, I looked for an employee. I found one man outside with a hand cart, ready to help people load their cars or trucks. Before we told him where our cabinet set was, Mel reached in her pocket and pulled out a twenty.

Mel winked at me and said, "You have to know how to tip well. Another thing I learned from being a Jersey girl."

There were too many cabinets to fit in our vehicles.

Mel told the worker, "We have to fit them in. We live four hours away, and can't come back tomorrow. We have to get everything in these two vehicles tonight."

He looked at her as if she were crazy, but when Mel pulled out more twenty dollar bills he climbed up on Powder. Then he waved two more guys over to help. Four cabinets went on top of my roof top carrier. They tied them down hard, and everything looked well placed. Then the men went to work on Bill's truck, tying cabinets here and there until they had all of them secured. At least I hoped they were secure. I tipped generously again, knowing we'd never have done this work by ourselves.

We were quite the spectacle as we drove away late that afternoon. Both vehicles were top heavy, but I thought we'd make it home. If we were careful. As we drove the interstate other cars with people inside looked at us, pointed and laughed. Soon I was laughing with them. Nothing mattered as long as we made it to Deb and Mart's barn.

An hour away from home a light rain started to fall. We stopped to put tarps over everything. Oh Lordy. "Just a little longer, I said, patting the tarp.

Mel called Bill, and when we got to the barn he was there to help. We made quick work of unloading everything. The moment we finished putting in the last cabinet, the sky opened and it poured.

"We made it just in time. No amount of tarps could have protected all that wood in this downpour."

I felt sheltered within the barn's dry and sturdy walls. Cared for by friends, by strangers, and God.

Working Days

Sunday morning I dragged myself to the field with the spotting scope under my arm. I was pooped from my auction trip, but I wanted to see the chicks in their nest. Kneeling down to take a look, I was astounded. The two babies were on the rim of the nest, walking its perimeter. And, they were beginning to get feathers. Now, a fuzzy gray/white, I could clearly see the new feathers growing along their sides.

One is getting a little too brave, I thought, but like most young raptors, they grow very quickly. He looked as if he were going to explore beyond the nest, and walk out onto one of the stanchions. In the end he changed his mind, and went back into the nest. That had to be pretty exciting for him. It was a long drop if he fell, but mom was close by, so I guess he felt more courageous. I could see her flying around the field, talking to them while she hunted for food.

Essentially, chicks are full grown by thirty-nine to forty days, and I knew they might outweigh their parents by the time they left the nest. Of course, all of that depended on whether or not they were well fed, and what kind of food they received. With the field and its small stream below, provisions should be bountiful.

But these two hawks weren't following the rules. They should have been larger by now, in fact, they ought to have fledged. Perhaps the first two babies didn't make it, and the mommy laid two more eggs. It did seem a long time before we saw their little heads peeking over the top of the nest. Hard to tell with nature, sometimes there were irregularities. But whatever happened, we still had babies to watch and that was exciting.

My mom wasn't much for having animals in the house. With babies on my mind, I sat for a minute and thought about that. I remembered rescuing so many different kinds of babies when I went for long horseback rides. I found eggs that had fallen from nests, baby bunnies that looked like they needed nourishment, and other tiny animals. I'd stick them in my saddlebags and bring them back. Mom didn't want them in the house so I kept them in the barn nestled in the hay loft with old towels to keep them warm, and fed them with eye droppers. Most grew up just fine, and then I'd release them back into the woods where I found them.

Walking back to the house, I began picking up trash. I didn't want to start the tractor until Mel was awake. She needed her rest. The ground was more littered than I'd ever seen it. I made a large pile of wood pieces for Kim's fishing trips, and a smaller one for us by our little fire ring in the park. Then, I stuffed trash bags full of odds and ends of building materials and put them in the back of our cars. By the time I finished, Mel came out to help. She was dragging herself around, too. Auction day had taken its toll on the two of us.

I walked over to the tarp to get a rake.

"Damn it to hell!" I said, kicking the dirt in front of me. "Mice have been in my grass seed. They've eaten most of it. The bag is almost empty. I should have put it in the basement or the shed."

"Dammit is right," Mel growled.

I was glad we had the kitties in the shed with us. I didn't want Toby or Eli to kill anything, but I didn't want any mice in my nest either.

"So much for grass seed," I moaned. Guess I was tired.

Our loud voices startled a fawn that capered across the field bleating for his mother. Several does had given birth in our woods early this spring, and fawns were everywhere. We had to be careful where we stepped. The fawns, even at two months, were fed early in the morning. Then the moms hid them either in the woods or field, for the rest of the day. Toward evening, the does came back to give another feeding and together they bedded down for the night.

Like the young hawks, it seemed the fawns didn't want to stay put anymore. Youngsters of all kinds were the same it seemed. Nature was a good teacher and I, the student, was taking it all in. As I worked, I saw several sniffing the air, and bleating for their moms. Each of them was unique, and so darn cute with their almond eyes. One had more white around its ears, and one had more tan around its nose. At night I could hear them crunching their corn at my feeding stations.

Mel and I took a break and sat down in our park chairs.

"Kim said the plumbing and electricity come next," I said, "but what comes after that?"

Mel thought a minute. "Kim mentioned he's going to call in the sub-contractor to pour the basement cement. It has to be done before the other subs can finish their work. We can expect them sometime soon. Then the phone, electric, and cable companies need to put in lines from the street to our house. Charlie will have to come back with the backhoe and dig the ditch."

"Still so much to do, Mel."

"It's okay, it will all get done. The plumbers are going to use a new kind of tubing, called Pex. It's the latest thing to have in homes now, and can be easily bent to go around corners and angles. Plumbers love it because they don't have to sweat the pipes or put in right angle fittings. It's not only going to be great and easier to use, but faster to finish the job."

"That means cheaper," I mumbled, more or less to myself.

After the Saturday we'd had, I felt we had earned a treat. Later on that afternoon, I jumped into Powder. "I'll be back, Mel."

"Where're you going?"

"You'll see. It's a surprise."

I drove to Roman Delight and picked up a nice Italian dinner for each of us. Eggplant parmesan for me, and pasta with marinara for Mel, and then I went on to the storage unit. I stuffed the VCR in my car, went to Blockbuster, and rented the movie *The Sixth Sense*. We had missed it in the theaters, and had been waiting months for it to come out on videotape.

When I got back to our shed, Mel was inside lying on her sleeping bag with Eli.

"Look what I brought."

"I can't believe you did this!" she squealed with delight opening the bag I handed her.

Mel loved movies. I did too. I never thought I'd have the capability to watch one in the shed. It was almost more than I could've hoped for. We dressed in pajamas, ate dinner, and watched our movie.

When the film was over, we walked over to the house in the dark. Soon there would be electricity, never looking quite the same again. I wanted to take advantage of these last few days of rusticity. Climbing upstairs with our flashlights, we laid on the floor looking out the skylights. Mel was in her room, and I was in mine. I tucked my arms under my head as I gazed at the stars.

"One day my bed will fill this space," I said.

Sometime after that, snow would be falling, and I'd see life on our land in another season.

———

Workers came up our driveway shortly after dawn on Monday of the following week. I walked out of the shed with my shovel, while Mel straggled along behind.

Mel had her tool belt on, but I had left mine inside the house. I ran to get it. Feeling a little hesitant, I stuck to nailing shakes on exterior walls for the day so I didn't have to interact with all the men. But I could have if I needed to.

"The basement floor will be laid tomorrow," Kim said, as he walked over to where I was working. "The cement truck will have to come up the driveway, and I'm a little concerned about it."

"We'll see what happens tomorrow," I said determined to stick to my guns. "I'm not taking that tree down. They'll just have to deal with it."

"It will be an interesting morning," Kim said, rolling his eyes for the hundredth time on this project. Somehow when Bob rolled his eyes at me it felt different in my heart. I think it was the intent, not the action. Something to think about as I nailed my way through the days.

I went back to work carrying bundles of shakes up the ladder and onto the scaffolding. I was content to let Mel talk to the workers while I nailed. A few minutes later, she climbed up to join me.

She wore a cryptic grin. "What?" I asked pausing to look at her.

"Charlie is coming this afternoon. He's going to dig the ditch for the phone, electric, and cable lines. It shouldn't take long. When he's done, I'll call the utility companies. Once they finish, Charlie will fill it back in. Kim will have electricity for his tools, and we'll have lighting for our house." Mel finished with a firm nod of her head.

I put my hammer down on the scaffolding and bowed my head. "Wow. Lights in the house. I can hardly believe it after all this time."

Mel nodded and grabbed a shake.

"And, it'll be nice to have it quiet after listening to Kim's generator for the last few months," I said, picking up my hammer.

We worked hard all morning, breaking for lunch with Kim and the rest of the workers. The only chairs available were the ones by the fire ring, so we were all together. That was rare.

"I saw an ad in the recent Penny Power for restoring your claw foot tub," Kim said, handing it to me from his lunch cooler.

"I saw that, too," I said, opening it up. "When the basement floor is finished, I'll call them."

"It'd be better to schedule now. They are one of the few companies that refurbish old tubs and are constantly busy, from what I hear."

Thanking Kim for his advice, I left to make the call in the shed. I spoke with the wife of the owner of the company. Her tone was nasty and angry.

"Why are you yelling at me?" I asked carefully, not to upset her even more.

"I'm not yelling," she said even louder.

"Yes, you are. Stop it, for heaven's sake."

When she calmed down I said, "I'd like to schedule an appointment. I have an old claw-foot tub that needs to be restored."

Not wasting a minute she growled, "How 'bout two weeks from today?"

"Fine."

I hung up, and went outside to join the others.

"Yikes, Kim. I talked to the owner's wife and she sounded so miserable, and annoyed. I almost hung up on her. What's the deal?"

As I looked at all the workers, I found the joke was on me. Everyone was laughing, even Mel. Kim had worked with these people before, and he had told everyone about this woman while I was in the shed making the call.

"Happy I can bring some joy to this group," I said a little embarrassed. "That was an experience I could have done without."

Kim sat back in his chair and lit a cigar. "The good thing is, her husband is a miracle worker. You'll never recognize your tub when he's finished."

Again we had gone as high as possible with the shakes, so after lunch I asked Kim to raise the metal scaffolding. When he was finished I climbed up and sat on the twelve-inch wide platform, and reminded myself not to look down. Sitting on it wasn't bad. Standing on it while nailing over my head was a different thing all together. The higher Kim elevated it, the more careful I knew I had to be. And, after a full afternoon of work, it was time to raise the scaffolding again.

"Kim's going to have to hoist it up again in the morning," I said, exhausted. The higher the scaffolding, the more difficult it was to carry shakes up the ladder.

"I know. He's always doing that for us," Mel answered.

The scaffolding was incredibly heavy. Kim's ladders were heavy, too, and they were tall and unwieldy. It was hard physical labor being a contractor. No wonder most of them had bad knees and wrists. Nothing about this work was simple. Swinging a hammer every day had to be very damaging on the shoulder, wrist, and finger joints. Fortunately, Kim was strong. He had to be to keep going.

"I'll have to have surgery on my knees one day," Kim said as he got ready to leave for the day.

I knew it went with the job, but I hated it for him. It made me feel terrible. "I'm sorry, Kim. You told me that your grandfather taught you how to build. Did he have surgery as well?

"No, but he had a lot of pain. Don't worry about Mr. Wonderful, though, he will survive." He said with a smile that looked a little forced.

Kim said he'd raise the scaffolding in the morning, so Mel and I were finished for the day. My arms ached, my back ached, and I was hot and tired.

Looking at what we'd accomplished, however, I was pleased.

"August sure is humid," I whined.

"Always is," Mel said, looking at our soaked t-shirts. "It's damp in the shed, too, in the mornings. Hate that."

We walked out to the chairs in the field to rest a bit, and I brought my spotting scope along. It was the first time that day I'd had time to look at the nest. Peeking through the lens, I could see one of the chicks far out on the stanchion. He looked as if he were going to fall, wobbling around back and forth.

Mel took her turn; it was hard to stop watching. Sometimes, I used binoculars because I was tired of kneeling. Again and again this little guy kept walking out and back, but the other chick stayed in the nest.

"Do you think the male is braver than the female?"

"Nah," Mel said, shaking her head. "I bet it's the other way around."

"Funny girl."

An hour later, I looked over at the house as I walked back from the field. I knew it would appear different by the end of the week. Plumbers and electricians were making great progress. Soon, we'd have to pick out our lighting fixtures for every room. We had the toilets and sinks for each bathroom, but still needed a shower. Despite all we'd purchased, more shopping awaited.

I hated shopping. It felt like wasted time. My daughter, Shelly, never had a mom who took her to the mall and if I did, I would have been cranky about it. I had to admit it though, shopping for lighting fixtures might be a different animal altogether.

Moving Scaffolding Again

"W"ow, what the heck was that?" I said, bursting out of the shed. Looking toward the driveway I saw a cement truck trying to make its way around the old oak. When I got down there, I could see the problem immediately.

"Hey guys, hold on a minute," I said to the driver and his passenger, "I'm going to make the driveway a little wider in that spot so you stop hitting the oak."

The driver looked at me with one eyebrow raised, and said very politely, "Thank you for helping out."

"No, thank you for being patient," I answered.

I brought the chainsaw down to the tree. I knew that the men in the truck were staring at me and I felt uncomfortably self-conscious, but regardless of my feelings I yanked the saw to life and took down three small trees. I cut them as low as I dared because I didn't want to dull the chain by hitting ground. Then, I used a smaller hand saw to take them down the rest of the way. I didn't mind taking the small trees this time, it needed to be done in order to save the one oak I loved so much.

"I have no extra fill for this space right now, I'm sorry. Would you like me to call for a load?"

The driver looked at me with his crooked grin. "No. What you've done is great. The ground is hard; I'll have no problem now. By the way, you're pretty good with that chain saw."

"Thank you," I said, still feeling a little self-conscious. "I've done it most of my life. Hate taking down trees I don't have to, though."

"I see that," he said to his helper, just loud enough for me to hear.

I smiled.

Up they came, clearing the oak by at least six inches. A few minutes later Kim drove in followed by the electricians and plumbers. Everyone went in different directions, all having their own work to do. Kim came over to the side of the house, and lifted the scaffolding another three feet. That would last for the rest of the day, and before he left for the evening he'd raise it again. It took longer the higher we went, more time spent climbing ladders with the shakes under our arms. This was hard work. The north side was almost done. Next, we'd move to the east side of the house—the one that faced the road. That was the longer, thirty-two foot side, but it was not as high.

Kim left to check on the sub-contractors before he began his work inside. It was a full day of construction on our land.

"We need to talk with Kim before we begin to do our own work," Mel said.

She went inside to find him, and I followed along behind.

"We are going to purchase a golden stain that we love and then stain the tongue and groove we're using for the ceiling, before you put it up." Mel said to Kim, hoping for no argument.

He looked at us as if we were out of our minds, but he listened. The ceiling was lofty; even with scaffolding it would be a difficult job. At the apex it was twenty-two feet high.

"Damn it, I hate working with stained wood. I understand, but it will have to be done soon—probably by the end of the week," he said. "I'll be starting that job on Friday or Saturday."

Mel and I looked at each other. This was Wednesday and we didn't even have the wood yet.

"It should be delivered in a day or two," I said. "But I thought we would wait and stain in the basement after the floor cures. That way no leaves or twigs or dust will get on the boards while they're wet."

Kim raised an eyebrow. "Ladies, that floor won't cure until the weekend. No…" he objected, but Mel stopped him.

"Couldn't you wait until next week to start on the ceiling?" she asked. "Then we can stain over the weekend, and have some of it ready for you on Monday morning. I'm sure we can stay ahead of you with the wood."

I looked at Mel's pleading expression and tried to match it with my own. How could "Mr. Wonderful" disappoint two such hopeful women?

"All right," he said, his voice filled with resignation. "Just be sure to put a lot of newspapers or a tarp down so you don't stain the cement."

"We will. Thanks, Dad." I said, winking at Mel.

"Pfffhh," he said, waving us away in mock exasperation. But I saw the twinkle in his eye and I felt like I had gotten away with something.

Now we were boxed into a weekend-long marathon of staining. I hoped the weather cooperated so the stain dried fast. It was going to be a race to get it finished. After a week of nailing shakes in the summer heat, I had been looking forward to a little time off. No such luck now.

It was another endless day of nailing shakes. When we finished for the afternoon, we had gone as high as we could—about twenty-five feet off the ground. This was really dangerous work, extremely hard on the wrists, knees, and muscles in general. Kim was going to have to do the rest. I didn't feel safe going any higher. I thought the east and west sides would be easier because the roof line was lower. Only the north and south sides had high gable ends. It wouldn't take Kim long to finish once he started. The extra cost would be worth it, and I'd save us money by carrying the shakes up to Kim while he nailed. I was okay going up the ladder and setting them on the scaffolding.

Before Kim left for the day, he moved all the scaffolding to the east side of the house. I wouldn't need to stand on it yet because I'd start out at ground level again. I planned to start first thing in the morning, and Mel would help when she returned from her studio.

Although we were tired from the day's work, Mel, Kim, and I all piled into my car and drove to Deb and Mart's barn. Kim wanted to look at the kitchen cabinets we'd purchased.

"These will easily fit the kitchen walls," he said after measuring the cabinets.

"Good. Going to Baltimore was worth the money," I said climbing back behind the wheel.

"Suddenly I feel rushed," I said to Mel an hour later when we were back on the land. "We need to purchase stain, and keep nailing shakes. The pine delivery is imminent."

"Why don't we go over to Buss's paint store in Emmaus," Mel suggested. "We might be able to find what we want tonight. I'm too tired to do anything else anyway."

"Ugh, I really don't feel like it." I whined, flopping forward like a collapsing plastic toy. Then my mom popped into my mind. She always said don't put off until tomorrow what can be done today. I hated to admit she was right, but I raised my aching body off the floor and stood upright regardless of the aches and pains.

We dragged ourselves into Powder again and drove over to the paint store. Luck was on our side and in minutes we found the stain tint we'd hoped for.

"We're going to need a lot of this," Mel said, ticking off on her fingers the sections of house that would need staining. "We'll need it for the ceiling, moldings, windows, and interior doors."

I knew she was right. I bought all they had in the store, and ordered an additional eight gallons. "This is one hell of a lot of stain. I'm tired even thinking about it."

By the time we got back to the house, it was too dark to see the hawk babies.

"I'm even too tired for ice cream," I said to Mel. "That's tired."

Walking back to the shed I noticed a light shining in the house. I went in to take a look, and Mel continued on to play with the kitties. It was the LED readout for the CD player. I turned the machine on, and sat in the dark listening to Bocelli. Now he had become a part of our project. I wondered how he'd feel if he knew he helped construct a house, and for some reason it made me feel good.

The next morning, Kim surprised us and brought everything he needed to build our stairway. He went right to work and any time I took a break from the shakes, I went in to watch his progress. By the time he was ready to leave that afternoon, the staircase was nearly done. He let us test it out.

Mel went first, running up the stairs. I followed before she had a chance to turn around and come down.

"I don't hear a single squeak." I said to Kim, scrambling down to stay ahead of Mel.

"That's how it's supposed to be." Kim puffed his chest out with pride. "I'll build the basement steps tomorrow. I've always loved making stairs," he said scratching the back of his head. "More of an art form, I guess. I'll need to put a heavy paper down on that oak so it won't be ruined."

"Amazing job, Kim." Mel said. "You'll need to think about the hand rail. Make one yourself so we don't have some old plain one."

"Yes, Boss."

John would be back in a few days for another building inspection. I knew the stairs would pass. Looking up from the bottom, I had to admit that they were as beautiful as they were functional. My only fear was that John would find out we were living in the shed when he came for inspection. I would have to keep on the lookout again.

Before Kim got back to his truck, I heard another vehicle rumble up the driveway. Our tongue and groove pine for the ceiling had arrived earlier than expected. It was Thursday and good timing for us. Kim helped us unload it, and we all tried not to knick any of the wood. We stacked it on saw horses near the edge of the driveway. We didn't want it to get damp from the ground.

"We can move it into the house tomorrow morning," Mel said looking at the clouds. "It isn't supposed to rain tonight. If it does, we'll get up during the night and bring it inside."

"We will?" I asked.

"Please don't rain," Mel put her hands together and looked skyward. I threw a tarp over the boards.

Mel and I worked on the shakes for a few more hours. It was almost dark when we stopped. While we were working, the phone and electric companies had come late in the afternoon and laid their underground lines in the ditch. Once the cable company came, Charlie could close it up. I hated that it was gaping open, and worried that animals might fall in.

Before going to the shed, Mel and I ran up and down the stairs again. After a couple of times we realized how tired we were, and called it a day. Sitting in my chair, I thought about my life as an outdoors woman and athlete. Despite being active my entire life, I felt as if I were in the best shape I'd ever been. I was tired every day from working hard, but I was strong and fit.

"Work hard for what you want, and do everything you can for it. Then trust it will happen. Life is all about effort," I whispered my personal motto into my pillow.

Oh No, They Fledged

Thankfully, it did not rain that night or the next. It was the week-end and the cement floor was cured and ready to walk on. It looked smooth and I couldn't have been more pleased. But I didn't have time to stand around admiring it as I was determined to finish as much staining as possible by Monday. Mel had other work to do in the studio, and only one person was needed for this job.

I hauled some of the tongue and groove pine into the basement and placed it on my two sawhorses, and then two more of Kim's. First though, I covered the floor with newspaper. I only stained two dozen pieces at a time, standing them on end between the floor joists to dry. Since I only had to stain one side, I felt certain I could stay well ahead of Kim. I had plenty of light during the day to work in the space that would soon be Mel's studio.

The tint of the stain had a golden glow. There was no doubt in my mind that it was going to look dramatic on the ceiling. Perfectly natural wood. Dad, would have loved it, I thought. My family home in New England was pine throughout, and looking at the tongue and groove now made me think of home.

While I waited for the finished pieces to dry, I wanted to nail shakes. Walking out the opening for Mel's French doors, I spotted a fawn walking toward the ground water bath. We had two baths, one was on a pedestal, and the other was on the ground. Birds drank from both, but used the higher one most often. Deer, turkeys, fox, raccoons, and other animals drank from the one on the ground.

Clearly the fawn was timid, but she stood close to it for a moment and stared. Then she touched her mouth to the water, gently moving it from one side to the other. Next, she stuck out her tongue and swished it back and forth through the water. Then she placed one of her front feet in the water, then the other, splashing around before deciding to step in with all four feet. Again, she stood quietly, as if her feet were sticky or frozen. She tried to walk around in this tiny bird bath top, slipping and sliding as if she had her own pool. It was so darn funny I had to look away to keep from laughing out loud. I didn't want to scare her. She was having too much fun, and so was I.

Twenty minutes later, all played out, she walked back to the woods. There, in the dappled sunlight of late afternoon, she took a nap.

I walked over to the pile of shakes, grabbed my tool belt, and buckled it around my waist. I was pleased to have provided the fawn with a safe playground.

It was late Saturday morning, Mel was here, and the electricians and plumbers were still on the land. Kim only worked until noon on most Saturdays and the sub-contractors followed the same rule. Charlie had come to close the ditch and when he finished, our utility services were buried and ready to use. He looked up as he drove away, and we waved our arms wildly. I could see him smile as he saluted back.

Shortly after he left, the plumbers stopped to say goodbye. "We'll see you in a week. The bathroom pipes are in, and everything but the shower is done. When we get back, Kim will help us carry the tub upstairs. He told me the restoration would be finished soon. Is that right?"

"Yes. Thanks guys," Mel said.

We still had to wait for the well to be dug in order to have water, and the kitchen would need to be plumbed once Kim completed the cabinets and sink.

"Wow, things really are moving forward rapidly," I said, as Mel and I climbed down. We wanted to talk to Kim before he left.

"How's the staining coming along?" Kim asked, as we approached. "Let's go to the basement and have a look."

"The color tint is perfect," Mel said.

Then Kim turned to me with a look of dismay on his face. "I'm sorry to tell you this, but you've stained the wrong side." I thought he was kidding, but his face said otherwise.

My first reaction was panic. How would I be able to stain everything all over again in time?

"Oh, I don't know," Mel said. "I like the look of the side Sal stained. The knots give it character." I looked at her and mouthed a thank you.

"You won't think so when it's up there," Kim said. "The plain surface on the opposite side will work much better for a ceiling. Knotty pine is too busy and will make your house look too rustic—more like a cabin than a house."

"It's a matter of choice, right?" Mel stood her ground and looked up at him.

"Well, there's the Ziegler way, and...."

"For us, Kim, the right way is with the knotty side out." Mel answered. "We made the decision and we're not changing it now."

"And besides, Kim," I went on. "This home is more like a bungalow than a house anyway. It's exactly what we want."

Kim just shrugged. "Okay, I'll start putting it up next week."

"I'm sure I'll be far ahead of you by then." I said confidently. "I have all weekend to keep staining.

As Kim left for his truck, later than usual for a Saturday, he turned back and said, "Oh, the owner of the well company will be here next week with his divining rods. He needs to determine where he'll dig the well." Kim looked upward and placed his hands on top of his head. I knew he didn't have much faith in dowsers.

Personally, I couldn't wait. I remembered my dad working with divining rods, so I was anxious to see them in action again.

"I'll get it all on tape, if I can," Mel said. "At the very least we'll get photos of him dowsing."

Mel headed to the field to check on the hawks, while I stayed in the basement. I needed to stack the dry wood in order to stain more. I had hours left of light and wanted to get as much completed as possible. Again, it was a one-person job. One brush, one pair of sawhorses, and only room for one in the basement with all the stacked pieces of pine.

Hours later, after I finished, I walked around the house, inside and out. I inspected every little thing in the fading evening light. Inside, the framing was complete and all the rooms were studded out. The electric lines were threaded through the studs and waiting. The plumbing was set in both baths. They couldn't do the kitchen until Kim started working there.

It would only be a few more weeks before it all disappeared behind dry wall. Kim had hired Tim, an expert with wallboard, to come in once the plumbers and electricians were finished. Once the wallboard was up we'd see how large our rooms really were. Right now they still seemed okay.

I stopped by the shed and picked up a sweatshirt for Mel, and then joined her in the field. As I approached, I saw she was sitting there looking off into space.

"They left," she said, a sad look on her face.

I kneeled down to look through the scope, and she was right. The baby hawks were gone. I couldn't believe it. I had missed the moment I so wanted to share with them. It was time for the chicks to fledge, and they weren't waiting around for me to watch.

"Well, all-righty then," I said, with a sigh. "I can't believe it's been forty-two to forty-six days already. Often their first flight is comedic, and I had wanted to catch a glimpse of it."

"Me too. I'm so disappointed."

We looked up and around, but didn't see any birds in flight. I thought they might come back to the nest in the evening. I intended to have a look first thing in the morning. If they survived their initial attempts at flying, they would improve rapidly. But it would take a while for them to leave their parents for good.

"I think we'll see them early tomorrow. Do you want me to wake you?" I asked.

"Please. I want to see the babies one more time." Mel said, looking a little sad.

Change comes, bidden or unbidden. I knew those babies were about to engage in all of life's adventures. While I missed them, I didn't feel too bad about their flight. I was living a new adventure. How could I do anything but rejoice in another creature doing the same? I was solid in my belief that you always want to go beyond what you think you can. It may be a solitary path, but most often the choices are worth the cost.

A Surprise Visitor

I tried waking Mel, but she wanted no part of it. I'm sure she will be sad to have missed this show.

There was a slight misty look to our field at dawn. Walking through wet grass, I felt the dampness of the air on my face and eyelashes. Through the haze, I made out three hawks above me, and from their relative sizes I could tell they were the babies and their mom. They flew back and forth among the treetops along the fence row. How exciting this must be for them, I thought, as I watched the flying lessons.

The sun rose behind me, evaporating the dew from the ground and eventually my face. The sky, full of puffy clouds, looked like a piece of fine art from Mel's studio.

Staring out into the openness of the meadow and beyond, I realized how nailing shakes onto my home made it stronger. The foundation of the house was, in and of itself, sturdy, but the addition of shakes made it more solid. While hammering each shake I felt myself becoming more unyielding as well. Felt myself coming together and gathering strength. Since my divorce everything mattered again. I was awakened to something old and precious, and I was escaping, finally, from the fear of "myself". My feelings of self worth and self esteem were returning, giving me hope once again. I felt alive and necessary. Earlier, during my marriage, I had an obsessive need to appear normal to all those around me. I'm sure that this was a carryover from my mom, and I was determined not to heft that load anymore. She was not at fault for that behavior; I was. I had a choice to live my own life. Now I lived in a calm, safe environment. Peaceful within.

Soon Stan, the farmer who sold us the land, would cut and bale the hay in the pasture below. I was anxious to see the large hay rolls standing in the field. The sun was up, and I knew the day was only going to get hotter. It was time to get to work.

"Wake up sleepyhead," I chided Mel, back at the shed. "Kim will be here any moment and you don't want him to catch you sleeping again."

"No more shakes," Mel groaned. "Why didn't you wake me earlier to see the hawk babies? Were they flying over the field?"

"I tried, Mel. You were adamant that you wanted to keep sleeping. But, they're out there now flying over the treetops in the fencerow."

"Oh. I don't even remember that conversation," Mel said rubbing her eyes with the heels of her hands. "I'm going out now, Kim can wait."

The weekend was over and we had accomplished a great deal. I was eager for Kim to see all we had done. "Kim will raise the scaffolding today, and think how happy he'll be that we did so much of the staining."

"Fine," Mel said, yawning.

By the time Kim arrived, Mel was ready to greet him. She had had a glimpse of the hawk babies in the field, and was satisfied with that quick sitting.

"Are the rest of the windows here?" Mr. Wonderful asked. Before we could answer, he walked inside to see, and turned on the CD player. Within a few minutes he was at work, hefting one of the windows into place. I joined Mel who was filling our tool belts with the nails we'd need for the next few hours.

"Sal! Mel!" Kim shouted. We looked at each other and raced inside, as a million possible disasters flashed through my mind. "Look up," he said, pointing to the highest living room window. A ruby-throated hummingbird hovered, trying to find its way out.

"Is that all?" Mel said. "I thought it was some disaster."

"No. It's a good luck sign," I said.

"It is?" Kim looked dubious.

"Hummingbirds bring happiness wherever they go," I explained. "Their vibration sings of pure joy, and an open and loving heart. They show you how to love the nectar of life and its pleasures. Didn't you ever hear that?"

"No." Amused skepticism was written all over his face.

The three of us worked to help the little guy escape. Kim went up to the second floor and, holding on to one of the studs, reached out as far as he could toward the window. I bit my lip in fear. He was leaning way out over the living room, waving a piece of cardboard. Unimpressed, the hummer flew down to the first floor.

"Don't hurt yourself little guy," I said.

Mel and I crept up behind him. He must have felt our presence because he flew over to the kitchen. It was the one area that wasn't yet filled in with windows. Out he went.

"There you go," I said. "Good job."

I watched as he flew around the house, ending up at the living room window again. He lingered there a while, as if he wanted back in.

Kim said, "I better get that glass in while he's still outside." All three of us hurried to lift the large casement into place.

"That was exciting," I said, brushing my hands together. "What a dazzling surprise visitor for our home." Even Kim had to sit back in appreciation.

After a few minutes, Mel and I left to work on the shakes. We moved faster now than when we first began the project. What had once been an exacting task had become almost mechanical. Several uninterrupted hours later we broke for lunch.

"It'll be scorching this afternoon. Why don't you two go shopping for your lighting fixtures and ceiling fans?" Kim took a bite of apple. "Once Tim is here he will move along quickly with the wallboard, and the electrician will be right behind him wanting to put the fixtures in place."

"You don't have to ask me twice." I said. I was eager to get out of the heat, but even more willing to choose the lighting that would add more of our own personality to the house.

Mel and I spent the afternoon and evening going to Lowe's, Home Depot, and other stores that sold lighting fixtures. We probably spent more time on the road between stores that day than we did looking at fixtures. I didn't mind. It was a relief to be sitting down.

By the end of the long afternoon and evening we'd purchased four ceiling fans, a hanging lamp for over the kitchen table, and lights for the bathrooms and pantry. We headed home. I hated to shop. Mel hated to shop. Enough already.

Driving in, I saw a note hanging on the front of the shed. I walked over and yanked it off.

"It's from Kim," I said, before reading it aloud. "He says the tub is in the basement." I made air quotes with one hand as I read. "The, scary woman, called saying they'll be over first thing in the morning to refurbish it. She says it has to be somewhere dry overnight, and in a place where it can stay for a week without being moved. Thanks for giving her my number."

"How did he get it down there by himself?" Mel said. "It's way too heavy to move alone." We ran inside to see where Kim positioned it.

There it was, sitting in the same area where I had left the stained pine for the ceiling.

"We will have to put a tarp over the tongue and groove while the man works on the tub," I said. "But my real concern is that woman. I hope she doesn't come along, but if she does, I'm going to leave. How will we ever get it upstairs and into the bathroom?" I asked, thinking it must be easier to take it downstairs than up.

Mel shrugged. "That's Kim's job," she said with her eyes squinted, and a smirk on her lips.

She was right. I let it go.

We went back to the car for the fans and lights. With all the windows installed, the house was tight and dry. Once Kim put the exterior doors on, we would be able to lock up at night. I wondered how long it would take.

⸻

The following morning I woke early, got dressed, and went outside with my toothbrush heading for the woods. Feeling as if eyes were focused on me, I looked toward the house and froze. John was standing there looking back at me while I gasped and swallowed the toothpaste.

He smiled and said, "I'm here to do an inspection."

Trying to compose myself, I shuttered, coughed and unsuccessfully suppressed a dry heave. I hated swallowing toothpaste.

"I'll be with you in a second, John," I said weakly, voice shaking. "Oh man, two surprise visitors in two days."

Palming my toothbrush and racing back into the shed, I woke Mel. "John is here and he saw me with my toothbrush!" I tried to keep my shriek down to a whisper. "He wants to do an inspection." I kept glancing over my shoulder as if John could see through the walls.

Mel jumped out of bed and stumbled around looking for her contacts. "Oh my God, I'll be out as fast as I can. Stall him so he doesn't ask to come into the shed."

"Good thing I'm in my jeans, and not my pj's," I said, shaking a bit from the close call. Many other mornings I would still be in pajamas.

I walked calmly—or at least I hoped I was walking calmly—to the house, and went inside with John. We laughed about how much cooler it was inside and he got on with his inspection. I meandered around the first floor while John walked to the stairs looking at everything along the way. With clipboard in hand, he returned saying the stairs looked solid and well done.

"I've seen Kim's stairways before," he said, "and they are always sturdy and tight. You'll never be sorry for paying extra to have oak." With that, he opened the basement door and started his inspection on the set of steps leading down.

By the time John was ready to leave, the man from the tub restoration company had arrived, thankfully without the scary woman. Mel took him down into the basement to show him the tub. I kept my fingers crossed and walked John to his truck.

"I am happy to see everything you've accomplished," John said. "It looks rock-solid. I'll give the written inspection form to Kim the next time I see him."

As John drove away, I heaved a sigh of relief.

Going down into the basement, I joined Mel and the tub man who were taping plastic sheets to the floor.

"We passed inspection," I quietly told Mel.

"Great," she said a little too loudly. "I never doubted we would. Together we walked outside, leaving the tub man to his work. Once we were alone, Mel grabbed my elbow. "Did he say anything about the shed?"

"Thankfully no." I said. "I had nothing to tell him if he did."

"That's good. You're a terrible liar." Mel looked at me as if that were a bad thing. I knew she was right. I could tease with the best of them, but an outright lie was something I'd never pull off. I felt too nervous to be convincing.

"The tub man will be here for most of the day," Mel said, hooking her head toward the basement. "He said he'd be done by early evening."

"This evening?" I couldn't believe that it was only going to take one day.

"He said someone else would be here soon to help and we could go ahead and do whatever we wanted."

"The woman?" I asked.

Mel shrugged. "We'll see, I guess. So, other than that, how did the inspection go with John?"

I told her the whole story as we walked back to the scaffolding. As I buckled my tool belt, Kim drove up.

"Good morning," Kim shouted as he got out of his truck. "Today I'm going to continue working on the ceiling, and I need you to bring me more of the stained wood." We dropped our tool belts and headed to the basement to grab some lumber. The tub man had not yet begun to spray, so I felt we could get most of the wood Kim needed up to the living room without delaying Kim.

It took an hour to carry enough lumber into the living room for Kim to use during the day.

"We'll bring another load up tonight and have it ready for you by tomorrow morning," Mel promised.

"Great." Kim fastened his nail apron, and we returned to the shakes.

Mel and I worked the entire day. All morning I was in the sun, and all afternoon I felt its heat coming off the house. Kim came out twice to raise the scaffolding, and he praised our progress. It helped us to keep going. By the end of the day I did nothing more than crawl next door to shower.

On the way back to the shed, I remembered the tub.

"Mel, let's go see how the tub looks."

"Sure. I forgot to look before. It's so dark. Do you think we'll be able to see much?"

"We can try," I said, waving my flashlight.

We hurried to the basement as fast as our tired feet would take us. Together we shined our flashlights on the tub.

"Oh," Mel said. "It's so dramatic. Look at the contrast in coloring." She grabbed me into a hug. "It looked yucky before, and now it's impressive. Thank you."

Back in the shed for the night, I had trouble falling asleep. Mel's steady breathing told me she was out, but I had a nagging feeling I had forgotten something important. I tried to ignore it, but before long I got out of bed and walked over into the house.

As I stood in the darkness I heard something. A buzzing sound. No, it was more like a humming. I directed the beam of my flashlight toward the noise and saw the hummingbird. He had come back in through one of the open doors and was again bumping against the living room window. Poor thing. He was trying to get back outside by following the moonlight.

I turned my flashlight beam toward an open doorway, hoping he would follow it. A moment later, he flew out into the darkness.

Something about the house had drawn him back. I felt doubly blessed by his second visit. The little feathered angel flew in to bring us joy and love.

"One day I will write about this," I promised him.

The Dowser Arrives

When Mel woke, I told her about our nighttime visitor. She listened with wide eyes, and a contented sigh. I held these small gifts of nature close to my heart, and Mel understood completely as she did too.

I was sitting on my sleeping bag when a truck drove up the lane. I peeked outside. "It's Kim," I said. I knew he didn't need us for anything, so I sat down and waited to hear the now familiar sounds of his workday. In a moment, the CD player poured sound into the woods, and soon after Kim sang to the morning light. I expected Stephanie to join him soon. She was helping him put up the ceiling, cutting the boards to Kim's specified measurements. They were a great team, and I loved watching them work. I hoped we'd get another concert. Mel had never heard them sing together, and I knew she wished she had.

As I scampered around to change out of my pajamas, I heard another vehicle coming up the driveway. It was the tub man. He wanted to be sure the bathtub was exactly what I wanted before he gave me the bill. I met him in the basement, and in the light of day the tub was even more dramatic.

"Let it sit there for the week," he said. "Then you can move it up to the bathroom."

"Easy for you to say," I said, handing him a check for his work. Mel, who was behind me, jabbed me in the ribs.

I thanked him for the great job he'd done and promised to recommend him to others. As he drove away, I was amazed how such a sweet man remained married to such a miserable woman. Perhaps he was blind to her anger; love is an astonishing thing.

That afternoon, Mel and I had plans to go to a kitchen cabinet shop in

Quakertown, that Kim recommended. We needed a countertop and wanted Formica with a maple edging. A complement to our kitchen cabinets. Built in one piece, it eliminated the need for seams that might catch dirt over time. The exact placement of the sink, corner, and ends was important. We went over the measurements again with Kim before we left. A mistake with dimensions was an expensive blunder.

It was not hard to find Country Crafters. We'd driven by it hundreds of times never noticing its existence. The showroom was larger than it appeared from the street, and Mel and I looked around until someone came to help.

"How can I help you?" the man asked, introducing himself. His name was Jim, and he mentioned he was the owner. He was bald, of average height, but on the heavy side. Even so, he swept around the showroom quickly and earnestly.

I told him what we had in mind. He showed us some samples, and made a few suggestions of his own.

"Here are the dimensions," Mel said, handing him the diagram she had drawn with Kim's exact measurements.

"Hmmm," he said, rubbing his hand over his smooth head. "This doesn't look too bad. We should be able to have this ready for you in three weeks. That work for you?"

"Perfect," I said.

We picked out a Formica color from sample chips. Sage green with neutral colors blending in the background.

"And this for our maple edging," Mel said, pointing to the wood chip we liked best.

"That will be fine," the store owner assured us.

We placed our order and Mel gave him a check for half of the cost. I'd pay the other half when I picked it up in three weeks.

Back home, we worked on the shakes again, getting into a rhythm and moving swiftly. We had used a lot of bundles so far that day, and Kim had to come over and raise the scaffolding again.

As those late August afternoons came to an end, I noticed how quickly we were losing our light on the east side of the house compared to the month before. The thick woods accelerated the arrival of dusk. When we moved to the south and west sides, we'd be able to work later into the evening. It was cooler now, too, and soon I'd need a sweatshirt in the evenings as well.

Kim and Steph gave us a concert as they worked. When they started to sing, Mel looked at me, her eyebrows lifted. "They sing like this every day?"

"When they're working together they do," I said, enjoying her amazement.

"They're even better than you said. Should we take a break and go listen to them?"

I thought about it. It was hard to hear them while we made so much noise hammering in the shakes, but I didn't want them to stop. I thought if we went in to listen it might make them self conscious. "Nah. Better to just enjoy it from here," I said. I could see Mel's disappointment, but noticed she took a bit more time between shakes after that.

Several days later, I awoke with a start. An early bird was pecking on the roof of the shed. Eli and Toby had their eyes trained at the ceiling, hoping it might make its way inside. I was sure no woodpecker wanted to find what was waiting for him in this shed.

After dressing, I went out for a quick peek. The red-bellied was still at work. It must have been hard on its beak, but didn't seem deterred by layers of shingles, tar paper, or plywood. I wondered what he was after.

I was up now and wanted to get something accomplished. Grabbing the lawn mower, I headed for the field. An hour to mow the grass wasn't long, but I didn't have any other time to do it that week. Just as I finished, I noticed Mel at the edge of the field wildly waving her arms and motioning for me to come to her.

"The well digger's here," she said. "Quick. Come see."

I followed her back up the path. Sure enough, a van sat in our driveway with the words "Wonsidler Well Company" painted on the side. Mel went to the shed to get her camera and I went in the house to tell Kim.

"Please stay inside while Mr. Wonsidler works," I begged.

"Why?"

"Because I'm sure you don't believe in finding water with a couple of sticks." I said, eyebrows raised. "I'd rather you leave him alone to do his work, leaving your skepticism out of it."

"You wound me," Kim said putting a hand over his heart. "But that doesn't matter because I need to talk to him first."

I watched Kim go out and shake Mr. Wonsidler's hand. The dowser was an older man of average height, slight and quiet. He had a helper along, a younger man, in his twenties. As it turned out, Kim had met them both many times while working on other construction jobs. He showed Mr. Wonsidler the large area he had in mind for the well placement and then left him to it. Of course, on his way back in to the house he turned toward Mel and me, quickly rolling his thin cigar from one side of his mouth to the other. He looked so funny I had to turn away to keep from laughing.

We introduced ourselves as Mr. Wonsidler walked back to his truck, retrieving two twenty-four inch switches. Mel and I sat down on the pile of shakes just off the driveway. Propping my elbows on my knees, I cupped my chin in my hands and watched, fascinated, as he carefully made his way around the area Kim designated. He held one stick in each hand, out in front of him, about six inches apart. Once in a while I saw the tips shift a little closer together. But then they moved back to a parallel position. He walked slowly over the designated area, meticulously focusing on the ground.

We observed for about twenty minutes. All of a sudden the tips of the sticks crossed over each other. He walked away from that area separating the sticks as he went. Slowly, he went back, and the sticks crossed over each other once more. He did this three times. On the last pass he held the sticks to the ground, exactly in the place where they crossed. He looked back at his assistant who came over and, without a word, hammered a spike into the ground and then sprayed it with orange paint.

"This will be precisely where the point of the drill will be located," Mr. Wonsidler explained.

Once the sticks were back into the truck, I asked Mr. Wonsidler if he minded responding to a few questions.

"Not at all. I'm happy to answer anything I can," he said, looking at me with warmth.

"What kind of sticks did you use, and where did you find them?" I asked.

"They are willow branches, and I cut them fresh this morning. There are small willow trees in back of my house near the small brook, and I use new twigs each day. If you wonder why I use new branches, I'd say it's because they are more light and porous, and I believe they better absorb vapors rising from buried water. " He cleared his throat. "The tips will cross each other when they sense water because of the slight weight they have picked up. I have no control over them when they are in my hands. I hold the branches loosely and parallel to each other, allowing them to move on their own if they want."

"That's very interesting," I said. "My dad used to use willows, too, when he helped our friends and family look for well sites."

Mr. Wonsidler nodded. "You actually have two veins of water beneath the spike where the willow branches crossed, and that's exactly where I'll dig. If I'm right, you'll have enough water for two homes and enough water pressure to go with it."

Time will tell, I thought.

He turned to leave and said, "I'll be coming back either tomorrow or the next day to begin the drilling."

"May we watch?" I asked.

"If you like," he said, climbing into the truck. "See you soon."

I went inside to find Kim, and when I looked up at him on the scaffolding, he was rolling those big baby blues of his and laughing out loud.

"You are so naive," he kept telling me. "You can't find water with a couple of sticks."

"Maybe not, but I'm still a believer," I said, walking away.

It was time for us to get to work on the shakes. The rest of the day went quickly as Mel and I spoke of nothing but the willow branches. I wanted to find some to see if I could do it, too, but I thought I might jinx it, so I decided to wait until the well was finished.

When I looked at the time it was almost five o'clock and Kim had not yet gone home. He usually left around four so I was a little concerned that he might have run into a problem. When I went inside, I found that he and Steph were still working on the ceiling.

"What are you two still doing here?" I asked. "Did you lose track of time?"

Kim laughed. "Nah, we want to get this one area finished." He gestured to the ceiling above him. "Then I can move the scaffolding before I go home and tomorrow we can begin first thing," Kim said nodding his head once.

"I'll have more lumber ready for you," I promised.

"Great. The electrician is coming in the morning to hook everything up to the box in the basement."

"You mean we're going to have electricity?"

"Yep," he said. "Tim will need electricity in order to work on the drywall. He does most of his work at night. It's a side business for him."

"Really," I said not feeling too happy. Will you let him know we're living here and to keep it a secret?"

"Oh sure, I'll let him know. I've known Timmy a long time ,and I trust him completely."

With that I went out to find Mel, letting her know the good news. We'd be able to switch on the lights when we walked in the house. What a concept.

I left for my nightly shower, and then took a walk to the field to watch the sunset. Mel soon joined me, and we sat there watching the baby hawks flying around with their mom. I loved watching those little guys learn to navigate. Often they flew to the old nest, but they never stayed for long. I felt like those babies were mine. As if one can own a wild bird.

Actually, I felt this way about all the animals and birds that walked across our acres. I wanted to care for them and find a way for us to live in harmony together. I hoped my work with nature empowered others, making the world a better place for the environment we all share. The world is large, but we can do our part by not being apathetic. We can start at home.

I thought of Dr. Jane Goodall. She said, "Only if we understand can we care. Only if we care will we help. Only if we help shall all be saved." I may not be fortunate enough to work with the chimps in Gombe, but I can define my own understanding of animals and ultimately myself. Nature has helped me with the largest part of my healing, and my spiritual self is nurtured by it each day.

Well, a Well

Labor Day had come and gone and still no word from the Wonsidler Well Company.

"Didn't the dowser say he would be here in the next day or two?" I asked Mel one morning as we hammered in siding. Before she could answer, I saw his truck pull into our driveway, followed by a larger truck with an attached drill. I must have had an inner sense about them coming.

Three men plus Mr. Wonsidler piled out of the four-door white pickup, and they all headed to the spike circled in orange paint. One of the men directed the driver of the drill truck toward the spike. When they were close he shut the truck off. The other men grabbed the drill, pulled the spike out of the ground, and placed its point exactly in the hole.

The men were enjoying themselves on this morning, laughing and joking, but all conversation ceased when Mr. W. turned on the switch to the drill. The sound was deafening. The men gathered around. One of the well diggers stood really close, hands on knees looking down, watching it constantly as it bit the ground. Others took turns with their shovels, moving the loosened dirt out of the way.

Mel and I went back to nailing shakes. I felt self-conscious, wondering if the men were watching us, but knew they were too busy with their own tasks to notice. My shyness always seemed to show up when men I didn't know were around, but I was winning this inner battle too.

Actually I wasn't sure if it was shyness or plain old lack of self-esteem. But I was improved from the earlier days and that fit well in my mind. The house and I were coming together, each at its own rate of speed, but damn, healing took time.

An hour after the drilling started, Kim waved us down from the scaffolding.

"I'm leaving for the day," he shouted over the whine of the drill. "I can't stand the noise and I already have a headache. I'll use this day to get the supplies I'll need for the rest of the week."

"See you tomorrow," I said, patting him on the shoulder. "Hopefully the well will be finished soon and you'll be able to work peacefully again."

"Don't count on it."

I walked over once or twice to see how the digging was going. It was interesting and I found it hard to stay away. I wondered how deep they'd have to dig. We knew from Bill and Heidi that their well was three hundred and sixty feet deep. I expected ours would be, too, especially since our land was at a higher elevation. When I asked Mr. Wonsidler about that, he said they were never sure. Just keep digging and the answer would show itself.

The afternoon wore on and we all kept working. Mel and I skipped lunch and kept on going. We watched the men work from the scaffolding on the side of the house. It was miraculous we didn't nail our fingers to the wall.

At the end of the day, they stopped the drill and locked up the truck. Then they all piled into their pickup, and started to drive down the driveway.

"Hey," I yelled leaping down from the scaffolding and chasing them down the driveway. When they stopped I peered in the open window. "Will you be back tomorrow?"

"Yup, we'll be here in the morning to pack up the drill and take it away," the driver said.

"Why? You aren't finished."

"We are," said the confident voice of our dowser.

"Really?" I said with my hands on my hips. "How deep did you have to go? That was so fast."

Mr. W. leaned out of his pickup window and answered, "Your well is only one hundred and forty feet deep. We hit the two veins I told you about earlier, and you have enough water pressure for two homes. You'll never have a problem. All we need to do is finish the casing and we'll do that tomorrow"

"Oh, wow," I said in shock. "Thanks."

Laughing, they all drove away. The drill truck stood where it sat.

I walked back to the hole. The drill was still deep within it. I wondered if they were kidding, but they looked serious. This was important. I saw a little water around the hole, and a lot of mud, but that was it.

"What's wrong?" Mel asked, walking over.

"Our well is finished. The guys will be back tomorrow to finish the casing."

"Stop messing around," Mel said.

"I'm not. They're done. They hit both veins at one hundred and forty feet."

"Whoohoo," Mel shouted. "It will be the only part of this project that has come within budget."

I was so happy that I pulled out my cell phone and called Kim, leaving him a message with the good news.

He immediately called back. "Thank goodness," he said. "I've been trying to think of ways to avoid coming over there while they finished the drilling. Now I don't have to."

"Good, because we need you to move the scaffolding again," I said, trying to put a scolding tone into my voice.

"I'll be there," he said, sounding contrite. "Those guys are really good. I've worked with them for years, and now you know why. But still," he added after a beat, "you know I don't believe in dousing. They just got lucky."

"Hmmmmmm, sure," I said.

As I entered the house at dusk, I almost forgot that the electrician had been there. I flipped a switch and reveled in the miracle of electricity. It was astounding to view the beauty of our home with the lights we'd purchased. I expected Tim to start the drywall sometime that evening. The electrician had finished just in time.

It was hard to believe that we had lights all over the house. Mel came in and we sat down on overturned buckets enjoying how our home looked. The wood glowed, but a part of me wanted the house to stay just as it was.

"I love this home," I said to Mel as I stood and walked around. "I think I'm in shock or something because it doesn't seem real."

She sat there staring at the ceiling. "Me, too. A lot of tough work was involved but look at the result. I just want to sit here a while longer. I'll be down in a second for my shower. You go first."

I left to go next door. After a few minutes Mel showed up. When we finished we walked back to the house and saw a shadow moving around. Someone was in there.

"I sure hope that's Tim," I said, walking into my study from the ramp.

"Me too." Mel said walking into the house with me.

"Hi. Are you Tim?" I asked the short man standing in front of me.

"I am. Kim's told me all about you two, and I'm sure we'll all have fun while we finish this gorgeous home." He bowed slightly, and put a cap back on his head.

"We laugh with Kim each day," I said.

"Most of the time," Mel said looking around at all the work yet to be done.

"I'll be working here some days, but nights will be constant," Tim said with a serious tone. "I have a lot of lights with me. I know this job is going to be challenging and I'll need extra lighting for the high walls. Also, I will need more scaffolding as well. Kim borrowed most of mine."

"You're kidding," I said. "All this is yours?"

"You bet. I'll borrow some of my friend's scaffolding until Kim is finished with mine. That's the way it is in my business," he said looking a little elf-like as he dashed toward the door.

Yesterday, at the end of the day, our wallboard was delivered. Mel and I moved it into the foyer so it would be accessible both to the upstairs and down. I showed Tim where it was, and he set about carrying pieces upstairs. Mel and I helped, but I thought for a small slight man, Tim was really strong. He carried twice as much as Mel and me together.

"I can't believe you'll be able to nail all that drywall by yourself," I said, studying the vast expanse of walls.

Tim shrugged. "I have a machine that helps hold the wallboard for me as I nail it in place. It allows me to work alone. Once in a while, I'll be bringing my son with me on the weekends."

While Tim began working, Mel and I went to the shed for dinner. I wasn't as comfortable knowing someone else was there at night, but I hoped I'd get used to it after a while.

I hardly tasted my dinner of microwaved cheese and bean burritos that evening. Mel watched TV while she ate, but memories of my marriage came flooding back. I wasn't sure why they came to me now. I told Mel I was going for a walk to the field, and she was fine with that. All she wanted to do was sit and watch her shows. She was exhausted. I left the shed and headed down the path to sit at the edge of the field. It was very dark, but perfect for letting my mind work out my anxiety.

For more than three decades, I'd been able to hold onto the love of my husband, but not my marriage. I honestly told myself I loved this man, but not as a partner. This taunted me for years until I unraveled it all with my therapist. Together, we sorted through the debris until I finally realized how one-sided my marriage had become. I never cheated in marriage, and I felt honest within myself. I had learned how to step outside of the guilt I'd felt, both with my children as well as my friends. And I was still learning. I'd lived in two separate worlds for many of those years. One was a marriage without intimacies and sharing, and the other world was one I hoped to fill with the promise and courage I felt inside my heart. A life I thought might be impossible to have.

But now I grabbed at that opportunity and felt that this was a love story of nature's gifts and me, the building of my home, Mel, and the meditation it encompassed. I was bringing a piece of the light of who God intended me to be to this space I now held. I was taking responsibility for it. I wanted my kids to do the same with their own lives; so far they had and I was proud of them.

God gave us a world full of hope for everything, and it was for everyone. I honored what was unfinished in Bob, and in me. I am not a lesser being for ending my marriage, and it's okay to retain what was private in my heart.

Two hours later we went to see Tim. When I walked into the house, he was seven feet tall. I gasped and nearly dropped the snack I'd brought for him.

"I always use stilts," he said, laughing. "They make me a foot and a half taller, and I don't have to climb up and down a stepladder each time I need to put up another piece of wallboard."

"You amaze me, Tim." He didn't take them off, even when I handed him a paper plate of cookies.

"New walls, what a metaphor," I whispered to Mel when we were in our sleeping bags for the night. "And a well, and electricity. What miracles."

"Shhhhh, I don't want it to be a dream. And your emotional walls are tumbling down quickly," Mel said.

Closer to Nature

By the end of the next day, the well was capped and finished. The men were pleasant, but I'd never forget Mr. Wonsidler and his divining rods. It was as if he lived in an earlier century, and I wondered if my grandchildren might ever be witness to events that were out of the norm, like dousing.

With that job behind us, I looked forward to the next item on the list. Mel and I needed to tile the kitchen floor, bathroom and foyer floors, and the area under the wood stove. But first, Tim needed to finish putting up drywall.

In the meantime, I kept working on the shakes, nailing and carrying bundles up and down the scaffolding until I was too tired to talk. When Mel was there we worked in a companionable silence, side by side, week after week.

The following afternoon, I was surprised to hear another truck approach the house. Glancing down to the driveway, I saw the electrician.

"Did you purchase the rest of the lights yet?" he called up to us on the scaffolding. "I'd like to get them in today."

I shook my head. "No, we haven't found what we're looking for yet."

"Have you tried Doylestown Lighting?"

I shook my head glancing at Mel.

"Don't think so," Mel shouted.

"You should check them out. You'll like what they have to offer."

"We'll do that," Mel said, bending over a pile of shakes.

"Would you please go today and have a look? I still have a few things to do while you're out. I'm hopeful you'll find the sconces for the stairway, the foyer light, the pantry light, and the downstairs bathroom fixture. I'd really like to finish this job today."

I looked over at Mel. She was elbow deep in the shakes, pulling out ones she thought would be perfect for the area she was working on.

"Will you go without me this time?" she asked, meeting my eyes.

"Sure. I'll try to be back within a couple of hours." Hating to leave the house, but wanting to get light fixtures for the electrician, I left for Doylestown. Normally, I loved going, but this was not a trip of leisure. I needed to get there and back, so I could keep nailing shakes.

Forty-five minutes later, I arrived at the store and was pleased to find that the electrician was right. The selection there was extensive and eclectic. I browsed for a while before someone approached.

"Here's a list of what I need," I said to the elderly woman. She looked it over, pointed out my choices and left me alone. I appreciated her consideration. An hour later, I had made my selections and paid for them. I purchased a ceiling light for the pantry, two attractive sconces for the staircase, one at the top of the stairs, and one for the landing at the bottom. A switch at the top and one at the bottom of the stairway turned on both. I also gravitated toward a ceiling light for our foyer. It was simple yet elegant, so I bought it. It held four candle-type bulbs, and would bathe the area with its soft radiance.

Anxious to get back home, I almost forgot to look for the bathroom ceiling fixture. I jumped out of my car and walked around the store again. Finally I found a Mission light fixture that showed an antique look that I loved, and then stood at the counter to pay for my final purchase. Back in Powder, I headed home.

Before long, I was on Deer Trail. I stopped at the bottom of the driveway to pick up our mail. It was fun having a mailbox. One of the things I would miss if I ever lived in the city would be a mailbox. I love the concept of having a mailman and a box to walk to every day.

I put our mail in the shed, the light fixtures in the foyer, and soon I was back nailing shakes. Kim had raised the scaffolding again to our final level on the east side of the house. When we finished he would move everything to the south side. That was going to be a challenge. Because the ground sloped away from the house, the south side was three stories tall. The north side was only two. It would be the highest I'd ever be off the ground on this project, for, unlike Kim, I wasn't used to working on roofs or scaffolding.

Five days later Kim moved the scaffolding to its highest level so far . "It's exceptionally lofty up here," I said, peeking down between my feet.

"Aw, come on." Kim laughed. "It's only twelve feet higher than you were before."

"But it feels taller," I swallowed, trying to calm my breathing.

"Yeah," Kim said. "I had a feeling you were going to feel the difference in elevation. You'll get used to it."

"Thanks," I muttered trying to sound annoyed. I helped join in Kim's merriment. "You realize that you will be doing the really high ones on this side, right?"

"I always get the toughest jobs," he said before walking away, his head hanging low. I watched him slouch his way to his truck, and turn with a smirk before climbing inside.

"I can tell he's really upset about that," Mel said, shaking her head.

"Yeah." It was clear he didn't mind.

In a second he was back and talking to us about the kitchen tile that needed to be finished. Perhaps he thought we forgot.

"The kitchen will be fun," he said. "I'll help start the project and then leave you two on your own. Mel will lay the tile and I want you, Sal, to mix the Quick Set. When you finish, you can buy the grout. After that, you'll wash the surface with the large sponges I stored in the study. It will be a gritty mess, but it has to be done."

"Okay, Kim. It will be our next job after the shakes," I said.

We worked for two more hours, nailing to the rhythm of the music that Kim had been kind enough to leave behind. As we climbed down, finished for the day, Tim drove up the driveway announcing that he'd be working for about the next four hours.

I glanced down at my watch. Mel and I had nearly run out of daylight. It was September now, and our life in the shed had gone on for more than four months.

After showers neither Mel nor I was ready for bed, so I built a small fire in the pit in our little park, or wood-chipped area, I had built in the spring, and cooked hot dogs on the same sticks we used back in May. The fire was especially nice in the cool evening. I ran to the shed and got our sweatshirts, and we sat out there until midnight chatting. Tim finally called it a day as well, and left.

"There might be a thunderstorm tonight," I said to Mel as we spent time making sure the fire was out.

"Did you hear it on the news?" Mel asked.

"Yeah, on Kim's radio. It's okay though; everything is either inside or outside and covered."

Back in the shed, I grabbed my toothbrush and headed for the woods. I think I'm going to miss this outside routine, I thought. Every night ended with going outside, and I wondered if I would continue the ritual. Not brushing my teeth out there, of course, but taking that last look at all that surrounded me. I felt close to nature as I fell asleep each night, and I didn't want to lose that connection.

I softened as I leaned against one of the oaks, gazing at the construction of my new home. My spiritual teacher has said that home is inside your heart and you can take that along with you wherever you go. I believe she is right. Finding a place to sit for a moment, closing my eyes in meditation; these two actions will bring comfort and a gentle peace. Even in chaotic circumstances.

But having this tranquility both inside myself and outside physically at the same time is the highest form of perfection. For me, nature equals this exactness. The night air smelled of late summer; corn husks, moss, and hay. The birds and animals were finished with having their families and a distinct calm had settled around my acreage. I wondered what tomorrow might bring.

AUTUMN

A Final Resting Place

It was time to find a resting place for my parent's ashes. They had both been gone for many years, but I had kept their ashes with me until the time was right to bury them. Once Mel and I had purchased this beautiful land, I knew the time was approaching. I hoped to find a spot in the woods that felt both significant and sacred.

Grabbing a mug of coffee, I began my search with a walk. A gentle breeze lifted branches and I listened to the sounds of wildlife. Birds sang, and I heard cricket music, apparently all orchestrated for my benefit. Each small chirp from the birds was pitched a little higher, and a catbird was following my every step. I sat and listened as they continued their concert. It was achingly flawless, filling me with appreciation and love.

A few hours later, I left the woods. Nothing satisfied me. I walked around the house and the park, my rocked in area, for a little while, and then the idea hit me. The park!

"Of course," I said, out loud. "No wonder I didn't find anything in the woods. They aren't supposed to be there." I had two huge oak trees in the park between which I had hung a hammock. I lay in its webbed bedding, thinking of my choices. Once I made my decision, I went to the fence row in the field. There were three huge stones that were perfect. I got the tractor and my come-along, and cart, and brought them back. It took hours to get them into the cart, the come-along only moves objects a few inches at a time. I was happy for the dump-down cart.

Digging the hole deep and straight, I placed the ashes into the soft damp earth, and it felt cool on my hands. I said a prayer of thanks for the life my parents had given me and covered the hole with dirt, along with a large flat stone. I pushed, with every ounce of energy in me, the three rocks I'd found around the flat one, and stepped back. A friend had once given me a concrete angel and I never knew where to place it; now it rests beautifully on top of the flat stone. In my heart I named this lovely resting place Poet's Walk. My mom loved to write poetry.

In spring I'd plant lilies of the valley in a semi-circle around it. Mom loved lily of the valley flowers, and she had carried them in her wedding bouquet. I wanted to surround her with those flowers. Dad, with all his love for wood, needed to be close to one of the oaks. He was the image of strength for me throughout my life, and I wanted to honor that force of his now, by giving him a special place on my land. Then when I walked by this natural grave, or swung in the hammock above, I'd have a little chat with both of them.

Bringing all of this together that morning also changed something in me. Again. I felt as if the corners of my own life were softening, allowing the transformation taking place within. I didn't need anyone patting me on the head telling me everything was all right. I knew I was okay here on my acreage, where I never felt weak. My fear of failing was disappearing along with the logjam that caused it in the first place.

Mel came out to see what I was doing. I showed her the gravesite for my Mom and Dad. She thought it was a worthy tribute and stood silently with me for a few minutes as I said another prayer for them.

Inside the house, Tim was making fast progress. Mel and I had a few more rows of shakes to nail on the south side of the house. Some time later in the week, Kim moved the scaffolding for us to begin work on the western exposure.

We worked for a few hours, but then took a break in the field. The earthy smell of mown hay in the pasture beyond gave the scene a pastoral feel.

Evening came, and with it a whiff of cool air. "Hey," I said, "let's go to the park and start a fire in the pit."

"Why not?" Mel said rubbing her arms for warmth.

As we left the woods, I nodded at the last lightning bugs of summer. They need moisture to survive and the humidity of those last summer nights gave it to them. Soon they'd be gone. I'd miss them, but it felt good to sit by the fire and watch their dance.

"I'm going to bring over the heater from my studio and put it in the shed. We don't want Toby or Eli to get too cold."

I nodded. "Good idea." The shed had no insulation.

We huddled together by the fire and I spoke of the little monument I had made earlier in the day for my parents. Mel agreed that the area had a special feel to it. As the night wore on we kept to the fire, trying to keep warm. Finally we gave up, and made our way down the path. I looked at my clothes stored in Heidi's spare room closet. I hadn't brought anything for cooler weather. I was sure all of my coats were in the very back of the storage unit. I didn't need them quite yet, but soon.

The chilliness reminded me to check with Grates & Grilles in the morning, making sure they were still holding our wood stove. I wanted to let them know we'd need it in about two months.

As I lay in my sleeping bag, I realized that neither Eli nor Toby had a warm enough kitty bed. Snuggling with us was one thing, but there would be cool days when they were alone in the shed. Toby was old, and I suspected she might have a touch of arthritis. She needed her warmth. I pulled Eli closer to me and Mel took Toby on her bed. I promised them something cozy in the morning. They snuggled even closer as if to say, thank you.

Autumn had come early it seemed, and a crisp chill was my constant companion. The following day I purchased new beds for Eli and Toby. I rubbed my hand across the fleece lining knowing it would keep them comfortable, and with the aid of Mel's heater we should all be cozy and warm.

After shopping, it was time to work more on the siding. I re-filled my tool belt with nails, discarded my sweatshirt, and climbed onto the scaffolding. Mel was up there already. Our work was constant and steady, from daybreak to dusk. Mel had finished her work in the studio and taken a few weeks off. We needed to finish the siding.

A few weeks later we finally nailed our last shake. Climbing down from the scaffolding we ran into the house to find Kim. He was upstairs in my bedroom laying hardwood flooring. Soon, it would be the first completed room.

"The shakes are now yours to finish," Mel said, with a huge grin.

"Great job, guys," he said, wiggling his cigar from one side of his mouth to the other. "But if you thought you'd handled your last shake, think again. Let's save money and time by having you stack shakes on the two gable ends of the house."

"We're on it," Mel groaned. "We can do it now so when you're ready to nail, they'll be there for you."

"Any word from Tim?" Kim asked us. "He hasn't bothered to come to work for the past few days so now we're running a little behind schedule."

I looked at Mel and she shook her head. "I haven't heard a word from him either. I guess you'll have to give him a call." I said a little disappointed.

"Don't you worry, I'll call him tonight." Kim said with a grunt.

It took us less than an hour to move the shakes. We'd used most of the pile, so there were just enough left for Kim to complete the job. Mel and I took off for Home Depot to get sanding sealer and sandpaper. I wanted to start working on the windows, doors, and molding. Everything wood needed to be stained and sanded. Also, we needed a water test kit. The state required that our new well be tested, making sure the water was potable and safe.

While we were out, we stopped at the market to buy food for the next few days.

"I'm getting sick of cereal and salad," I said sticking out my tongue. "Let's skip to soup and sandwiches for these cooler days."

"Cereal is easier," Mel argued.

"I know, but we'll feel better eating warm food at night. Perhaps we could buy some instant oatmeal; it's an easy thing to make in the microwave." I said.

"Whatever. I'm so tired by that time it's hard to think of food prep." Mel answered, with a shrug of her shoulders.

We got back at six o'clock and Kim was gone, but Tim was there to work on drywall again. I guess Kim must have called him earlier rather than later. His absence recently was starting to push us behind, and it was upsetting. Kim left Tim a note to finish the bathrooms first, because the plumbers wanted to complete their work.

I unpacked the car and brought the food into the shed, while Mel brought the items from Home Depot into the house. She stored them in my bedroom because that was the first room Mel and I would stain.

Mel was waiting for Tim to finish the kitchen and bathrooms. She needed to start laying tile, and I was anxious to help. Kim was laying hardwood flooring, then he'd follow it with the molding. That was his sequence. When he finished a room, we were to go in and start staining. This job seemed easier to me than nailing shakes, but perhaps it was only a different type of work. In any case, the change was nice. Also, there wasn't as much climbing.

When I came back from the shed, Mel was in the kitchen measuring and taking notes.

"I'll have it easy choosing a color for the grout," I said. "With your fine art background, I defer." I shrugged my shoulders and grinned.

"Okay, not a problem." Mel said. "That will be simple. We tend to agree on most of our color choices anyway."

"We have on this entire project," I said. "I wonder how odd that is; I've heard that a lot of couples have strong opinions with this kind of venture."

"Not us. We both agree on an earth-tone palette."

"None better," I quipped.

Colder

One crisp morning in late September, Kim surprised us. We walked in the back door, and he called us to come into the living room.

"You need to bring the kitchen cabinets over today," he said, turning to us from the bottom rung of a stepladder. I felt my stomach do a flip. This was the part of the project I had dreamed about for weeks.

"Couldn't you have given us a little warning?" Mel chided.

"I don't care," I said, excited. "I'll go right now. I can't wait to see how they'll look."

"They'll be perfect when I'm done," Kim said, with his usual attitude. "Now get going!"

Yikes. He's being bossy this morning.

We went to Bill's and borrowed his truck for Mel to drive, and I hopped into Powder. We made six trips, and by noon we pulled in with the last load. Mel hauled one cabinet through the door and I pushed another, resting one corner on my foot as I hobbled across the living room. Kim was almost finished framing the half-wall between the kitchen and living room.

"Oh my God, Kim, this looks astounding." I said eyes wide and hands spread out in front of me.

"I know. I'm amazing." He struck a heroic pose, showing off his muscles.

All afternoon, Kim worked on mounting the cabinets. He started with the top ones, above the counter, and then worked on the sets underneath.

"I'll finish this job tomorrow, and then you can work on the flooring," Kim explained.

We moaned. "We were just at Home Depot yesterday, and could have picked up the grout," Mel said. "Why didn't you tell us?"

"Don't bother with that yet," Kim said, with his cranky pants on again. "It will take a few days to finish the tile. After that you can go for the grout. I'll help you begin the process in the morning. I'm going to purchase a new tile cutter on my way home." The tile cutter Kim owned was broken, and he wanted to replace it with a larger one. "Sal, I'm going to use your study. I need a place to cut the tile and your room is close to an outside door, and the water spigot. You'll need to bring in one of the hoses from the field when you have time."

All tile had to be cut with water so the blade didn't get too hot. It would be a messy job, and my study floor would pay the price. I knew water sprayed everywhere during the process, so I'd try and wipe up each evening. It was my plan to keep it as dry as possible for the duration.

When he left, I went to the field and grabbed one of the hoses and hooked it up to the outdoor faucet on the north side of the house. It was only a few feet from my study window.

"Wow, we have water," I said. Although it had been weeks since the plumbers finished, I marveled every time I turned it on.

"Kim will finish your bedroom flooring in the morning after he shows me how to lay the tile, and use the cutter," Mel said. "Then he'll start in my room."

"Okay, sounds good. I hope you don't mind, but I want to watch while Kim teaches you how to use the tile cutter. I love stuff like that."

"Of course, no problem. I'm sure it will be easy enough. Besides, you have to learn, too," Mel said, getting back to work.

Giving more effort than you ever thought possible continued to motivate me, but I was getting exhausted. So was Mel. Each day brought something new, and I learned a little more. I was fit and strong after months of physical work, making it easier to lift and carry boxes of tile and hardwood flooring. But I couldn't imagine doing this full time.

I walked into the shed for the night, drained but happy. I could see Mel was thinking about cutting tile as she climbed into her sleeping bag. Her brow was scrunched up, and her eyes were staring at nothing I could see.

"Just wait," I said to Mel, bringing her attention back. "We're going to be experts at so many different jobs before we're finished with this house."

I stayed silent for a long time and, as I was falling asleep, Mel said, "You're going to have to go to Lowe's or Home Depot tomorrow to purchase a stove. Let's get a microwave with a hood to go above it. I think it would take up less space than if we have one sitting on the counter."

"Okay. I think it makes the kitchen more balanced. I'll take off first thing in the morning before Kim comes," I laughed, throwing my pillow at her. "Stop waking me up when I'm almost asleep."

"Yep, got it." Mel yawned, turning on her side.

When I opened my eyes, I saw my breath floating in the cold air in front of me.

"Not good," I said, climbing out of my sleeping bag. "Not good at all."

Looking around, I found Toby curled in her little bed. I grabbed a towel and covered her up, wishing I could move her closer to the heater. "I'm sorry, girl. It wouldn't be safe." It was clear our arrangement wasn't working for the kitties, and I didn't know what to do about it.

"Brrrr," Mel groaned, waking up. "Oh boy. Here comes the hard part of shed life. Good thing we bought new coats and sweatshirts."

"Good for us, but what about Eli and Toby? We definitely need to do something before tonight," I said. "We can't let them get this cold again, Toby's too arthritic. I can't believe it's this cold so early in the fall."

I shivered and wrapped my fingers around the coffee mug for warmth. When I looked over at Mel, she was doing the same thing. I saw my breath hanging in the air, and when I went out to brush my teeth, I was even colder.

"Now we'll really see how tough we are," she said, shivering. When I walked back in, the shed felt a little warmer than it did before, but maybe it was just by comparison with the air outside.

"I'm going to go to the pet store to see if I can find something else for the kitties to sleep in," I said wrapping my arms around my body.

I took off right away. When I got into Powder, I turned the heater on high, and once I looked at the clock, I realized I'd have to wait a little before the stores opened. "At least I'll be warm."

As I entered the pet store, I didn't have the faintest idea what to look for. I'd had dogs all my life, never cats. Now I was in love with Eli and Toby, too, and wanted to keep them safe and warm.

Walking up and down the aisles I found some thick pads made from synthetic pile. "This is great for Eli," I said under my breath, "but there has to be something warmer for Toby." As I went around to the next row, I spotted something blue on the top shelf and found a step stool to reach it.

"Oh, how cute!" I said, climbing back down. It was a little blue tent, and it resembled the larger ones sold for campers. Taking one of the pile pads and placing it inside the tent, I knew immediately it would be perfect for Toby. I'd find something special for Eli, too, with his new pad.

On my way home, I stopped at our storage unit. I needed to find the box with our bedding. It sat in the back corner. I moved everything around until

I could crawl back there, then I opened the box slowly, hoping I wouldn't find any mice. Thankfully, it was clean and undisturbed so I grabbed two of the heaviest blankets. I started to close up the box, but I reached inside and pulled out two more.

"You never know what we're all going to need in the coming weeks," I said. These blankets will give us all extra warmth and they will feel cozy at night. One will be for Eli to snuggle in on our bed, and the other I'll try to stuff in and around Toby's tent.

Once I got back to the shed, I felt better. I laid the blankets over the sleeping bags, and set up the little blue tent. Then I positioned it near the heater. Toby crawled right out of her bed and into the tent. No problem there. She knew it was hers the minute she spotted it, and I felt sure she loved it. I had high hopes the tent would trap her body heat. When I looked back to find Eli, I noticed he had crawled underneath one of the blankets on the sleeping bags.

"All righty then," I said to the kitties. "We're in good shape now."

Grabbing an energy bar, I walked over to the house. I was still all bundled up and Kim belly-laughed when he saw me.

"Hey, what are you going to wear when winter gets here?"

"Shut up, Kim," I grumbled. "You sleep warm at night."

Everyone was there. Tim was working hard on the wallboard upstairs, the electrician was doing his thing in the kitchen, and Kim was laying flooring. I climbed upstairs to see Mel. She had put the first coat of stain on the skylight in my bedroom, and it looked so dazzling it took my breath away.

"I love it." I sighed, admiring her work. "The color is just what we hoped for."

"The stain is very thin and drips easily," Mel said, as it trickled down her arms when she lifted the brush to the skylight. "We'll have to take off the doors and bring them to the basement. Then we won't have to worry about spilling stain on the hardwood floor. We'll also continue to use the tarp that I found in Kim's truck."

"We'll have to repeat the process for each door?" I asked.

"Yes. First we stain, then we use sanding sealer, then another light sanding, and finally we apply a coat of polyurethane. Of course the windows and molding will be done in place." Mel finished.

"Sounds like a plan," I said, letting go of a deep breath. "Lordy. This is going to take some time."

I told Mel what I had done for Toby, and she was tickled with the tent. "What a great idea," she said pleased with my purchases.

"I know you'll like it when you see it. Toby barreled right in. She knew it was hers, and Eli had no interest in it," I said.

"Are you talking about how cold it was last night?" Tim asked, pausing in the hall. He was bending over on his stilts so he could peer at us through the open doorway.

"Yes we are," I answered.

"I have several small heaters that I use on my various jobs. There are four that I could spare. How about I loan them to you?"

"Thanks, Tim."

Mel and I looked at each other. "We have the most caring group of guys helping us build our home," I said exhaling.

"Did you remember to pick out a stove and microwave while you were out?" Mel asked.

"Yeeeesh," I said rubbing my hands through my hair. I had forgotten all about it, my whole focus had been on the cold.

"Do you have any thoughts on the stove before I leave?" I asked Mel.

"Propane," She said flatly.

"I know that!" I said hands still in my hair. "We already discussed it a million times."

The previous week I'd picked out the refrigerator and dishwasher. All I needed to do this time was match the color of the stove and microwave with the rest of the appliances. I wish I'd taken the time then to get these two items.

"Back into Powder again."

"Hello, Sal." A heavyset, middle-aged sales clerk greeted me by name when I entered Lowe's. "How's the house coming along?" I struggled to remember how I knew her, but realized I always seemed to end up in her checkout line.

"Fine thanks," I said with a wave, moving with a purpose to the appliance section in the rear. "I should buy stock," I grumbled, shaking my head. "Everyone in here knows me."

When I got to the appliance section I was pleasantly surprised. They had lots of choices. I narrowed it down to two. One was the bisque, or light tan, I needed but the other had the features I wanted.

Fingers crossed, I walked over to a salesman nearby.

"Do you have this one in bisque?" I asked the salesman.

"I do," he answered.

"In stock?"

"Yes."

"And do you deliver?" I asked again.

"Sure do. Will tomorrow work for you?"

"Perfect!" I was batting a thousand.

I looked for a microwave in bisque, the light beige color I loved, but

I didn't see any. I paid for the stove and then drove several miles to Home Depot.

My heart jumped as I caught sight of the perfect microwave, but it looked like I had competition. Another woman was looking it over, too, when a clerk walked over and said, "We only have one in stock."

"I'll take it," I shouted, louder than I had intended.

"Well, now," the woman huffed, eyebrows raised as she walked away.

The salesman lifted it into my car as I put the receipt in my wallet.

I drove back to the house. Mel seemed pleased when I showed her the picture of our new stove on the ad sheet I picked up while I was there.

"I can't wait to see it in our kitchen." She said, paintbrush in hand.

Kim went out to my car and carried in the microwave. He took it out of the box and said, "It'll work."

"May I help you with the staining?" I asked Mel.

"Actually, I was about to grab a little lunch before Kim shows me how to do the tile." She headed back to the shed to make a sandwich and I followed. When Mel walked in she saw the little blue tent.

"I love it," she said, laughing. How cute it was, and Toby was nestled in the back of it.

"She's smiling at us," I stuck my hand in and rubbed her back. "She seems warm." Eli was still under the blanket so I knew he was okay, too.

"No screened porch for them today," Mel said, "it's too chilly to leave the door wedged open like we usually do. Even a couple of inches will make it too cold. They'll have to cope with staying inside."

After lunch, Kim showed us how to lay tile. It took an hour. First, we each painted a thin sealer on the plywood sub-flooring. Next, I mixed the Quick-Set while Mel measured the area. Then she spread the Quick-Set, and placed a few tile pieces. I was able to keep up, and our work looked amazing.

Kim and Tim both left for the day, and we were half-finished with the kitchen floor by sunset. The tile looked different than it had in the boxes, and the subtle color became more obvious. It drew in tints from the cabinets, woodwork, and appliances. Our kitchen had the look of an interior designer, rather than the pieced together impression one would expect from construction auctions.

"It's better than I expected," Mel said, snapping off her knee pads.

"I know, and it has the warmth I wanted." I stood back so I could see the entire room.

We didn't expect to see Tim again for a couple of days. But as late evening came, there he was, driving up our driveway.

"I can't stand to see you two so cold, or the kitties. I'm on my way to my other job, but I wanted to drop these off. You need be more comfortable tonight."

"Thank you."

"You're welcome," Tim said, a little bashful as he climbed in his old station wagon.

"What a dear man," I said, with two of the heaters tucked firmly under my arms.

My Inner Strength is Emerging

The air in the shed was a good ten degrees warmer than the day before. Hefting the five-gallon water container off the floor, I noticed the outside of the jug felt tepid compared to yesterday. I poured some into the coffee pot, stuck my finger in it, and smiled. It was definitely improved.

"Thank you, Tim," I said quietly. "We're good to go now."

I scrambled into my jeans when I heard Kim driving in, and, as I walked toward him, I felt that he seemed more calm and content than usual. I wondered why, but let it go. Not my business.

"How's your progress coming along with the tile?" he asked.

"Come in and find out," Mel said, as she came running up behind us.

"Looks great guys," Kim said, swallowing a gulp of coffee from his thermos. "Keep it up."

I mixed Quick Set again, while Mel cut more pieces of tile. I hated seeing water from the tile cutter spilling on the floor of what was to be my study, but I knew it was the way it had to be. It was a messy job. Water on wood was never a good thing, I remember my dad telling me. Those words stuck with me through the years, and I hoped this project wouldn't take too long.

As I worked I thought about Dad and what he had meant to me. Had I compared Bob to him as I lived my married life? Perhaps. I may have used Dad as a model for all the men in my life. If so, that was unfair. But Dad was so reasonable in every situation or discussion I'd ever had with him. He was the same way with others as well. Respected and loved by so many. Bob, too, was loved and respected. It was only at home that our life together didn't mesh. I married a man I never should have married. He never met me halfway, and I was angered by not feeling or being treated equally. I had my kids and grandchildren, but I wanted more. I wanted to write. I needed to write. Books, short stories, or poems that were powerful, subtle, raw, moving, beautiful, pain-filled, joyous, or sordid. I wanted to use the gifts God gave only to me, but Bob laughed at my efforts. Once, at a dinner party with friends of ours from New York, he boldly stated that my work was to put a few words down on a page each day. And then he snickered meanly, glancing my way. At that moment I felt painfully inadequate and embarrassed. Our friends laughed too. I'll never ever forget it. My plan ever since has been to use that awful feeling of inadequacy as propulsion for my future writing.

I saw my dad in each of my sons. For Shelly, it was more difficult. She saw the daily judgment and often asked me why I allowed it. I had an answer, but I didn't want to tell her I was fearful at times. I didn't want to tell her I was mad about her dad's anger and that it held me back in all that I'd attempted in life. I guess I wanted her life to be different and better. Shelly grew into a competent woman regardless of no answers from me, and she opted to be stronger. She became adamant about what she felt, and no one was going to make her feel less than anyone else. I'm proud of her.

Yes, I made mistakes, but they were my mistakes. I accept myself well enough to know why I made the choices I did. I now take accountability for all of them. I may appear passive to others, but I have seen agony and madness, and the menace that it invokes. The ugly world has not clung to me, so I will do as I want with words from this point forward. I will not leave anything out.

Mel and I worked until mid-afternoon, and then took a break. I saw how well the tile was coming along and thought we'd be done by evening. Once we were finished, we needed to shop for grout. I would leave Mel to pick the color, while I shopped for more latex gloves.

As Mel washed the tools, I cleaned and dried the floor of my study. I picked up the small pieces of tile that had fallen, threw them into a bag, and headed out to tidy-up around the rest of the house.

"It's amazing how fast everything gets disorganized," I said, shaking my head.

"Tim is really messy," Kim said, overhearing my words as he came around the corner and headed for his truck. "It drives me crazy. I like everything planned and in its place."

"Mel and I do too. Guess we're on the same page with that. But Tim does good work. Of that I'm sure."

I resolved to neaten things a little more often until Tim was finished. Three full garbage bags later I was done, and Mel and I were ready to go to Home Depot. It was eight o'clock and we were tired, but were going nonetheless.

It wasn't on our way, but we stopped at our friend's dumpster with

Powder and another full load. While throwing our bags inside, a police car drove in behind us, lights flashing. The officers kept their headlights shining on us, and I had to shield my eyes with my arm in order to see. There were two officers in the patrol car.

"What are you doing here?" one asked, getting out.

"Emptying our trash," Mel answered as she squinted up at them.

"Is this your dumpster?" he asked, with a sarcastic air. His partner was equally annoying, and with arms crossed over his chest, he threw us a condescending look.

Mel was so tired she didn't care how she sounded. "Of course not! It belongs to a friend of ours. We work for him from our home offices." She was stretching the truth, but only a tad. Mel did jobs for our friend's company, and every so often I helped them out, too.

"You're making us feel as if we're doing something wrong," Mel said with a sharp tone, "and we don't like it."

Yikes, you go girl.

We showed them our company ID cards, and they seemed satisfied.

"Okay," they each said, shaking their heads and smiling as they walked back to their car.

I didn't see anything funny about the situation. I wanted to ask them if all they had to do at night was "dumpster patrol," but I was too tired and hungry to get into an argument. We still had to go to Allentown for grout and gloves.

Mel and I stumbled through the doors of Home Depot, exhausted but determined. Mel chose the grout color while I grabbed two more boxes of gloves. Soon we were on our way home.

The shed was cozy when I got back, and finally I rested. I fed the kitties their canned food mixed with kibbles, and our dinner was burgers made in the toaster oven. After peeing in the woods, we settled in for the night.

Hoo-hoo, Hoo-hoo. It had been a while since the owl last sang to us. The sound was comforting, and in my half-sleep I felt content.

"Oh damn it," I said, sitting up in my sleeping bag. "I forgot to put out feed for the deer." I looked over at Mel. She was already asleep so I slipped quietly out of our bed. Putting a sweatshirt and jacket on over my pajamas, I went out intending to keep the promise I made when I first walked this land. The one where I gave my word to the animals that I would care for them always while we shared this land. The owl hooted again. The large garbage cans behind the shed held corn and sweet feed. The latter is a mixture of various grains and molasses, mixed with the corn it makes the perfect combo for animals. The corn keeps them warmer in cold weather. Opening the tops of the cans I inhaled the fragrant aroma.

"No wonder the deer like this," I said quietly, putting two scoops of corn into a bucket. I mixed in a slight scoop of sweet feed and whistled for the deer. Over the past few months I whistled the same tune each time I fed them. Soon they knew my sound and scent and came out of the deep woods to eat. I usually heard them before I saw them, and chuckled to myself every time. I felt they knew the feeding stations were a safe place.

Back at the shed I sat down for a minute on the porch, listening to the owl, and other sounds of nature surrounding me. I was cold, but it felt good. I felt the palpable presence of my dad as I sat there. In my youth, when our work day was over, we would sit on the stumps of the trees, listening. He'd explain the animal and bird sounds we were hearing, and I took in every detail. I loved those times. Laughter requires company, and we had a lot of that together.

Unlike the easiness of my dad's nature, my ex-husband, Bob, seemed stressed most of the time. Rarely were we at peace. One year, on our anniversary, I purchased new swim suits for each of us, and reserved a room in a Philadelphia hotel. I thought it would be a grand get-away place for us to renew our life together. We never went. He thought it was a frivolous gesture, and I became embarrassed in front of our kids as he stuffed the gifts back in the box. The next day I returned the bathing suits with a ready excuse and more doubts.

At the end of our marriage, we rarely argued any more. I was never good at it in the first place. But when we did, I wanted Bob to answer two things. Did you hear me? And, did what I had to say mean anything to you? My dad told me once, that after any argument or discussion, no one should feel in a one-down position. I felt sad that I wasn't standing up to Bob's words. I allowed myself to feel in that one-down position again and again.

Unless we were sharing a bottle of Pinot Noir, Bob's anxiety never fully left. To him, I lived too much in my heart. I saw a man who was unhappy about his life and did not want to change. A curtain came down between us. Perhaps I tried too hard to please, but I was too proud and needy to quit.

An hour later I tiptoed back into the shed. Eli had taken my place in my sleeping bag, keeping it warm.

"Thanks Eli, you're a little sweetheart. How about if you and I stay in here together, keeping each other toasty tonight?"

It was almost fall, and soon our cottage home would be ready. I had come a long way, and I felt strong emotions of commitment, courage, and compassion. I held tight to Eli, and snuggled.

Getting Colder

Once again, the shed at dawn felt like the inside of a meat locker. I stepped over to Mel's large heater, and decided it was doing its best. Then, I checked Tim's smaller ones. They were working hard, too, but the shed lacked insulation making these attempts at warmth ineffective. I turned on the coffee pot and sat in my chair wrapped in a blanket, shivering until the coffee finished brewing. After a couple of mugs, I got up, changed into heavier clothing, and walked outside with my toothbrush and cup of cold water.

Strong gusts of wind on this late October morning made the tree tops dance. That explains why it's so cold. I looked at the naked shed while I brushed, shaking my head. Tar paper and insulation would help. The question was, should we make the time or work faster?

Contemplating that, I walked over and went inside the house. It was cold there too, but stronger and sturdier than our little shed, and it had a different feel. I knew I'd be warmer once I started working, and Kim had promised to bring his huge industrial heater this week while we all worked. *Hope it's today*, I thought, walking over to the kitchen to look at the floor. It was lovely. I did a little jig, happy that Mel and I had done such an excellent job.

I heard a truck coming up the driveway and, as it paused near the old oak, I knew it wasn't Kim. I ran to my study and looked out the window. The Lowe's truck was pulling up in front, and I knew it carried our kitchen stove.

A tall slim man and his helper unloaded it on the driveway, and then took it out of the box. They started wheeling the stove towards the house on a dolly and it occurred to me that I had no idea where it should go. I wasn't a hundred percent sure if Kim wanted it in the kitchen seeing it wasn't finished.

The tile wasn't completely dry so the kitchen seemed out of the question.

"Where would you like us to put it?" the tall guy asked, carrying his end.

"In the living room," I answered. "I think the plumber still has to run in a line of propane." How had they managed to beat Kim to the house?

No sooner had the men left, than Kim walked in.

"Will you go to the barn and get the toilets, and pedestal sinks? I'll need to put them in today before Mel can tile the bathroom floors. The plumbers will be here by the end of the week to hook up everything, so you'll have indoor plumbing."

"Lordy," I said, sighing. "This is too good to be true. It has been a long time coming. May we use the sinks too?"

"Sure," Kim said. "Then, after the tile is finished, I'll help the guys bring up the tub."

He turned and walked into the kitchen, while I made a bee line for the shed. Mel was waking up and I was talking so fast she couldn't understand a word I said. She sat there blinking her eyes. Breathing deeply to take the edge off my excitement, I grabbed another cup of coffee and repeated the good news.

I was giggling when I said, "Mel, we're going to have indoor plumbing by the end of the week. We have to go to the barn right away and get the sinks and toilets. Oh, one more thing, Lowe's brought our stove this morning and it's gorgeous."

"Whoooohooooooo," she whooped, as she jumped up to get dressed.

Before we left for the barn, Mel went in to see the stove.

"Great job. It looks great; I knew you could do it."

"I'm so happy I can't stand it," I said to Kim. "Don't eat anything this morning, I'm bringing egg sandwiches and donuts home in celebration."

"I know you don't eat eggs, but you eat donuts? I thought all donuts had eggs in them." He asked with his eyebrows raised.

"We sure do eat donuts." I answered, happily. "Almost all raised donuts are made without eggs. It's the cake-like donuts that have eggs in them. The Yum-Yum Donut shop in Quakertown has the best around."

We left in my car and drove over to the barn happy and excited. On the way, Mel said, "How about us having our own toilets and sinks? I'm really sick of brushing my teeth in the woods."

"No more peeing in the woods either." I said. "Of course we'll have to use the bathrooms before the workers come each day because there are no doors on them yet."

"That's okay," Mel said. "We can do that."

When we returned with the sinks, toilets, and breakfast, the stove was already in place. I handed Kim his sandwich, grabbed a couple of donuts, and raced upstairs to mix the Quick Set.

"Give me an hour to put in the sink and toilet up there, Sal, before you mix anything," Kim shouted.

"We're going to start in the back where the washer and dryer will go."

"I never have the last word," Kim mumbled.

Even though the amount of tiles needed for the bathrooms was less, the job took longer. Mel did a lot of intricate tile cutting, and that took time. God, she was doing a great job.

By late afternoon, Kim came up to say goodbye.

"Wow, guys, you're getting good at this. Keep it up," he said. "You'll be done by the end of the week even though you have to grout."

We worked long and hard, and by midnight we were finished. We washed out the tools and headed for the shed.

"Darn it," I said walking in, "we forgot to turn the heaters on and it's freezing in here."

"Toby seems warm in her little tent," Mel said, reaching in to feel her body.

I fell into bed with no dinner and I was cold. Really cold. Exhaustion had taken over, and I had no desire to eat anything, let alone make it. I'd eat in the morning.

———

Daylight came more quickly than I wanted. I woke feeling as if I'd been drugged. No energy, dusty brains, but still I tried my best to get moving. Kim was standing outside playing reveille, and we weren't responding. I felt my body straining to get some warmth. After some coffee, we finally made it over to the house.

Kim took one look at us became concerned. "Are you guys okay?"

"We are, but we need more rest and warmth," Mel answered, voice subdued.

"Not today. You've got to grout the bathroom. The plumbers will be here first thing tomorrow morning and it must be finished by tonight. It needs to dry for at least twelve hours before we can install the tub."

I got to work mixing grout, which was a lot like the Quick Set.

"Can you get me more of those egg sandwiches today?" Kim asked.

I looked at him. Had he listened to what he had just said? "No! We're too busy. I'll get some tomorrow but not today. You're going to have to eat leftover donuts for breakfast just like us," I said like the grump I was. "Didn't you hear us say we were really, really tired?"

"Okay, I'll go out instead. I'm more than hungry." Kim said walking toward the door.

"None for us," Mel said, wrinkling her nose.

Teasing us a little, Kim said, "Eggs have protein, they'll be good for you."

While Kim was away, Mel and I fell into a rhythm. As soon as she finished grouting one area of the bathroom, I would come along and wash it down with the large sponge. Again I was learning a new skill. When applying grout, I learned you rub it over the entire area, not only in the spaces between the tiles. It worked well, but it was hard to remove the grit. I sponged it over and over again. It took hours and was hard and tedious work, but valuable as well.

I heard feet on the stairs, and looked up. "How are you coming along?" Kim asked, sandwich in hand.

"Great," Mel answered without looking up.

He went to work on the flooring in my bedroom. "I think I'll make a nice thick steak tonight for dinner."

"Shut up, Kim." I yelled from the bathroom.

"I'll bring the bones over tomorrow and leave them in the woods for the animals to gnaw on. That okay with you guys?"

"Kim," I shouted. "Shut the heck up. I mean it."

We joked back and forth between the two rooms for the rest of the afternoon.

"Goodnight," Kim said, around four o'clock. "I'm headed home."

"Have a great evening Kim," I said, stretching my shoulders.

I still had a mountain of work in front of me, so I kept at it. Hours later it was dark, and I was starving. Neither of us had eaten anything all day except stale donuts, but we were almost finished with the floor.

"I'll finish in here if you'll go out and get some dinner for us," Mel suggested.

"You have a deal," I replied, happy to get off my knees. "I'm ravenous."

"Me too. I'm going to turn on the heaters that Tim left here for the night, so we can be sure the grout will dry by morning,"

As she went back to work, I walked over to the shed to get my money and driver's license. I turned the heaters on for the kitties and left.

Everything looked appetizing in the store, but I settled on frozen veggie lasagna, a baguette, and some salad from the salad bar. I dragged myself home and when I got back to the shed I stuck the lasagna into the toaster oven. It would take a while to bake, so I went back into the house.

"All I have left to do is turn on the heaters, and wash out the tools," Mel said with her hands on her lower back.

"I already did that before I left."

With the two of us working together, it didn't take long. Our hands were freezing from the cold water, and I was so tired that everything seemed funny. I needed food and rest.

Finally, I headed back to the shed for dinner. The hot food and soft chairs were like a little piece of paradise.

Plumbing

The next moring my coffee mug was cold to the touch, but the liquid inside was hot. I drank it quickly craving its warmth. After two cups, I shook off my blanket, dressed, and walked over to the house.

I looked for Kim on the first floor, but he wasn't there. He was working somewhere on the hardwood flooring. The second floor was nearly finished, and that's where I found him.

When are the plumbers coming to hook up the bathroom fixtures?" I asked. We had stopped going to Bill and Heidi's in the mornings, taking care of our personal business in the woods. I was more than exhausted and more than cold. Trying to keep warm most of the time required all the strength I had to keep going. Walking up and down the path several times a day took too much time and energy.

Kim looked up from his work. "I called them again last night after I left. They'll be here soon."

"Soon seems so far away."

"By afternoon, the upstairs flooring will be complete," Kim said rather proud of himself. "You'll need to finish staining the woodwork, and Tim still has to put up more drywall. He has to stuff insulation in around the studs, but it won't take him long once he's here for a few hours."

"Maybe he'll be able to do it this weekend," I said looking to Kim for confirmation.

After Mel woke and dressed, we began to stain the wood around my bedroom windows, and floor molding. Despite Kim's loud music, I heard a truck coming up the drive. We dropped our brushes, and rushed to the window to see who it was.

"Zippity-doo-dah. It's the plumbers," I yelled, jumping around. I was so excited I could hardly contain myself, and raced across the room hugging Mel as hard as I could.

"Whoa, girl."

"About time." Kim left Mel's room and went downstairs. "I'll find out what has been keeping them."

Mel and I decided to stay where we were. Kim had his own technique of keeping his sub-contractors honest, and we didn't want to get in his way. An hour went by before we heard them coming up the stairs, huffing and puffing.

Looking out my bedroom door toward the bathroom, we saw that the plumbers were attempting to carry the claw foot tub. Two young guys were on one end, and Kim was on the other. It was the two young guys making all the noise. Kim was walking up the stairs with his end of the tub in one hand, and a cigar in the other, grinning widely.

"These two dudes can't handle this job by themselves. How sad," he said yawning.

We knew enough to go back to work and say nothing. It took three more hours for us to finish staining everything in my bedroom. We needed to wait for it to dry before we could move on to the next step in the process, so we moved all of our paraphernalia into Mel's room.

Later I would apply sanding sealer. I wanted it ready to sand in the morning. What a long, arduous process.

At three o'clock, Kim walked in. "The plumbers are finished for the day. They'll be back tomorrow to plumb the kitchen. All they have to do is connect the pipes to the sink, attach the stove to the propane line, and tie in a copper pipe to the ice maker in the refrigerator. It will take a few hours because only one man can come back. The others guys have to work on another job they're doing, but we'll be fine."

"Okay. We trust you."

Kim went back to work on the living room flooring. He needed to cut out the area where the wood stove would sit.

"Why didn't you leave that area without flooring, instead of cutting it out now?" I asked Kim from over the upstairs railing. "Seems like a waste of wood."

"It's easier to lay the flooring first, and then cut out the pattern. I wish Stephanie was here to help. She's such a good worker." He looked a little sad.

"I miss her too, Kim. How does she like East Stroudsburg University? All three of my kids went there too."

"She loves it. It will be a long four years for me, but at least she'll be home during the summers." He went back to work.

Upstairs, Mel and I continued to stain in her room. I loved how the house was shaping up for us. As I listened to more of Bocelli, the effort seemed easier.

"I'm leaving. I'll see you tomorrow," Kim called upstairs, two hours later. "Come to the railing."

Both of us stood looking down at him in the living room. The wood floor was nearly finished, and he stood proudly, hands on hips.

"Congratulations. Thought you'd like to know the plumber got the hot water heater in. Not sure why I waited to tell you, but you are now the proud owners of a working tub, sink and toilet. I'll get to the shower first thing next week, but the downstairs bathroom won't be done until Friday." With a wave of his hand, he left.

I stood there with my mouth open before it all sank in. It was hard to believe. Tonight we could take baths in our new tub. And, use the toilet and sink. Oh Lordy, now I was really excited. I ran into the bathroom and turned on my new fancy-dancy tub-spray faucet, the sink spigot, and finally flushed the commode.

"Yippee," Mel sang out. "No more long walks up and down the path."

It was very loud on Deer Trail Road for the next hour, while we finished our work upstairs. Every once in a while, one of us would run in the bathroom and wash our hands, just because we wanted to.

Later, I asked Mel to take the inaugural bath in the new tub. She was delighted.

"It will be my honor."

I left, and went to the shed to spend time with the kitties. For once it felt cozy in there, and I fell asleep in my chair while I waited for Mel. She came back an hour later, smiling.

"It's absolutely perfect." It made me happy to see her so radiant.

Finally, I left to take my turn. As I climbed into the tub, I realized the house was cold on this late-October night. I ducked down into the steamy water to get warm. As I washed, I felt cleaner than I had in months. Ordinarily I hated baths, but knowing it was ours, all ours, made me happy. I brushed my teeth in the new pedestal sink. It seemed larger than I expected.

"Wow," I said, out loud. "We have a bathroom."

By the time I got back to the shed, Mel was asleep. Having a hot bath made me feel better than I expected. Slipping into our bed, all warm and cozy, I marveled at all we'd accomplished. For the past six months we'd been living in a cramped, twelve by eighteen foot shed with no bathroom or running water. But that was soon coming to an end.

I am a tough old soul, after all.

Long Days...Still

All it took was a hot bath to change my feelings about life in the shed. Just knowing the tub, sink, and toilet, were only twenty yards away made my existence easier. Early the next morning I scrambled to the house, and brushed my teeth in the new sink.

"Good morning, Kim," I managed to say around a mouthful of toothpaste when he walked up the stairs. "You can't believe how good it feels to walk over here in the morning, instead of going down to our neighbors. It's made our small world a little larger, and we're so grateful."

"You're welcome," Kim answered. "I figured the whole routine must be getting old."

"Yeah, it's been hard going lately. I'm so tired at night I don't even want to eat. I'm beginning to understand hermit life."

He got to work, and so did we. Mel had walked in while Kim and I were talking, and she waved a hand as she went by. I needed to keep moving, so I began in my room. I did a light sanding on everything, and then wiped the freshly sanded wood with a soft cloth. After that, I applied the finish coat. It glowed.

Two weeks later we were almost done with my bedroom. Except for the closet door, my room was complete. I stayed a little longer making sure I looked at every detail, before moving on to Mel's.

Kim kept working with the hardwood flooring in the living room and foyer.

"It's supposed to be exceptionally cold tonight," Kim yelled to us upstairs.

"Okay, Kim. Our heaters in the shed are already on," I shouted down. I wanted to get a jump on the cold for ourselves and the kitties.

"We can do this," I said, pumping my fist in the air.

"Yes, we can," Mel answered, over and over like a mantra.

After an hour, Mel went downstairs to talk with Kim about Tim. "He's keeping us waiting on so much work."

I walked down while the two of them were talking. "Tim seems to have disappeared," I said to the two of them. "You're almost finished with the living room flooring. Tim said he'd be here to work along with you, and none of us has heard from him in days."

"I'll call him tonight and give him an ultimatum. He can work on this house or not. If he doesn't want to be here, I'll hire someone else to finish the job or do it myself." Kim said.

"I'm so damn exasperated and frustrated with him." I said, stomping my foot on the floor. " You have to work around the scaffolding, and then move it every other day. I've even tried calling him but his phone always goes to voicemail. I've left three messages telling him he's putting this whole project behind. Mel and I are getting colder by the minute in the shed. I'm sorry, Kim" I continued, "I know it's not my place to talk to him like that. And he's your sub-contractor, but when it comes to our well being, I'm inflexible."

"He'll be here. He only needs a push," Kim said.

I hoped inwardly he was right and wanted to give Tim the benefit of the doubt. We all got back to work. Mel and I skipped lunch in favor of an earlier evening for a change. I wanted to sit in the field and watch the sunset. We were having gorgeous fall evenings, and I was missing out on them. The plan was to keep working until six o'clock, and then, together, we'd watch the sunset.

Although I went back to work my mind kept busy. I had become triggered by Tim's lack of completion of our home. It brought me back to the ending of my marriage and how incomplete I felt as a result. Bob and I had an opportunity, both then and now, to show our grandchildren that our love for each other did not stop because of the divorce. We needed go on as two adults, living life as a divorced couple, but in a loving way. An example for the kids, in case divorce showed up in their life one day.

I had desired a period of time for discovery and growth, to re-create myself into the person I knew I was born to be. Bob said he needed to stay in familiar territory. I wanted to re-establish my potential as a woman who felt "unfinished" and find the confidence I'd lost. Bob was happy in his own skin. Or was he? Regardless of our differences we could still give our grandkids an opportunity to see love in action. But it was not to be.

By the end of the day, my arms, neck, and back ached. I was staining and sanding over my head on the wood surrounding the skylights, both in the bathroom and Mel's room. It was hard work, and I was ready for a break. I fed the kitties, bundled up, and headed for the field. On the way out, I put corn on the feeding stations. I loved that part of my day, mostly because the natural world's magnificence sang to my heart. In my chair, the cold nipped my face while I watched a red sun disappear from the sky, leaving burnt orange and other fiery colors in its place.

"Doing this work makes me feel alive and inspired about my life." I said to Mel who had followed me out. "When we finish the house we should keep living life a little out of our reach. It's too easy to stay safe all the time."

Hawks were flying overhead, and I recognized them still. How beautiful they were with their rust-colored tails glowing in the evening's twilight. They flew over our heads as if to say hello, then soared into the tree line for a moment before shooting out again at top speed. It looked like a fun pursuit.

"Let's sit here until we're freezing, then we'll run in for hot baths and dinner," I suggested.

"Sounds like a plan."

Within an hour, the glow had gone and darkness was complete. As I walked by the shed, I stopped and turned on the lights for later, and then went into the house.

I hadn't heard Tim come up the driveway, and I was pleased to see him. He was working hard and fast, trying to make Kim, and us, happy.

"No bath for us tonight," I said to Mel, laughing. "Not without a door on the bathroom. I'll try to take mine early before Kim arrives in the morning."

"How daring. You never know when he might turn up." Mel said. "One thing I know for sure. I won't be up in time."

"Maybe we can get Kim to put the doors on tomorrow, or at least the one for the upstairs bathroom."

I awoke the following morning to hammering from the house.

"Oh no," I said, sitting up quickly. "Kim is already here, and I wanted a bath." Rubbing sleep from my eyes, I got up, pulled on jeans, a tee-shirt, a sweatshirt, and, finally, a jacket. "Lordy, it's even colder." I heard the sound again and looked at the clock. It was only six-thirty. Kim never arrived before seven. As I ran toward the house, I realized the noise was behind me now, and coming from the shed. Confused, I looked for the source and found a female Pileated Woodpecker on a nearby tree branch. *Oh God, you are so gorgeous. Thank you for being here with us, I hope you have babies on our land.*

I turned my head toward the driveway, and it was empty. I could take my bath after all.

Rushing into the house, I climbed the stairs two at a time, ran into the bathroom, turned the water on in the tub, and stood there shivering. Once it was full, I took the fastest bath ever, hopping out just as Kim's truck pulled up the driveway. I ran in my bedroom with no door, jumping into my clothes along the way.

"Are you decent?" Kim yelled, from the bottom of the stairs. "I can hear you up there."

"Yep, all done." My hair was wet and messy, and Kim laughed out loud.

"Are you cold?" he asked coming up the stairs.

"It's chilly in here, but its okay. Better than going next door. Takes half the time." I grabbed my sweatshirt and coat, and walked back to the shed. As I went in, Mel woke up. She didn't look too happy when she realized her bath time would have to wait. I poured a cup of coffee, and enjoyed the short time I had before work.

I went to the house to begin my day. Rounding the top of the stairs, I guessed Kim was in the bathroom because the door was closed. The door! The bathroom had a door! He had told us he wouldn't put it on because Tim wasn't finished, but I guess he knew we'd love having it.

"If you want it to lock, you've got to go out for a door knob. In fact, you should be making all your hardware selections now. Perhaps tonight? In your spare time," Kim teased.

We said yes, and then got busy again with the never-ending task of staining and sanding.

A Bit of Heat

By the first week in November it was even colder. At noon the outside thermometer said forty-eight degrees, and our small shed home was hard to keep at a livable temperature. We were healthy, but the cold was affecting my mood. The kitties were still okay, and we were too, but sleeping in the frosty air took away most of my energy, leaving me stiff and tired when I woke.

"I feel guilty," I said, frowning at my sandwich.

"Why?" Mel asked.

"Because living in the shed was my idea," I said, swallowing my last bite of lunch.

Mel held up her hand. "Living in the shed was a choice. I, alone, am responsible for my decision to be here."

I found the hardware I wanted, Kim hung the rest of the doors. It had been fun making our choices, but we had to go to four stores in order to find the brushed chrome look we desired. Mr. Wonderful liked our selections, and nodded his approval. Mel and I loved the way the doors had turned out for us.

Finally, he gave us the go-ahead to grout the kitchen floor. It had been weeks since the tile was down. I didn't think we'd ever get to that project, but at last, that job, too, was complete. And it was damn tiring. Everything was in the cold.

Tim was finished with the drywall upstairs, and was now working in the living room. Kim told me that he'd had another heated conversation with

Tim over the weekend, and he had decided to stay with us and complete the job. Tim felt bad that he had let us down, but it seemed that he had this pattern of not completing things on time. Everyone had moved on, and now he was making great progress once again.

When Kim finished the hardwood flooring in the living room, Mel and I helped him tape heavy brown paper to the floor. We wanted to protect it from scratches and dirt, along with the legs of Tim's scaffolding that now reached to the ceiling. What a job. My back was sore and my muscles tight. Straining from the act of cold versus effort. With more heat my soreness might not be so ever-present.

Tim must hate us by now, I thought, as I looked at the height involved. Kim handed the heavy drywall to Tim, who was waiting on the second tier of the scaffolding, and he hefted it up the rest of the way. Painting everything was our job. For a minute, even I hated our decision on the high ceilings as I thought of what loomed ahead. We had designed an attractive home, but painting at that height would be complicated. But then, so was everything else. We could do this, too.

Thanksgiving was two weeks away and I didn't know how we'd get through another month in the shed without extra heat. I was staining the molding in the upstairs bathroom, feeling the leftover warmth from the morning's baths. I closed the door while I stained, hoping to hold onto it a bit longer. Once the electrician was finished putting in the electric heating system, we'd bathe in a warm room. What a pleasure to look forward to.

It was the year 2000, and I wondered why electric heat was so much less to put in our home than an oil system. We wanted the cheapest heat available, but didn't plan on using it. Our heating system was only a backup for the wood stove.

I wanted to use the wood stove, but the house wasn't ready. Kim had to fireproof a space for it, and Mel and I needed to select the surface that would go underneath it.

"You need to shop for tile, guys," Kim yelled upstairs.

"It's on the list," I answered, bending over the railing and looking down into the living room. "Along with selecting our paint colors. Is that a light I see at the end of the tunnel, or is it an oncoming train?"

"Glad you can see it," Kim frowned. "It's too far around the bend for me to view. Are you really warm enough in the shed? Why don't all of you move into a motel?"

"Hell no!" Mel protested, from her bedroom. "We can't afford it for one thing, and what about the kitties? Let's work hard and see how far we get. Not too many things are left to complete, and if we work late each night we can move in soon."

I knew she was right, but only if John agreed. We still needed our occupancy permit.

The following weekend I suggested we shop for paint and tile. I wanted a
larger tile for under the wood stove than we had in the kitchen, and a blending
color to match the furniture we had sitting in our storage unit. Mel agreed,
and we knew it was getting us one step closer to that coveted permit.

"I'm surprised to see all this variety," I said to Mel at Rocca Tile and
Marble in Sellersville. "I'm so used to the limited selection of auction tile. It
makes it harder to choose."

"It really is difficult," Mel said, carefully handling each piece.

An hour later, we'd made our choice, and workers loaded up Mel's car
with the boxes. There were so many choices that we had to keep the selection
process down to the top three we liked best. Then we each chose the one we
liked from them.

Then we went to Buss's paint store in Emmaus. We brought sample chips
of various colors home and Mel taped them on the wall. Mostly they were
soft shades of off-white, cream, faded sage, and pale yellow. I would look at
these in the living room each time I walked by for the next few days. After a
week or so, I hoped one of them would stand out and become my preference.

Later that afternoon, the electrician's truck was in the driveway. It was
Saturday, and I was amazed to see him.

"Kim must have told them we really needed heat," I declared, lifting some
boxes out of her car.

"Damn straight. We do need it," Mel blurted out hefting her share of the
boxed tile.

I high-tailed it inside and found he had some of the heating elements
hooked up and running.

"It's warming up fast," I said, rubbing my arms. It was downright toasty
in there, but then I thought of the cost. I looked out to the field at the rows
of stacked wood. *There must be four or five cords out there,* I thought. Soon we'd
be using it, costing us nothing but our own labor to heat the house. What
was the old adage? "She who chops her own wood warms herself twice. But
actually, it's thrice; they forgot about the stacking it part.

I worked on staining the railing overlooking the living room, and the
molding coming down the set of oak stairs. It had been a couple hours already.

When the electrician was done for the day, he walked over to report his
progress. "The upstairs bathroom is complete, and the bedroom over the
kitchen is hooked up too." he said. "I'll be back next week to finish the job."

I nodded my head. "Great. Thank you."

After he left we reveled in the warmth of our home—or at least a small
part of it.

"I'm expecting John sometime next week," I said to Mel, looking up from my work.

"Yeah, he'll need to come over and take a look around. No reason to worry though, we're doing a good job," Mel said as she worked.

A second later I heard a truck. I looked out and saw Charlie. He had brought his dozer.

"I'll be here on Monday," he said looking happy to be back with us. "I'm going to bring over a few loads of modified stone for the driveway, and then I'll grade it. We always wait until the end of the project to put down the final layer."

"Thanks, Charlie," I said, with a little pout. "I'll miss seeing you. I feel as if you've become part of our family. It's hard to believe the driveway will be finished. You've helped us so much."

"It has been more fun for me than you'll ever know," Charlie answered with a smile. "I never thought I'd say I loved working with two women. Call me any time you have more egg sandwiches, and I'll come over."

"I'll have some for you on Monday when you're done with your work. Make sure you come with an appetite," I laughed. "Mind if I give you a hug?"

"I'd love it, thank you." He blushed. It must be hard to be a sweet guy when you're trying hard for the grizzled look.

I hugged him hard and my eyes immediately filled with tears. Perhaps I was thinking a bit about my dad.

Downright Cranky

I woke again to the freezing cold of my shed. Again, it was an effort. I knew Toby's joints must be stressed. Both cats had thick coats, thanks to Mother Nature, but Toby's fur was finer than Eli's. It might have been due to her diabetes or insulin injections. Mel and I were handling the frosty air, even though it was sapping most of our strength. The stress of getting the house finished was taking its toll. Working in the dry, cold air made the tips of my fingers crack and bleed. It seemed, too, that I was feeling uneasy most of the time.

As I walked to the house one of these mornings, I knew something had to change. Inside, there was a little heat, so I took off my jacket and sweatshirt. The old New England custom of layering clothing had stayed with me.

"Good morning, Kim," I said, not wanting to talk.

"Morning," he answered, not looking up.

I worked in the kitchen, staining, sanding, and sealing. The windows, floor molding, and pantry doors, all needed to be finished. "Oh, hi Mel. I didn't hear you come in," I said, standing up from my kneeling position. Placing my hands on the small of my back, I leaned back a little to take out the kinks.

"Hi guys. Does your back hurt?" Mel asked.

"Oh, you know how it goes. The cold and sixty years of hard physical work makes the back weaker," I said, grimacing. I was impatient with my body not doing what I wanted it to do without complaining.

Kim was laying flooring in my study. After a few hours, he came over to talk with us.

"I'm going to cut more out the area on the living room floor for the wood stove before I go home. It's not quite large enough."

I was glad, but it was hard for me to get too excited. "Good, Kim. Thanks."

"I thought you'd be more excited, Sal. You've been waiting for me to do this for weeks." Kim said a little disappointed.

"I guess I've been too cold to get any enthusiasm going, Kim. I go to sleep cold, wake up cold, and work all day in a chilly house. I hope Mel and I can keep this up. We're getting bitchy and tired, and our energy level has dropped, but I'm really pleased you're focused on the wood stove area."

"You girls are tougher than any I know. I'm sure you can hang on a little longer." Kim said grabbing his circular saw.

The masons were scheduled to arrive the following week. The chimney and stone walls behind the stove needed to be built. When they finished, Mel had to lay the tile floor. After the grouting dried, the wood stove delivery was next.

"I'm not looking forward to the new chimney masons coming, Mel," I said, looking her way.

"Me neither."

"Why not?" Kim asked, from my study.

"Neither of us like this new guy, Kim, not even a little. I don't trust him for a second," I said, with total disgust. "I've felt that way from the very first day you brought him here. Why do we have to have a different mason?

"There are guys who only do chimneys, and they do a better job because of it."

"Okay, but this man is not someone I'd like on our property for very long. I want you to be here while he works. I just don't get a good feeling when he's around."

"Yeah, I understand," Kim said. "I wish my usual mason wasn't injured; I'd be using him."

"I'm going to call Grates & Grills. They ought to get our wood stove out of storage," I said to Kim, "and have it standing by to be delivered as soon as we're ready. It's been months since I ordered it."

I heard footsteps, and looked out to see the building inspector standing on the porch.

"Hi, John," I said, opening the door.

"Wow, guys, you're really making progress. I need to inspect again."

My stomach clenched every time I saw this man, but for once, I was happy to go upstairs and work. Everything had to pass inspection, it just had to.

A half-hour later, he went out the front door and I walked downstairs to get the news.

"Everything passed," Kim said. "Just as I said it would. You still have to get the water tested. He also said the swale at the end of the driveway needs to be paved. There isn't any hurry though and he can give us a temporary permit until we finish it. You can wait until spring if you want, or longer. Oh, and I have to build steps up to your study door."

"I'm leaving to pick up the water test kit," I said, to Mel and Kim.

"That's a good idea," Mel said.

While you're out, will you please pick up some more egg sandwiches?" Kim added, as I headed for the door.

"Sure," I mumbled. "Why not. I've wanted to do that all morning." Wow, I was becoming a certified grouch.

The crisp air felt good, but my fingers were stiff from the chill of the house. I felt glad to be by myself for a while. Alone time was in short supply. Maybe that was why I felt so out of sorts. Mel, Kim, the sub-contractors, and I had been working side-by-side in close quarters for many months. I needed space to bring balance to my world. I always had.

Driving to get the test kit, I thought about the women in my life. My daughter, granddaughters, daughters-in-law, sister, and friends. I wanted to empower them and show, by example, how strong women can be. Did that include pain? Oh yes, but growth is the result.

When I got back, egg sandwiches in hand, I put the testing kit by the kitchen sink. I had to draw the water first thing in the morning after it had settled overnight. I sighed and returned to staining wood. We worked, stopping only to eat a cold sandwich, until ten o'clock that night.

"Mel, why don't you take your bath first?" I said. "I want to go to the shed for a while."

"Okay, but I'm going to soak for hours," she said taking the stairs up to the bathroom.

As I walked into the shed, Toby was sitting on my sleeping bag, shivering. I opened it up and stuffed her down near the bottom, covering her entire body. She seemed content for the moment, but I was sure she was tired of being in the little tent. Both Eli and Toby needed some exercise.

When Mel came back I said, "Let's take the kitties to the house and let them walk around. It will be good for their legs, and they need to see where they're going live."

"Okay."

We each grabbed a kitty and made our way to the house, putting them down on the floor of my study. Eli took off, scampering around the place at a run. Toby walked around looking stiff, and then climbed the stairs as if she knew she would be sleeping up there one day soon. Mel let them get their exercise while I took my turn in the tub. When I was finished, we carried them back to the shed.

"Sorry guys," I cooed, as I nuzzled Toby, "but you'll have to stay in here a bit longer."

Toby licked my nose and Eli squirmed to get out of Mel's arms, eager to expel more energy.

"They seem better, don't you think?" I asked, as I set Toby on the floor. I felt guilty about putting them through life in such a cold, confined space.

"Yea, I do," Mel laughed. She looked at Toby, "You know you just saw your new home, don't you?"

They seemed warmer, and more settled. They had a good work-out and I promised them we'd do it more often.

Our First Thanksgiving

The shed was still freezing cold. Despite the blankets and heaters, I was huddled in my sleeping bag and didn't want to come out. The cold felt icy and sharp on my face and ears, as I peeked around for a moment. Toby was curled up tight in her tent. Eli slept very close to Mel, snuggled half-under her sleeping bag. Mel's breathing rose and fell in little white puffs over Eli's head. I inched back down in my bag, feeling lethargic, and hoped it was because of the glacial feel to the air.

After another hour, I made the leap from sleeping bag to clothes, hopping around, pulling them on as quickly as I could manage in the cramped cold space. I smacked the start button for the coffee pot, sat down, and realized, with a start, that it was Thanksgiving Day. We had accomplished so much, and survived in the shed to the end of November. I have much to be thankful for, I thought. Why haven't I felt like it lately? What's wrong with me?

Pulling my feet up, I grabbed one of my blankets and wrapped it around me while I sat in meditation. Only a year ago, building a house and living here on the land like this was just a vision. Despite all my fears, all the work on healing myself, I pulled it off.

After coffee, I pulled on my coat. I wanted to walk to the house and call my kids, wishing them a Happy Thanksgiving from my new home. Quietly, I let myself out of the shed door and onto the little screened porch. "Oh my God!" I said. Four inches of snow had fallen during the night. It gave the woods a look of freshness and enchantment, and I was in awe of its beauty. The world was bright and glittery as I hiked in the snow, and I felt my spirits lift. When I got to the house, I turned and looked back at the shed. It resembled an igloo and gave me the giggles. It was a wet snow and it had stuck to the shed like the shingles on the house. Totally white. Totally frigid.

I entered the house through my study and pulled off my wet sneakers. "That's it," I announced to the house, arms stretched to the ceiling. "We're all going to move in today. Permit or no permit." Eyes closed, smile wide, I continued my dialogue, "I declare this Thanksgiving morning to be the day."

I called my three kids, wished them a happy Thanksgiving, and told them how much I loved them. Then, I called Bill and asked if he would help us carry our things from the shed to the house.

"You got your permit?" he said, sounding surprised.

"No, but we're moving in just the same."

"Okay," he said with a laugh. "Finally had it with the shed, eh?"

"Oh, yeah. It's time." I told him to give me an hour to wake Mel, and get the kitties ready.

I turned the heat on high in my upstairs bedroom and closed the door. Then I turned on two of the other heaters downstairs, as well. Thanksgiving was going to be a warm celebration.

Back on the shed's porch I stood still for a minute, looking again at nature's beauty. The snow was gleaming and lustrous. It was a clear day with an arctic feel, but the sun on the snow made everything sparkle. Each branch glistened, waving slowly in the quiet, gentle breeze. Nature was so giving. Both Flora and fauna enhanced my spiritual growth these past six months.

I dashed inside and woke everyone from their sleep. When Mel opened her eyes, she looked around and began to groan and shiver.

"I have an announcement," I exclaimed, dancing from one foot to the other. "Today is moving day. We are taking everything and everyone into our new home this morning. We'll all have a warm Thanksgiving Day together. Eli? Toby? Mel? Do you hear me?"

Mel was a tornado of movement as she got herself together. She jumped up and scrambled into her clothing just as I had an hour earlier.

"Woohooooo!" Mel bellowed. I laughed at her enthusiasm.

We sat down and had coffee together. For the first time in months, neither of us felt the cold.

"This will be our last morning cup of coffee in the shed," I said feeling nostalgic. As we sat there, the kitties looked at their food bowls. "Let's wait to give them their food until we bring them over to the house. They can eat their first meal in their new home, and be warm at the same time."

Anticipation was growing the longer I sat, and I enjoyed the thought of what was to come.

As Mel gathered what she needed for herself, I sat back and closed my eyes for those few minutes. I'd been grateful for this shed. In my heart, the moments spent within these walls had become bountiful gifts. Life here had become more spiritual than any place I'd lived, and with it came a new significance. I'd felt the presence of a Higher existence on this land. Nature had given me the sacred feeling that we are all One, together. That there is no soul, human or otherwise, that has more worth than the other. I had created a space for that to happen, by letting go of expectation. Everything passes in its time. Our shed life was over.

That decision of living months in a tool shed was a choice. It was the beginning of my new awareness of finding God in uncommon places. The parts of our lives where you'd never expect God to shine so brightly, and I was gratified each day as I looked at our meager shed. It had been my honor to live there. I had learned so much, not as a traveler, but as a resident. And there is a difference. Everything was first hand there; you didn't read about it in a book or listen to the experiences of others. I felt equal to those who lived here, and my prayer was that one day the human race would stop eating its animals, and instead realize that we are more blessed to do without. I intended to grow older, meeting and living my life in thoughtful quietude.

So, on the first Thanksgiving Day of the new millennium, Mel, Eli, Toby and I, moved into the only room that was finished in our new home. My bedroom, or our bedroom. Four of us in one room. We had been doing this for months. The house would welcome us with that one warm space, its silence, and the promise of a hot bath.

Mel and I stood together, each holding a kitty in our arms. We had to bring them to the house first, as we were afraid they'd escape the shed during the transition. Plus, I didn't want them to feel cold one more minute.

I walked up the stairs ahead of Mel, opened the door to our bedroom, and stood there in its warmth for a moment. We put Eli and Toby down on the floor, watched them scamper around, closed the door and then walked back to the shed. Bill arrived, and we moved the kitty things first, then the mattress, dresser, and finally our clothing and food. Mel grabbed the toaster oven on the final pass, and I grabbed the coffee pot. We left the microwave for now; we already had one in our new kitchen.

I turned to close the shed door, but something stopped me. Walking back in, I felt the emotional impact of the last six months. Tears filled my eyes, and I had to leave before I completely fell apart. Slowly, I made my way back to the house.

As Bill left to go home he asked, "What are you doing for the rest of the day?"

"Working," I answered. "Andy asked Mel and me for Thanksgiving dinner, but I said no, not this year. We need to stay here and work. This house needs to be finished."

"I understand," Bill answered. "See you later. Happy Thanksgiving."

We painted Mel's bedroom that afternoon. The soft cream color we'd chosen complimented the wood. Warmer and more energized, I enjoyed a new strength and passion for what I was accomplishing. I felt renewed, as if a huge gift had just been given to me.

I worked until mid-afternoon and then walked downstairs for a drink. As I took a glass from the shelf, I heard a knock at our door. It was our friends, Heidi, Bill, and Christel. They had brought us a Thanksgiving meal.

"Thank you for this feast, and for your love," I said, eyes brimming with fresh tears. "Wow, it looks and smells delicious. Want to come in and stay for awhile?"

"You're welcome," Heidi answered, "but no thanks. We need to go for a walk after all the food we just ate." We hugged them, and they went on their way.

After they left, we took our paper-plated dinners upstairs to my bedroom so we could be with Eli and Toby. Before we sat down to eat, we gave thanks for the gift of love in our new home. Our chairs and knees made a good table for our meals, and I could hardly wait to eat. As I removed the foil, I found a yummy meal of faux chicken pieces, mashed potatoes and gravy, cranberry sauce, broccoli, and Christel's famous stuffing. The day was cold and clear, but our food was hot. A blessing, really.

In the evening, I walked upstairs and put our sleeping bags and pillows on the mattress. The kitties had their beds, too. Mel hooked up the TV, while I put more fresh food and water in the kitty bowls. I closed the bedroom door to keep the heat in, since I had turned the downstairs heaters off for the night. Eli and Toby were not allowed to wander around the house without us. There were too many dangers lurking.

Mel went to take her bath, but I decided to wait until morning. It all seemed surreal as I sat in my chair to watch TV. As I looked around the finished room, I realized that the shed and our bedroom were about the same size. We traded for heat. Well worth it, in my opinion. When Mel came out of the bathroom she was smiling, and I felt her joy. But I was a mess.

"What's wrong?" Mel asked, concern written all over her face.

"It's all too sweet, and I don't feel worthy," I said, reaching for the box of tissues. "I love this home so much."

"Me too, and we've worked hard for it, Sal." Mel said sitting down on the mattress.

It was almost midnight. We were all snuggled in, warm and cozy on this first Thanksgiving night.

Wood Stove Arrival

Thanksgiving settled into a memory. Now I was focused on Christmas and finishing our home for the winter.

Kim was almost done with the flooring. Meanwhile the masons had completed the chimney along with the dry-stacked stone walls behind the wood stove. The electrician and plumbers were finished as well. And, at last, Mel was going to lay tile under the wood stove.

I expected John again, too. The water test results were back, but he needed to inspect the chimney. We were not supposed to be living in the house, so of course, each morning we picked up the bedroom, making it look as if we were using it for storage. We'd been living on our land for six months. This was certainly not the time to get in trouble so close to the end of our project. Christmas was coming soon, and the one gift Mel and I wanted to give each other was our living room without scaffolding. Tim was still working, but promised he'd finish well before Christmas. We still needed to paint—all the way up to the ceiling.

When Tim showed up for work, I broached the subject with him. "Is there any way you can leave the scaffolding up when you finish with the drywall? We'd like to use it when we paint the living room." I stood in the kitchen, paint brush in hand, shifting my weight from one foot to the other in anticipation of his answer.

"Sure," he said, gesturing toward the "metal monster" close by. "I'll leave it up as long you want. Call me when you're done, and I'll come by and take it down."

I let out a deep breath. "Thanks, Tim."

The painting went smoothly, and hours flew by as I worked hard to complete the walls, along with the half-wall separating the kitchen from the living room. When I finished, I wrapped the roller cover and paint brush in plastic wrap. Doing so kept me from having to wash out the brush each evening. Anything to save time, I thought. As long as I came back to them within the next few days, the bristles would be soft and flexible.

"I'm done with the tile," Mel said, as night fell. "I have to wait a couple of days for it to dry, and then I'll grout."

"I'm done for the day as well," I said, feeling bone tired. I finished cleaning up and went out to the shed. The home I'd had for six months now held Bluebie, deer and bird feed, and our own tools and equipment. Kim had packed up most of his gear, saying he'd bring what he needed with him in his truck from now on.

"Tomorrow I'll bring wood in from the field, and cover it with a tarp," I said when I came inside the house. "It will be ready and waiting for the stove. The owner of Grates & Grilles told me we had to cure the stove first, building small fires for the first two days. After that, we can increase the heat each time we use it. There are tons of small wood pieces leftover from this project. I'll bring in a few wedges from the initial oaks we cut on our land. We promised the trees we would, remember?"

"Of course I do. Those small pieces will be burned with respect," Mel answered in her softest voice. "It seems so long ago."

I went to bed excited again that night, feeling cozy and comforted.

As usual, I was the first to rise. I went down to the kitchen and made a pot of coffee, realizing how easy it was now that we were in the house. Dressing warmly, I went to the field with Bluebie and brought back a load of wood. I stacked it beneath the sliding glass door, realizing that I was more than ready for the stove to arrive. The last electric bill had been a shocker at well over five hundred dollars for the month. I knew there was a reason we decided to heat with wood. All of the workers had used their tools and our electricity, Kim especially. It drove the price up beyond what I'd imagined.

After putting Bluebie back, I took a walk through the snow-covered woods. It was a cold December morning because of a breeze coming in off the field, but it felt good on my face. I found the six wedges we had cut from the first old oaks. They had weathered in the field over the summer, and then I'd wrapped them in a tarp and placed them behind the shed. Those pieces would be the first to burn once we had a hot fire.

Mel was up when I came in, drinking coffee in her chair upstairs.

"What are you thinking about?" I asked, knowing the look on her face.

"Finishing the grout. It won't take long," she said, wiping sleep from her eyes. "Then we can finish painting the living room."

"I think we can have it completed by tonight if we keep at it," I said, kneeling down to pet Eli and Toby. "Yesterday, I finished the west wall and the half-wall between the kitchen and living room."

"I think we can, too," Mel said as she closed the door and headed toward the bathroom.

By late morning, Mel was done with the grouting and could help me paint. We both worked all afternoon and evening until eight o'clock. As I cleaned up my brush, my cell phone rang. "Mel, it's Grates & Grilles," I yelled, excitedly. "They are driving onto Deer Trail now with our stove. It's dark for heaven's sake. Good for them."

Mel rushed to look out the window, "Wow. I didn't expect delivery until tomorrow."

"They said because Christmas is almost here, they're trying to get everyone's delivery to them as soon as possible." I looked out my study window and saw them coming up the driveway.

A minute later, they knocked on the door. "Hi," the taller of the two men said, entering the room. "Where is this going?"

"I just finished the grouting this morning," Mel said, as she walked him to the drying tile.

"Good timing," he said looking around the room. "It will look beautiful here. We'll be very careful. Once it's down, it's down. You won't have to move it again. We'll attach the stove pipe, hook it up, and then we'll start a modest fire for you. After that, you're on your own."

It took less than an hour before our handsome, green-enameled stove started to heat the room. As the shorter, burly man walked toward the front door he said, "I love your home. May I come back when you're done? I'd love to see the finished product."

"Of course you can," I said.

Closing the door, I turned back and could see the tiny fire from the entryway. It looked warming and cheerful. Mel had a smile on her face as she turned from the stove, and went back to work. The last bit of painting needed to be finished in the topmost corner of the living room.

Mel crawled up the scaffolding. "I'm not tall enough," she said.

I climbed up behind her. "I can't reach it either," I said, my arm waving over my head. "I'll get the small step ladder, and put it on the top of the scaffolding." After nailing shakes, nothing scared me anymore.

I won the "rock, paper, scissors" bet for who was to be on the stepladder, so with me holding it, Mel stepped up.

"I still can't reach that little spot," she said, laughing from the top most step.

"Here," I said handing her the long aluminum pole I had taken off the paint roller. "Let's fasten a paint brush to the end of it with duct tape."

"Okay. Good idea." Mel climbed up again after securing the brush to the pole, and reached up as high as she could manage. I held the stool tight. She was on her tiptoes.

"I think I have enough height now...maybe," Mel said, standing twenty-five feet above the living room floor. "There, I got it!"

"Whoohoooo" I sang out.

We were done with the living room. We climbed from the scaffolding and called Kim.

"We've finished painting. Should we call Tim to get the scaffolding, or can you take it down tomorrow?"

"I can be there early if you'll have coffee waiting for me. Do you guys know how late it is?"

"Oh my God, Kim," I winced, glancing at my watch. It was almost midnight. "I'm so sorry. Good night, sleepy head. See you in the morning."

After cleaning the brushes, I made my way upstairs. It was a little after midnight and I was exhausted. I knew it wouldn't take long to fall asleep, especially in the warm bedroom.

"Almost Christmas," I quietly said to Eli. "Almost Christmas."

All is Well

M el and I stood together admiring our living room. I knew we weren't getting much accomplished, but I was having fun. A second later, someone knocked on the door.

It was John. "I hope to give you your occupancy permit this morning," he said, smiling. "Let's do a final walk-through." We had picked up our mattress yet again, and my bedroom had the look of a storage room. I wasn't as nervous this time.

"Come in," Mel said shivering, as the cold wind nipped at our ankles.

John unzipped his jacket and pulled out his small pocket notebook. "This will be a temporary permit until you pave the swale at the end of the driveway. However, there's no hurry," John said, with a positive tone to his voice. "Kim said he completed the few items left on the list, but I need to look at them anyway. I want to check them off."

I looked forward to showing John around. His last inspection was the week before Thanksgiving. At that time he told Kim to have the slider door in the living room nailed shut. A simple two-by-four across the outside would be fine. It was a safety hazard. We'd run out of money to build the deck, so now there was a five-foot drop to the ground. It would have to be secured. The same applied to the ramp Kim had built to my study door. It wouldn't pass code, but in the past week Mel had made time to build a sturdy stairway. Now it was a delight to come in and out the back door.

We proudly walked him around the house. He looked in every room, upstairs and down, except my bedroom. We invited him in, but told him the kitties were behind the door so we had to be careful that they wouldn't escape.

"I don't need to go in there. They'd be afraid of me anyway," John said.

"I'm happy you brought them in where it's warmer."

"Thanks. We thought they'd get lonely all day at the old farmhouse, so we've had them in the shed. Besides, Toby is diabetic and we need to keep an eye on her," I said.

"It must have been a lot of work bringing them here each day," he said, with not even the slightest hint of irony.

"Not really," I responded off handedly.

Mel and I walked downstairs smiling. "Thank you for everything, John," I said meaning every word. "You've been very kind to us, and extremely easy to work with. The township is fortunate to have you as their building inspector."

"Thanks. I'll tell the town supervisors. Maybe I'll get a raise," he said looking over at Mel.

He looked at all our work and said, "I am so pleased to authorize this permit. I've never seen anyone work as hard as you two during this past year. Good luck," he said, as he handed us our temporary permit. Walking out the door he turned around, "Oh, there is one more thing." I held my breath, and then he grinned. "If you'd like to move in to your new home, you can do it anytime."

Neither of us moved a muscle. I imagined we looked like two women sculpted out of stone. His eyes held a jovial look as he turned and walked to his truck. We closed the door, and looked at each other.

"He knew all this time," I said. "He had to. What do you think?"

Mel grabbed her head in her hands. "I'm not sure. Maybe he did, maybe he didn't. Did he wink at us?"

"It looked like a wink, but it was so subtle, I don't think it was. Who knows? Who cares?" I said stretching my arms toward the ceiling.

"What a game we all had to play," Mel said, with exhausted effort. "All for the sake of a temporary occupancy permit."

"But it's ours now," I said, waving it in the air. "I think we should frame it and then it can be our first wall hanging."

"Let's celebrate," Mel said walking over to the living room windows. "I'm going to call Kim and ask him to come over tonight. Let's have some fun together and give him his Christmas gift. His work here is almost complete. The scaffolding is gone, and the ugly brown paper is off the floor. It's celebration time."

"Sounds like a good idea," I said. "He has to come back yet to caulk those two high living room windows. As far as I know, that's his last job."

"I'm sure he'll tell us if there's more." Mel grimaced.

After a quick sandwich, we headed to the storage unit for our living room furniture. We had Bill's truck and my car. It would probably be enough. We lifted the sofa into the truck along with a few other items. The lamps, coffee table, and ottoman, went in my car. It took over two hours, and we were tired from the heavy lifting.

"I'm happy it isn't snowing yet, " I said closing the door to the storage unit.

Mel looked at me and asked, "Is it supposed to?"

"Not sure, but maybe it will. I want it to," I said, slamming the car door.

At home, we carried in the sofa. It was heavy, but seemed easier than when I lifted it in the spring. I had grown stronger from this project, and it felt good. We each brought a chair down from upstairs, and brought them into the living room. I set a lamp beside each chair. The coffee table came in next, and we placed it in front of the sofa. Mel went back upstairs and brought down the TV. She positioned it on the same table we had used in the shed.

"Here you go, Mel," I said, dragging a new area rug out of my study.

"When did you get this beauty?" Mel asked.

"I went to Quakertown yesterday shopping for food and extra paint rollers, remember? And while I was at Lowe's, I saw this carpet and thought you'd like it. It's an early Christmas gift. You mentioned it was something you wanted."

"Wow." Mel said, unrolling a rug covered in earth tone colors. "It's just what I would have picked out. Thank you."

"You're welcome," I said, pleased that she liked it.

When we finished, we returned Bill's truck and walked up the path one more time. Dusk was fast approaching, and Mel stopped short and stared at our windows.

"I love the candles," Mel said, as she looked up at the soft radiance coming from our cozy cottage home. "When did you put them in?"

"Last night when you took your bath," I said. "I turned them on earlier when you went upstairs for the TV, but you were too preoccupied to notice. I love the little soft bulbs; they look like real candles burning."

Radiance surrounded our home, and we stood there in the cold evening admiring it.

Our living room was charming and felt inviting. Mel and I went upstairs, got the kitties and placed them on the sofa. They jumped down and sniffed their way around the living room, then did the same in the rest of the house. Finally, Toby scurried over to the little blue tent we had placed by the wood stove, and crawled in. She peeked out, let go of a huge sigh, and settled in for a nap.

Eli jumped back onto the sofa, and looked around. We sat beside him, sank back into the welcoming cushions, and admired our work. Cozy and comfy, just as we'd hoped.

"I think I hear Kim's car in the driveway," I said, walking toward the foyer.

"Good," Mel said running for his brightly wrapped gift in the kitchen.

Opening the door with a grand gesture, I said, "Hi, Kim. Welcome to our little abode. Come into the living room and see how remarkable it feels." I stood beside Kim, crossed my arms over my chest, and gazed up at the ceiling's soft glow from the light of the wood stove.

"Thanks, guys," Kim said quietly, for the first time in months. "I've loved working here with you. I'd like to bring customers by to show them your home. For advertisement, if you're okay with that."

"Sure," Mel said. "We'd love to help you out."

"Thanks," he said bowing his head a little.

"Have a seat," Mel said, handing Kim his Christmas gift. He unwrapped it as a knowing grin slowly covered his face.

"Ha!" he grunted. "I'll make this last a long time and every morning when I drink a cup of this hazelnut, I'll think of our project. We all worked hard. Here's to us," he said, lifting the bag of coffee into the air.

"Here's to us," I said with a soft voice, filled with emotion.

Kim stayed for an hour and then stood and walked toward the door. "I'll see you after Christmas. I'll be over to finish caulking the windows." We shared a group hug for a long moment, and then he left.

"He really is Mr. Wonderful," I said to Mel as she put another log in the wood stove.

"Yes, he is," she said, closing the lid.

"We're warm now, Mel. Both inside ourselves and here in the house." I walked toward Mel, eyes wide and filling with tears, and rested my head on her shoulder, feeling the strength and age-old comfort between two tired, but confident women.

"All is well," Mel said.

And though I knew how hard I'd worked during the past year, I felt for the first time that perhaps it was.

A Sense of Completion

Wstayed in bed a little longer, knowing it was Christmas Eve morning, and reflected on why the twenty-fourth held such tenderness for me. Regardless of how many ups and downs I'd had in my life, this day remained precious. Smiling, I thought of my children. They were grown now, and had families of their own. Thinking of them, I faded back in time. Our Christmas Eves had always been extraordinary. There was wide-eyed expectation as the five of us shared time and love for one another around the tree. Gifts were shared on Christmas morning, but Christmas Eve held a distinctive gentleness. I loved those times together.

Life in the shed had shaped my future, I thought as I laid there. I would re-build my counseling practice in the coming year, along with other projects I wanted to complete. I was different now. A woman full of grit with an earthiness. My life, from this point forward, held even more of a story. And every story has a lesson. It was time to live mine.

I slipped from my comfortable refuge and headed to the kitchen for coffee. Mel joined me soon after I sat down.

"You're up early," I said, gazing evenly at her.

"Excited," she answered.

"I feel different. Somehow, very different. Clear, immediate, vivid." I said, immensely satisfied in the easy companionship between us.

We held steaming cups of hazelnut coffee, and looked forward to the day ahead. We promised to stop all work by four o'clock, in celebration of Christmas Eve.

I climbed the ladder, once again, to stain the windows in my study while Mel worked in the foyer. It was quiet, except for my Christmas music playing softly in the background.

It felt like an extraordinary day, and I sensed the difference. As I worked, I thought about spending Christmas morning with Andy and his family. I also wished that Chris and Shelly along with their families lived closer, so we could be with them as well.

"Want to go to Andy's with me tomorrow for part of the day?" I shouted to Mel.

"I'd love to. Thanks for asking. Kathy and Andy always make me feel so welcome, and significant. I think they truly understand our life together." Mel yelled back. "In fact, all of your kids are caring. You've been a great mom."

I smiled and felt proud of my kids.

"I didn't enjoy Christmas with my family as I got older," Mel said walking into the room. "As you know, my family was torn apart in my high school years. I do enjoy spending the holidays with my sister and my nieces, and I do that a few days during Christmas week. But Christmas Day seems more special with you. Wherever you are is where I want to be."

"I share that feeling, sweetie."

We stopped work at four o'clock as planned. Mel took her bath first. I went out to the shed for corn. "I want to give the animals their food early. After all," I said, "if legend is to be believed, this is the night the animals talk. We have to fill their bellies now, so they'll enjoy Christmas Eve, too." When I returned I was blowing warmth onto to my fingers. "I'm eager to jump into the tub. A nice long soak will be perfect."

Looking back at Mel I said, "Tonight will be a special celebration of our achievement."

It was dark outside when I came down from my bath. "I feel renewed and relaxed. Let's begin the evening." I said, feeling full of joy. "Open the refrigerator, Mel. I hid a bottle of Martinelli's sparkling cider deep in the crisper drawer. It's under all the veggies."

"Oh, how fun," Mel answered, her face beaming.

"Let's make a toast to the finished living room. Then we'll have another celebration when the rest of the house is complete. We're almost there," I said.

Holding her glass high, Mel said, "Here's to the departure of the scaffolding."

"And here's to our physical stamina," I laughed, holding my left arm like a body builder. As we drank, we talked about preparing our Christmas Eve dinner. It was the first "real" meal we'd made for ourselves in many months.

"Let's get to it," Mel said. "I'm starving."

"Me, too. Can you believe we actually have "real" food in our brand new refrigerator?" I said holding the door open and viewing all the items inside.

We made a luscious meal together that night, each laughing and pushing the other out of the way with our hips as we worked. Side by side, we shared our first Christmas memory in our new home. Dinner was roasted potatoes and asparagus, faux chicken strips sautéed in a garlicky oil, herb stuffing, and buttered rolls. It was hot and delicious. We ate on real dinner plates, and shared it in our living room in front of the glowing fire, which had the earthy smell of woodsmoke. Eli and Toby sniffed our plates, and licked their lips. Mel jumped up and gave them each a couple of kitty treats for being so good all those long months.

But before we sat down, we looked around the home we had built together. We hugged hard for a minute. Tears fell as we held calloused hands, and said grace. I thanked God for the strength I'd been given, the land around this home, the trees that gave us warmth, and the animals and birds who'd taught me so much. Our gift to each other was fulfilled.

The spiritual journey of rebuilding my life had been remarkable and I was grateful for not feeling unfinished as a woman any longer. Love and nature helped me feel reassured and assuaged, giving me the courage and determination to confront whatever came next. My surroundings allowed me to understand time and to feel the power of life that each one of us possesses. No longer damaged and afraid, I moved forward with courage and felt honored by the challenge.

We ate our dinner amongst tears and laughter. No one else would ever understand the effort it took to build this home, the cold we felt, the exhaustion we'd endured, or the sense of completion we now shared. It was simply enough for us to know, with God as our witness.

It was midnight. Candles, woodstove, and kitty eyes, all glimmered like magic. The night had the feel of a fine symphony, performing its masterpiece in the theater of our hearts. A sense of peacefulness surrounded me, and with it a delicious glow of gratitude.

"Merry Christmas, Mel."

"Merry Christmas, Sal."

Author's Note

Building a house was a stepping stone. A challenge that caused me to expect more from myself each moment, day, and week. I accepted that dare and found strength buried within. I knew it was there, but kept it covered.

To write this memoir I relied upon my house receipt file, personal notes, and consultation with several people who were close to the project. But most of all I have used my own memory. I have changed the names of some, but not all of the people in this book. My wish for those who read these pages, by this author of imperfect words, is that you walk away with hope. If you are passionate about something in front of you, a skill you want to learn, or a trip by yourself for the first time, or a challenge in your personal life, you can do it. It might be the one experience that changes your life.

There is nothing in our lives that can't be done with greater understanding, love, and patience. Take a deep breath. Take another. It is time to go forward, you can do it.

I, too, am wary at times. What am I wary about? Wary about my children reading this book and finding discrepancies with what they thought my life was like, wary of whom I have become since I took my life into my own hands, and wary that I will never give enough love. Love, where we begin and end.

CPSIA information can be obtained at www.ICGtesting.com
Printed in the USA
BVOW02s1556201115

427561BV00001B/5/P